THE SOUL'S JOURNEY

THE SOUL'S JOURNEY

EXPLORING THE THREE PASSAGES OF THE SPIRITUAL LIFE
WITH DANTE AS A GUIDE

ALAN JONES

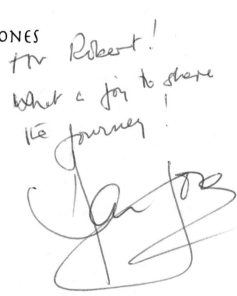

for Robert!
What a joy to share
the journey!

HarperSanFrancisco
A Division of HarperCollins*Publishers*

Book design by Jaime Robles. Set in Octavia type with Herculaneum.

FIRST EDITION

Library of Congress Cataloging-in-Publication Data:
Jones, Alan W.
    The soul's journey : exploring the three passages of the spiritual life with Dante as a guide / Alan Jones. —1st ed.
        p.   cm.
    Includes bibliographical references (p. 231) and index.
    ISBN 0–06–064253–X (cloth: alk. paper)
    ISBN 0–06–064254–8 (pbk.: alk. paper)
    1. Spiritual life. 2. Dante Alighieri, 1265–1321. Divina commedia. I. Title.
    BV4501.2.J5855   1995
    248.2—DC20   95–1345

95 96 97 98 ❖ HAD 10 9 8 7 6 5 4 3 2 1

This edition is printed on acid-free paper that meets the American National Standards Institute Z39.48 Standard.

MATER DEI, ORA PRO NOBIS.

ৠ৵ঀ৶

FOR JOSEPHINE, WHO HAS LOVED ME INTO LOVING

"To see Thee is the End and the Beginning
Thou carriest me and Thou goest before.
Thou art the Journey and the Journey's End."

·

It is difficult
to get news from poems
yet men die miserably every day
for lack
of what is found there

WILLIAM CARLOS WILLIAMS

CONTENTS

ACKNOWLEDGMENTS

There are many people to thank who encouraged me to write about the journey of the soul as it is illuminated by Dante's *Divine Comedy*. I walked with students through the poem several times. Many of them helped me understand Dante's soul's journey and myself more fully. I would like to thank Dr. John Ogden, the senior pastor of First United Methodist Church in Wichita Falls, Texas, for inviting me to deliver the Perkins Lectures in 1994. These lectures form the basis of this book. Such gracious invitations gave me the impetus to put on paper my version of Dante's journey. I would also like to thank my sometime editor Ronald Klug for helpful suggestions in organizing the manuscript. John Shopp at Harper San Francisco guided the book through the various stages to publication. My wife, Josephine, read the many drafts and gave probing comments when difficulties of interpretation came up. My colleagues at Grace Cathedral made it possible for me to take some sabbatical time to finish the writing and I am deeply grateful to them. Above all, I am thankful for Dante's many brilliant interpreters who led me through the circles of desire.

Alan Jones
The Feast of All Saints, 1994

ONE

THE SOUL'S ITINERARY

This book is an invitation to a journey of life as seen through the eyes of the poet Dante. Most people have heard of Dante's famous three-part poem called *The Divine Comedy*. According to his vision, human beings have to pass through three stages of life—more than once, and at different levels in a lifetime—in order to understand themselves as full human beings. The three passages are hell, purgatory, and heaven. They represent three states of the soul that most people can recognize as three common experiences. Many, if not all, of us experience from time to time the frightening feeling of being stuck in a depressingly downward spiral of hopelessness. This is hell. Most of us know something of being sorry for things we have done in our past and experience the possibility of making a fresh start. This is purgatory. Some of us have occasionally caught a glimpse of what it is to be a free person in a free society. This is heaven. Dante's three passages correspond to those places where we feel stuck, where we can move, and where we catch sight of our home or spiritual destination.

We can, of course, make reference to such common experiences without speaking of God. Dante would claim, however, that we cannot understand the true nature of these passages without understanding what it is to be a human being. To be a human being is to be in relationship with God and with one another in a commonwealth where everyone is included. The poet's vision is as intensely political as it is personally spiritual. We get stuck in hell when we are out of relationship with God and with one another. We begin to move through the second passage, purgation, when we start reaching out to one another. Heaven is the "place" where we are at home not only with ourselves but with other people too.

The first passage is hell or the inferno. It isn't easy to persuade people to take the passage of hell seriously; to look inside themselves and explore the possibility of damnation and perdition; to entertain the idea that even if hell, purgatory, and heaven are not real places, they at least describe actual human experiences and point to genuine human fears and aspirations. These may be unfamiliar words, but they describe common states of mind.

The idea of going to hell is a distasteful one not only for skeptics who dismiss such talk as superstitious and perverse, but also for sophisticated religious types who believe they have outgrown what they think of as the kindergarten kind of religion—of the bogeyman who will come and get us if we misbehave. We rightly criticize vindictive religion and spiteful moralism. For a few, I suspect, the thought of damnation or eternal lostness might be a bit exhilarating. If there is nothing to look forward to and if my future holds either torment or simply nonexistence, I might as well live it up now. "It doesn't matter how we behave now. Death cancels all debts." For some, hell is the only passage there is. The possibility of perdition can act as a kind of stimulant to an already corrupt and decaying life if we believe that we live in a world where nothing matters in the end. Life is cheap. Life is fleeting. For many, there is no binding moral authority. Wouldn't it be exciting if we found that our actions really mattered, that movement out of our particular hell were possible? Wouldn't our lives have more energy and focus if what we did had consequences—some of them dire? Wouldn't it be amazing to discover that we had souls and that they were forged in the imagination and revealed in the unfolding of a story that pointed to a homecoming?

Not long ago, the word *soul* was looked down on in intellectual circles and for mixed reasons. It was rightly thought that the tradition that had divorced the soul from the body had done a lot of harm to people over the centuries. But some went too far and dismissed altogether humanity's deep longings, which we associate with the word *soul*. Although the word is now back in fashion, it remains almost impossible to define. A working definition might be "the true self," or we might use the word *heart* to describe what is essential about a person. But all definitions are inadequate if they do not take into account our vulnerability as persons as we move through time to our eventual death. The soul (whatever it is) is revealed through the unfolding of a story. Dante believed that the soul (the self, the person) is on a journey with high stakes. It is possible to get hopelessly lost. Not to take the possibility of damnation and perdition seriously is to be spiritually and morally dead. There is nothing more difficult than knowing who we are. There is no greater adventure than trying to find out.

It has been said that religion is for those who fear and want to avoid hell, while spirituality is for those who have been there. I find it hard to imagine anyone awake to the realities of the world who hasn't seen hell in its personal, social, and political manifestations. I am asking the reader to walk with me because I believe that the old story of the journey through the three passages of hell, purgatory, and heaven is a hopeful one, a story that has much to teach us as we live in a world falling apart and move into the confusions and opportunities of the next millennium. My hope is that we will recover the art of dreaming big dreams that will reveal to us the mutuality at the heart of everything—the meaning of all that we have to pass through.

My soul has been shaped by a story learned from various sources as I was growing up and constantly reworked in my imagination. My story had to do with a perverse if romantic view of myself as someone from humble beginnings who, nevertheless, was blessed with being white and not some shade of black, brown, or yellow. Add to this my personal needs to be liked and loved, mix everything together into a confused ambition-vocation to be a priest, and you discover a soul on the way to getting lost— on the road to hell. We can maintain a vital fiction for our lives for years. We can be in hell and claim that we are in heaven.

A man once showed up at the cathedral where I work and convinced my colleagues and me that he was an ordained deacon. He knew all the churchy jargon and spoke the language of our tradition. We were completely taken in. He was attractive, intelligent, and articulate. One day he went too far in his charade by telling someone that he and I had been roommates in seminary in England. Not only had I not met him before but I had been trained in a monastic setting with simple rooms or cells where there were no roommates. His story began to unravel and when I called to confront him with his lying, he disappeared. I wonder where he is now. He must be perpetually on the run and yet stuck in a fantasy about himself, which means that he can never be really at home with himself.

Finding out that one is lost can take a long time. Many of us discover we are lost somewhere in the middle of our lives when the soul has gotten used to its own little drama and the imagination has become sluggish because it thinks its work is done. I came to the end of my rope as a "religious professional" right on schedule—in the middle of a story that I thought I knew and that, on the whole, I liked because it gave me a place of privilege and power. I found myself in unfamiliar territory where the rules of my own world didn't count. The poet Dante (1265–1321) called the place a dark wood—*una selva oscura*. I also became scared of others. What if they found out that the story of my soul was unraveling? And what of those who, unable or unwilling to face their own particular hell, made life hell for others? I saw some of my contemporaries who had suffered pain and humiliation in their early lives ladle it out to others as if it were in the natural order of things. I didn't like what I saw of myself in them.

THE DRAMA OF CHOICE

At some moment in the middle of my life, I realized three things about the making of the soul: stories have to be questioned and reviewed all the time because of the possibility of error; the imagination has to be reawakened to open the soul up to new possibilities and unimagined futures; and what little freedom we have in choosing one path over another is *the* thing that makes us human. I came to see that my own soul-making was a drama of choice. I had to choose and risk making a mistake. And the stakes were high—the choice between good and evil, right and wrong. In my choosing I have found deep and lasting joy (heaven). I have also found pain and torment (hell). And the drama isn't over.

The journey to hell and back can sharpen our awareness and make the conscience truly alive. Christianity has often been castigated for insisting on some form of self-examination, for emphasizing sin and guilt, for holding individuals morally responsible for their actions. We are beginning to see what human beings are like without these humanizing restraints. A human being who isn't morally alive, available to the pain of a guilty conscience, capable of amendment of life, has closed down his or her imagination and is cut off from new possibilities because the soul story has already been written. Dante blew apart the fixed stories of his time and contributed incalculably to our vision of the morally aware human being living freely in a just society. He saw the soul as political and social as well as personal and interior. He showed his contemporaries that the future is not fixed, that their choices mattered and mattered for eternity, and that they were part of a love story that has no end except in God. He opened up the soul to new possibilities.

In forging his poem of the soul's journey, which he called the *Comedy*, Dante used three great images: the dark wood (the *selva oscura*), the mountain, and the rose. They describe his experience of lostness and home-coming. The wood leads into the funnel of hell—the place where the soul gets stuck. The mountain is where purgation and healing happen—the place where the soul gets unstuck. The perfect circle of the unfolded rose is a sign of homecoming—the place where our exile comes to an end. Dante speaks to our wounded imaginations. He helps to heal the soul by provid-ing it with an itinerary through the painful and joyous pathways of its experience.

Experiences of exile, lostness, and homecoming are predominant themes in contemporary life. Carl Jung wrote of the poverty of modern spirituality, which lacks wholeness and vision. People lose something deeply human when they are cut off (or cut themselves off) from their spir-itual depths. At one point in my life, I became such a terror to myself that I wasn't at home even in the outer vestibule of my soul, let alone in the dark-ness of its interior recesses. I found myself in the dark wood that leads to hell, spiritually bankrupt and confused. I lost my orientation. I was adrift. Jung writes, "The need for meaning in their lives remains unanswered, be-cause the rational, biological goals are unable to express the irrational wholeness of human life." He goes on to point out that the way back "de-mands concentrated attention, much mental work, and, above all, patience, the rarest thing in our restless and crazy time."[1]

People aren't likely to turn to poetry (let alone to Dante's) for their souls' health, but I wonder how many of us realize that we are always turning to a kind of text or script (a novel, a movie, a TV show, a conversation, a trip, an illness, a death) to help us revise and interpret our lives. Many have liter-ally made the journey to Tibet or India to look for a new way to understand themselves. Others hunt for clues to who they are and what they are about in following the fortunes of the glamorous and wealthy. A text can be as easy to pick up as those in the checkout line at the supermarket. *People* magazine or *TV Guide* can serve as texts, as can "Star Trek: The Next Gen-eration" or "Roseanne." Advertisements promise itineraries for opening the mind and heart to new experiences. One recent TV ad asked, "Where in the world would you go if there was no Las Vegas?"

We need something to help us make sense of our experience. Sometimes the things we make use of in this way are trivial and accidental. Sometimes they are heroic. In the city where I live, AIDS has become the prism through which many come to see what their lives might mean. A friend of mine

transformed her dying into a voyage of discovery and in the process transformed those around her. I visited her only a couple of times. Her hair was
gone and tubes were everywhere. We cried, laughed, and prayed. She, in
her dying, gave all those who saw her an unexpected joy. Another friend
has "found herself" by working among the poor in Central America. Yet
another has, in giving birth to her son, changed the way in which she understands herself and her story. In the first case, dying was a kind of text
that demanded to be read and understood. In the second, working with the
poor became an interpretive key. In the third, a pregnancy fairly late in life
gave my friend a new vision for herself.

The various texts we pick up along the way help us to endure and enjoy
our lives. They offer different ways to understand who we are and what has
become of us. These *alternate* readings we give to our lives after watching a
TV drama or sitcom should tell us something of the power of stories. As restricting, stupid, and short-lived as they often are, they are a method by
which we find our way out of or into the "hells" of everyday life. They even
give us glimpses of "heaven." We need stories that take note of our frailty
and foolishness and yet honor our deepest longings and highest aspirations.

I want a story that will heal our wounded imaginations. The surgery of
reimagining the story of the soul is demanding, and, at first glance, an ancient poem would seem a frail and futile (some would say effete and elitist)
weapon against despair. In a crude sense, however, we are all poets. The
architecture of heaven and hell is built by and in our imaginations. The
trouble is that the poetic images conjured up by the imagination lie as well
as tell the truth. We resist poetry and metaphor because we tend to look at
life with a literalist squint and believe not only in the myth of objectivity
but also in the easy accessibility of meaning. We want to move straight
past Go, collect our two hundred dollars, and move on. We want unequivo-
cal answers to our deepest questions. Is there a God? Do I matter? Does
anyone give a damn? On one level, clear answers to such basic questions
are a matter of life and death. On another, a quick and easy response could
short-circuit the work of the soul in its struggle to find its true way. As a
teacher, I have often irritated a questioner by posing another question instead of giving a "straight" answer. When a physician asked me recently if
I believed in hell, I made the mistake of saying, "It all depends what you
mean by hell." He got angry with what he saw as my equivocation. I should
have said, "Yes! Absolutely!" He wanted me to be a Bing Crosby or a

Barry Fitzgerald priest from one of the old movies, but I couldn't play the role of the man with all the answers.

The wisdom of the ancient mystical paths tells us that while we may have occasional flashes of insight and significant moments of conversion, there are, in the long run, no shortcuts. We make the descent into hell not to stay there but to learn what it has to teach us.

Many of those who have heard of Dante's great poem are familiar only with the juicier bits of the *Inferno*. Hell is the realm of Satan, the Father of Lies, and is therefore the place of deception. Hell is able to make itself appear more interesting than heaven. Some have heard of the lovers Paolo and Francesca, forever wind-tossed in a clinging but passionless embrace. The rest of Dante's cast of characters are, however, largely unknown. We know little or nothing of Dante's poetic vision of the soul's journey, his passion for human community focused in religious commitment and political and social justice (what he would have called church and empire). Apart from a fragment of a quotation or two, such as the opening lines of the *Inferno*— "In the middle of life's way . . . " and "in His will is our peace" (and isn't there something about "love and the stars" at the end of the poem?)—even the most literate know very little about its overall vision. Yet the themes with which Dante struggles are startlingly contemporary. They are part of our story.

THE POWER OF TEXTS

The journey of the soul always comes to us in the form of a story. At first sight, Dante's version of the journey is determinedly uninviting—too much work, too inaccessible, too dense. Besides, who wants to go to hell? But there comes a time in one's personal life when one is ready for the inner work, and sees it not merely as a private quest but as a way of responding to an inner longing for community, a desire to be in communion with others. Something forces us to take notice of three basic human desires: for the common rather than the merely private good, for engagement in the world around us, and for dependence on one another in commitments of shared responsibility. Occasionally, outward circumstances make the work doubly urgent. Someone we love dies suddenly and unexpectedly. We lose our job or find ourselves out of love. A local atrocity or a distant catastrophe hits us between the eyes with the fragility of life and the futility of human evasions. As we move toward the end of the millennium, the journey of the soul modeled in *The Divine Comedy* becomes a pilgrimage of hope in a world where, for many, hope is lost.

When I stumbled into Dante in the course of my teaching spirituality, I was disturbed by the gap between what I knew academically and what I knew (or didn't know) in my soul. The Christian spiritual tradition speaks of the *cognitio experimentalis Dei*—the experiential (experimental, too) knowledge of God. I wanted experience. I wanted to experiment. I longed for an integrity I knew I didn't possess. I had read extensively in-depth psychology and had a little experience in Jungian analysis. Jung introduced me to the inner world of the psyche. What was I to name these states I discerned, not only inside myself but also in the body politic? Dante called them hell, purgatory, and heaven. Jung further identified my interior hells, purgatories, and heavens and provided me with two things. The first was a working acquaintance with some (although not all) of my inner monsters, demons, angels, tricksters, wise old men and women, children, and clowns—that community of actors who live, acknowledged or not, in one of the three realms in the depths of the soul. The second thing that Jungian analysis gave me was the rudiments of an honest approach to the inner life. I could not only try to tell the truth, I could also trust it.

Each of us is living from a text we received or learned as we were growing up. I learned that the world was unfriendly and that, in the end, no one would look out for me and that I would be alone. The presenting pathology in my own itinerary is common—a pattern of self-sabotage and even self-contempt. I sometimes feel the urge to make the story I received when I was very young come true. I've looked for alternate readings in, for example, the Bible and in any form of literature I could get my hands on. I have valued the corrective readings of my life by many friends and even an occasional enemy. Dante's poem gave me a new reading of my life. He taught me that texts can and should be abandoned and that new stories can heal the imagination. Marriage has been by far the most powerful text in my life: a spiritual roller coaster of crashes, disasters, and hurts, but also of rescue, forgiveness, and healing—a wondrous garden of renewal. Because of the version of the human story I picked up in early childhood from worn-out parents recovering from the stresses of war, I find the world a wonderful but untrustworthy place. How can it be both? As I was growing up, I dreaded the possibility of the wonder being snatched away from me. How stable was it? Would it overwhelm me and swallow me up?

It's not so much a matter of trusting individuals as a question of trusting society, the cosmos, life itself. The roots of my anxiety are still too deep for me to understand. But when I don't trust, I find myself in hell. Dante's poem helps me to explore my own particular inferno and find a way through.

I am now convinced that a merely therapeutic approach to life isn't enough. This book is about getting out of the hell into which our fears often drive us. Gandhi once told a fellow Hindu how to do as much after his son had been killed by a Muslim. "Find an abandoned Muslim child and bring him up as your own." The path isn't easy and we can find plenty of reasons to cling to our rage and disappointment and not make the journey.

In part, I took to Dante as an antidote to both biblical and psychological "fundamentalism," and as a way of honoring all the levels of human experience inside me that demanded attention—the bad stuff as well as the good. The Bible has only recently come alive again for me. It had been killed by the double onslaught of the literalists and the critics. I know many for whom the Bible is a dead and deadly text. They have turned to other traditions looking for a map to guide them through life. Bookstores cater to the search by stocking their shelves with books on alternative spiritualities. One of my friends literally feels sick to his stomach on entering a church because of early experiences of a joyless and repressive religion. He has found a way through his life by reading the "text" of nature. He is now an ardent environmentalist and blames all our ecological ills (to my mind, unfairly) on the Bible.

There are, of course, forms of fundamentalism other than biblical ones. Psychological fundamentalism (of any school) has never attracted me. I am suspicious of attempts to make the work of the soul merely clinical and scientific. I resent and resist having my longings reduced to addictions and my searching explained away as neuroses. Dante was a poet, not an analyst, and the liberating thing for me about The Divine Comedy is that it is neither the Bible nor a compendium of psychological reductionist explanations. I find it in tune with the writings of the great religious traditions, but it has the advantage of not carrying the dead weight of a sacred text (in my case, the Bible) made harmful by centuries of abuse by many of those who have interpreted it. This, of course, is a one-sided view. I know others have not had this negative experience of the Bible, but I, at a significant time in my life, needed an antidote. Dante came to the rescue.

The Bible is, nevertheless, a key text for the telling of the human story (for believers and nonbelievers alike) in the West. Because it is often appropriated for partisan purposes, I find that its great message can best be received indirectly through, for example, poetry. I wish people who quote the Bible would admit that they are puzzled by it. Anyone reading it today *should* be mystified by it. Dante is my way back into the drama of the sacred texts, not just the Bible but the texts of the other great religious traditions as well—into texts of depth, difficulty, and diversity in which I find disturbing and puzzling challenges to my interpretation of things. There is always more than one way to tell the human story. Poetry is liberating because it does not lend itself easily either as an instrument of spiritual technology or as a set of dogmas and rules by which to live. It breaks us open with metaphors that invite the retelling of our stories in a different way.

I felt liberated when I learned that Dante's poem was *una bella menzogna,* a beautiful lie—not a literal fact—bearing deep truths. But this is not everyone's reaction: some people still want to ban and burn books, not simply on moral grounds, but because they indulge in flights of the imagination. The power of our dreams is neither recognized nor acknowledged, let alone honored.

Dante invites us into a different world to find the truth—the ambiguous and ironical world of dreams where heaven and hell are the realities. But the truth of dreams is not easy to discern. Error, as we shall see, plays an important role in Dante's description of the soul's journey through hell and purgatory and on to heaven. Acknowledgment that we might be mistaken and on the wrong track is both a sign of grace and an antidote to moralism and self-satisfaction.

In the late 1960s and early 1970s, while I was struggling with the Bible and with my own inner dreams and longings, religious and secular institutions were going through their own midlife crises. The present age seems rather like the sixties without the idealists who believed in the birthing of a new world. The church is still deeply involved in reinterpreting itself to itself—often painfully and sometimes hilariously turned in on itself around issues of sexuality, liturgy, and scripture. People outside the church couldn't care less, and many are discovering that they can have a spiritual life without the trappings of what seems to be an irrelevant institution. Believers and nonbelievers, traditionalists and New Agers—all of us together face intractable political and environmental challenges. The growing population pollutes the planet, children starve, the homeless populate our streets. Tribes are reforming. Old destructive texts are being dusted off. Hell.

APOCALYPSE MEANS REVELATION

We need practical help to interpret the apocalyptic times in which we live and to choose the way of love over the way of crude power fueled by fear. The words *apocalypse* and *apocalyptic* are now part of our everyday vocabulary. They are catchwords in the media, and Francis Ford Coppola's movie *Apocalypse Now* (about the Vietnam War and based on Joseph Conrad's novel *Heart of Darkness*) captured the imagination of a generation of moviegoers. In the popular imagination, "apocalypse" suggests the destructive end of everything in a blistering holocaust. From the ashes of the old will spring a new and cleansed world. But the word means more than this. In its primary sense it means a revelation, an uncovering. In uncovering its destiny, the soul may have to experience a fierce cleansing and endure bitter discoveries about itself. For Dante, the soul's apocalypse involved not only a journey to hell but also his enduring and enjoying the deepest truth about himself as one destined for heaven.

For most of us, however, "apocalypse" suggests hell on earth. We see our dread come alive on the nightly news. Only the most naive no longer believe in one inferno or another. Hell is all around us and we understandably seek shortcuts to heaven. It is not always easy to tell which road leads to the inferno and which to paradise. The key issue in the spiritual life is always discernment. The role of error and deception in human affairs cannot be overemphasized. When we are frightened and anxious, discernment becomes even more difficult. Fear clouds the mind and clutches the heart. We don't make good decisions when we are frightened.

As we move through the end of one millennium and into another, our imaginations are bound to be caught up with visions of rootlessness and homelessness—of hope and fear, of heaven and hell. The closer we get to the year 2000, the greater the expectation becomes for upheaval and change. There will be a sense of enormous relief when we come out on the other side. Secular as well as religious voices are heard predicting contrary "ends": one of doom and destruction (perhaps through a technological holocaust); the other, the birth of a New Age. We feel caught up in events beyond our control, yet it is impossible to be a mere bystander to the drama

of the world. We have to get up in the morning. For some, who have no reason to do so except bare survival, that is a daily heroic act. Yet there is also
a lot of simply waiting around, hoping that something significant will happen. We fill the waiting with busyness to no purpose. We live in between
acting and waiting. Such it is to live in apocalyptic times. Our culture is
even capable of exploiting the coming millennium, making it into a minor
industry of chic doom and gloom. Through the centuries, there have been
those, inflated with grandiose plans to shatter the world as it is and usher
in a brave new one, able to exploit people's apocalyptic fears. In one sense,
of course, the year 2000 is simply an arbitrary date. At another level, however, the date captures the imagination with terrors and expectations of gi-
gantic proportions.

Apocalypticism, as ain't-it-awful-ism, is easily dismissed as crazy
talk—the playground for religious fanatics, end-of-the-worlders, and
Monty Python fans. Sectarian believers gather, from time to time, on the
tops of mountains to wait for the End. We think of the victims of Waco and
Jonestown who were sucked into the restricting fantasy of a cult leader and
led into the maelstrom conjured up by his diseased imagination. True believers hole themselves up on a farm or in a compound and engage in either
an apocalyptic conflagration or an ecstatic mass poisoning. The End never
comes and the survivors have to make their way back into the "real world"
with their tails between their legs. They can either hang onto their fantasy
of the End by adjusting (yet one more time) the schedule, or go through the
painful process of debriefing, of giving up their cherished dream. I feel for
them. They are so easy a target for fun or contempt that we miss the fact
that they may be onto something. They might not be as crazy as we
thought. They disturb us because they see, albeit in a distorted way, the
inner truth of our basic instability. They know that the world has a history
and that it will, one day, come to an end.

The apocalyptic end of everything is ironically ever-present. Human life
is inherently unstable. It *always* ends in dissolution—death. Most of the
time we are able to suppress our uncertainties and pretend we are living in
a solid and dependable world. We are now, however, living in a period of
history when it is extremely difficult to pretend that we can carry on as
usual. At such moments, we are faced with a choice. The choice can be
framed in various ways. One way is to juxtapose love and fear.

There are only two feelings. Love and fear.
There are only two languages. Love and fear.
There are only two activities. Love and fear.
There are only two motives, two procedures,
two frameworks, two results. Love and fear.
Love and fear.[2]

One way or another, we are challenged with choosing love or fear as we get in touch with our amazing psychological and physical fragility. It's difficult to find something to cling to. What can we believe? Whom can we rely on? What is permitted? What is forbidden? In apocalyptic times there is both moral confusion and a sense of exile. We feel homeless. Many people are literally homeless; many more are spiritually so. Questions haunt our imaginations. Why do we feel lost, empty, unfulfilled, anxious? Are we entering a period of "a new world disorder"? In the face of planetary disaster, hunger, and homelessness, can one have spiritual life without it sounding silly and escapist? How can we face the future? The uncertain times make me unsure of myself. I want to be accepted and recognized. I'd like to know that I and those I love have a place in the world and that my life matters, that I can make a difference, that I will be missed when I'm gone. What challenges me to live with hope in this in-between time is that I am driven to look for companions, to search out others and learn to trust them. Others, I know, have been wounded so often that they avoid companionship as much as possible. But this is no way to live. We are not meant to be isolated from one another. In spite of the cultural mess that has led to our chronic uncertainties and to the dismantling of our sense of self, there is hope.

I'm in a bit of a fix, though. I don't want to choose between love and fear. I want to sit on the fence. I want to live but I don't want to take risks—especially in these times. A friend of mine is a good diagnostician of what troubles me. She writes, "Intimacy is never totally safe, and it's understandable why many people choose comfort over aliveness." But in order to be fully alive and aware (to have soul), I have to reach out in love to others, form personal attachments, and belong to communities over which I have no control. I am attracted by this and at the same time repelled. I know that life is not worth living unless I reach out to others. In apocalyptic times, though, it's hard to know whom to trust. We are vulnerable to hosts of unknown "others" who may or may not be trustworthy. Some are so hurting and lost that they surrender themselves to cults and communities that invite them to *find* themselves in the so-called safety of the group. They go seeking heaven. They find hell. We need a revelation to light our way. Apocalypse as the revelation of the new and hopeful is, however, frustratingly inaccessible. There's a sense that things are coming to an end, and yet the future is pregnant with possibility. When we think about the political challenges, the breaking down of old boundaries, and the building of new ones with programs of ethnic cleansing and retribalization—issues of ecology, health care, and economic dislocation on a global scale—it's hard to deny that ours is a time of the shaking of the foundations. The instability of the political order is reflected in the uncertainties of our personal lives. The global becomes personal. Will I lose my job? Will this relationship last? What is this pain in my chest? Our lives are constantly challenged by these little revelations, these minor apocalypses—these day trips to hell. Does it make any sense?

IS THE UNIVERSE A STORY?

Dante believed that the world is a story. Many people I talk to don't believe that the world is a story and don't even know that people once believed this. There's a technical term for our living in a universe without a story. It's called postmodernism. Giving something a name helps us to understand it. When I first came to live in the United States, I was intrigued by our need to name and categorize. There were no alcoholics when I was growing up, but there were plenty of drunks. I never had any allergies in the summer. I just sneezed a lot. There were no homosexuals in my community in the 1950s. There were confirmed bachelors and old maids. Today, everything seems up for grabs politically, socially, and ethically. The chaos can be the prelude to madness and dissolution or to the joy of new possibilities. Postmodernism is a technical way of talking about what it's like to be a human being *without a story*. Our world faces a crisis in storytelling. It is so much a part of our everyday experience that we barely notice it. But it raises questions about the kind of world we are and will be living in.

We cannot face the future without a story, but what kind of story do we need? Is there a universal story that sees all other human beings as our potential companions, or are we left to make up our own tales (based on the divisive energies of race, gender, and class)? We need help in interpreting the times. We need an apocalypse, a revelation. When our nerves are raw and on edge, we experience wild anxiety and deep stress. We look for guidance and are vulnerable to exploitative storytellers. Perhaps there's a Waco or a Jonestown out there somewhere that will really deliver what it promises. We can't not join in, can we? Trying to stay above it all is no answer. We need to be bound together somehow.

We cannot live without stories, narratives, and symbols. Here is where discernment is crucial, because stories can exclude as well as include and the way they are told can make all the difference. What *binds* people together can also put them *in a bind*. Stories can imprison as well as liberate. We long for an overarching, inclusive narrative that will hold us together in one community, because human beings are, in Lewis Thomas's words, "all of a piece, a single species, and our present situation will not do."[3] But we are wary of stories that make totalitarian claims. The claim that we live in a reality in which there is no *one* story is an understandable corrective to those who think that they have the only story and insist on our finding our place in *their* narrative. The stories we tell have to be incomplete yet coherent if we are to be free. The stories we tell have to point to a fulfilling end if we are to live in hope. That is why the journey through hell is important. It reveals to us the way some stories inevitably end. We need cautionary tales to show us just how daft the notion is that we make up the rules of living as we go along. Our choices are always made in the context of the stories we tell. Our moral life relies on the narratives we inhabit and live out. They give shape and direction to our personal and communal lives.

I love living in California. The joke about it being a state of mind has some truth to it. I see it as a laboratory of the soul and know people of great integrity and courage who are pioneers in searching for the outline of a new but noncoercive story for the universe. Some experience a sadness because of their own incurable agnosticism. For many of my friends, belief has ceased to be an option. They are, however, distressed at having lost something valuable. They even admit that their imaginations are impoverished. But they believe the sense of deadness inside them is the price one has to pay for giving up childish hopes. Yet we respect and love one another. They are puzzled by my attachment to the old story of God's passion, and I am distressed by my inability to share it convincingly with them. I am saddened that the Bible—the storybook of much of our civilization—has gone dead and sour for them. Many for whom the fire of belief has gone out still drift in and out of churches, synagogues, and temples. I meet them every day. They are my friends. They show me my own confusion. They sometimes have the distracted look of someone who has just mislaid something.

Can we reawaken the imagination to retell the old story? How can we make universal claims to universal sympathies without sounding totalitarian? Can we tolerate the contradictory and conflicting stories of others? Having experienced cruelty and repression in communities that told only one story in only one way (in families, churches, synagogues, temples, and cells), some people think that they can find refuge only in fragmentation and disintegration. It is thought that if we give high value to discontinuity and difference, the validity, freedom, and dignity of "the other" will be safeguarded. We know that Big Stories have sometimes served a terroristic function. We know what happens to people who won't be part of (or are assigned the role of outcast in) the story of life as told by a Hitler, a Stalin, or an Idi Amin. The destructive irony of totalitarian explanations or narratives can be clearly seen in the French Revolution. In 1793 the Jacobins wrote a new Declaration of Rights—rights of the principle of individual liberty—even as they instituted the Reign of Terror. Theirs was a political correctness gone wild and bloody. In their scheme, all people were free and equal but some people were good and some were bad. Liberty was for all, but there was to be no liberty for the enemies of liberty. As one ironically put it, "Be my brother or I will kill you!" Utopias can lead to the repression of those who will not conform. That is why we retreat from the struggle to find a story that builds community and nurtures communion. The best we can do is agree to have mutual treaties of noninterference: I'll leave you alone if you'll leave me alone. Many have suffered because of the arrogance of an enlightened modernity that presumes to speak for others and know what's best for them.

How pluralistic can we be and still claim to be a community? It is no more possible to represent the world in a single language than it is to describe our inner lives in one sentence. Some kind of pluralism is a given, but does the Tower of Babel have to be the location of international politics? If we are deaf to other people's stories (no matter how repellent), we move into tribalism and polarization. We need to find a story that is able to pay attention to those who have been silenced.

The hellish side of the vision that we live in a world with no story is its relativism and defeatism. Such a point of view is, however, useful for reading the maps of hell. It provides us with some infernal cartography. Hell shows us the danger of romanticizing schizophrenia, fragmentation, and instability. Those for whom life is not a story have no strategy for working for a radically different future. The only time is now. I am disturbed by our lack of drive to sustain continuity of values or beliefs. Even our disbelieving is unstable. All attention is given to surfaces, and the idea of progress seems laughable. When we abandon all sense of historical continuity and memory, we make a patchwork quilt out of the bits and pieces of the past that happen to be lying around—rather like the casino architecture of Las Vegas with its Arthurian Court and Caesar's Palace. I can remember when a uniform with its attendant regalia meant something. What were once meaningful symbols become fashion accessories. Nowadays, designer crosses are in fashion, be they simple wooden pieces or extravagant aquamarine-and-yellow-sapphire crosses. When symbols (which are the building blocks of stories) become fashion accessories, we are on the road to hell.

Are there universal truths that, while they refuse to be tied down, can be inferred through a certain kind of storytelling? Is there Absolute Truth that can never be spoken fully but only glimpsed in prayer, ritual, and silence?

THE STORY THAT HAS NO END

There are other images that might lead us out of the particular hells of our wounded imaginations—images of purgatory and heaven, antidotes to hell's poisons. For the other images to work their healing power, however, we would have to face up to and acknowledge the hell in which we find ourselves. The wisdom of the spiritual traditions suggests that to get out of hell we have to go through it, not around it. We have to look apocalypse in the eye if we are to be surprised by joy. Does this sound naive? The promise of joy in apocalyptic times lies in the invitation to let go—to abandon the old securities that are letting us down. We are to give up our faith in the old political machinery and in the dead certainties of a fixed religion to find new faith as an orientation of the self toward God, others, and the world. To move from faith as a profession of belief in set formulas to faith as a genuine leap into the unknown is to move more deeply into our relationship with uncertainty and mystery. We are the protagonists in a story whose end has yet to be written. This is our hope. We live in a historically evolving world. The universe has a history and time travels in one direction only, with a beginning, a middle, and an end. Yet while the end is important, it is still to be written. Meanwhile, there is a vista of promise, terror, and opportunity. There is terror because what we choose to do, avoid, or not do has irreversible consequences. The past cannot be undone. But there is hope because the past can be reinterpreted and its impact on the present altered. Tragedy and error can be an opportunity for the birth of new life. The story has an "end," but the end is God who has no end.

Dante understood that we cannot live without surrender to a supreme loyalty. But to what or to whom should we submit? Stories locate our loyalties and provide us with much-needed images of self-recognition. We read or hear a story and we say, "Ah! Yes! That is what my life is about. Here is where I know who I am. Here is where I will make my home." The actor Cary Grant (who started life as Archie Leach) said toward the end of his life, "I have actually grown into the person I wanted to be." Insofar as this is true, here is a glimpse of heaven.

Apocalyptic times demand the revival of a particular kind of storytelling that takes the old, familiar material and weaves a new and generously inclusive narrative for the planet and its people. We need storytellers and mythmakers who can show us the way by finding a story that sees the planet as a holy place and includes everybody. The crucial question for the storyteller today is, What about the stranger, the alien, the poor, the weak—the other? What about the rage and pain of those who say No! to every attempt to tell a common story?

Our own reality depends on our being able and willing to include others. Thomas Merton wrote, "The more I am able to affirm others, to say 'yes' to them in myself, by discovering them in myself and myself in them, *the more real I am*. I am fully real if my own heart says *yes to everyone*." This, in fact, is precisely Dante's vision of heaven—the celebration of mutuality in a place where everyone is his or her unique self. I am reminded of James Joyce's famous definition of the Catholic Church as "Here comes everybody!" Merton goes on: "If I affirm myself as a Catholic merely by denying all that is Muslim, Jewish, Protestant, Hindu, Buddhist, etc., in the end I will find that there is not much left for me to affirm as a Catholic: and certainly no breath of the Spirit with which to affirm it."[4] Denying the stories and presence of others is to be on the road to hell.

Affirming the mutuality of heaven does not mean allowing others to trample over us. Someone once said, "We're on earth to help others. What others are here for I have no idea." *Others* have responsibilities, too. The old maxim is: We are here to love and to be loved. We might put it another way: I'm here to love you. You're here to love me and don't you forget it! We cannot be truly ourselves without being in relation to others. Those mysterious and often threatening "others" are not only to be loved by us, so that we may come to full birth as persons; they also are called to love us in return so that they can become more truly themselves. Hell on earth is to be found where the strange and mysterious other has to be ethnically or socially cleansed and his or her stories eliminated from the public memory.

Meanwhile, the others are crowding in and taking over our space and demanding attention. The hitherto voiceless are demanding to be heard. Stories of heaven and hell revolve around our attitudes toward others. Jean-Paul Sartre's famous phrase from *No Exit* is "L'enfer, c'est les autres" (Hell is other people). But what will God say to us when we go to him without the others? What about these others with whom we share the world? Hell is other people! Heaven is other people! It all depends on the tales we tell—the stories that shape our experience.

One of the great images from the New Testament is peculiarly apt for our apocalyptic times. The cosmos is in labor with a new birth (Romans 8:18–25). Paul writes of the sufferings of this present time and of the glory that shall be revealed. What a place to get caught—in labor. Creation waits, he writes, for the revelation (apocalypse) of God's children.

Sometimes the heart requires a special kind of suffering in order for it to come to fullness of life. Suffering, not in the sense of being masochistic or quietist but rather of allowing things to be by permitting, consenting, and submitting to life's processes, assists in the birth of the soul. As a friend of mine, Dr. Paula Reeves, once put it, "If we don't accept our destiny it will return to haunt us as fate." The soul is something with which we are in labor. Stories are needed to bring it to term.

Where might we find a story that speaks to our situation and need? We get to the truth only by inference—through myth and poetry, through metaphor and storytelling. We cannot trust in the world of bare fact alone. We need instructions on how to feel—although not in the sense of what is derided as the touchy-feely. I am tired of being told to "get in touch with my feelings." Getting in touch with them is no easy matter. In this sense, the poet Dante is one of the great physicians of the soul in that he performs radical surgery on our imaginations so that we can think and feel again.

The great stories give us a sense of identity. They locate us in time and space; they order our desires. The great myths are always pushing us into community by challenging us to find and accept a moral framework for our life together.

We cannot understand Dante apart from the love story that he believed held the universe together. He was driven by a desire for communion. The technical word for this drive is *eros*—a tricky word for us because it suggests a narrow vision of sexual love (our culture is overeroticized as it is). But *eros* is much more than sex. It is the desire to reach out and connect not only with others but with everything. *Eros* makes us tick. *Eros* gets us into trouble. *Eros* pushes us into forming stories around and about our hungering longings. Dante has no equal in helping us reimagine (realistically and hopefully) the world in erotic and narrative terms. His genius lies in his ability to tell a story with definite form and structure and yet leave it all open. The ending is left in the hands of the One in whom all endings meet. There's a word for God in the Jewish mystical tradition that would have appealed to Dante. God is *Ain Soph*—Being Without End. God's name is No-End. The name speaks to the overflowing generosity of the divine in unimaginable openness.

THE NEW LIFE BEGINS

Dante's hopeful words to me are "Incipit vita nuova"—The new life begins. It is always beginning because, for him, God makes all things new. *Ecce, omnia nova facio*—Behold, I make all things new (Revelation 21:5). Even though I feel that I know little about the interior terrain of which Dante writes, I have known something of the terror and miracle of newness. (In some ways, his poem is as opaque to me as my own life with its blindnesses and dead ends, its pattern of misery, conversion, and delight.) I've made various expeditions into one or two particular circles of hell, climbed a cornice or two of the mountain of Purgatory, and been given an inkling of what Dante means by heaven. But my understanding is woefully thin. Why then write a book about something about which I claim to know so little? Either my modesty is a literary device, as unnecessary as it is annoying, or it is genuine and I have no business wasting the reader's time. There is, however, a third way of looking at this attempt to give an account of our shared spiritual journey as we approach the end of the millennium. It is the way of personal testimony to the power of a text, however imperfectly understood, to heal and transform the soul and lead it from hell to heaven and into communion.

This book is the story of how a text can become a companion for the educating of our wills, the refinement of our desires; particularly of how an ancient poem, in a language other than one's own, speaking in a different time to different people with a different consciousness—a text that is at once inaccessible and accessible, a text like one's own life—can do things in the soul that the soul cannot do for itself. The process is breathtakingly humbling because something overtakes the one who makes the double journey of self-knowledge and knowledge of God, of inner transformation and communion with others, of personal and social integration. The paradox is that when the will is truly surrendered to God, we are more free to act.

In this book I seek to mirror the path set out in *The Divine Comedy*, a threefold pattern of hell, purgatory, and heaven—ways of talking about real-life experiences of misery, conversion, and joy. Each section is preceded by a brief outline of the story of Dante's descent into the funnel of hell, his climbing up the mountain of Purgatory, and his being shot like an arrow into heaven. I've used various English translations because I know only a little Italian, although seven years of grade- and high-school Latin have helped a bit when I have the Italian text open in front of me. I like to think that I *feel* the language just a little.

Several editions of *The Divine Comedy* are available in English.[5] For a straightforward translation I have used John D. Sinclair's version. I have also enjoyed Helen Luke's *From Dark Wood to White Rose*.[6]

I make no claim to be a professional Dante scholar, but I've traveled with students through Dante's spiritual adventure several times. What follows will not introduce the reader to many of the characters in Dante's poem. It is, rather, a personal testimony to the power of texts, words, narrative, poems, to form the soul and heal society—particularly in times of stress. They allow the soul, from time to time, to surprise the mind. My hope is that readers will be driven to the source and discover Dante's genius for themselves—to find that they are part of a love story that has no end.

TWO

DANTE, THE SOUL'S GUIDE

What is the human prospect as we straddle two millennia? How can Dante help us understand ourselves? What was his peculiar vision? These three questions begin our journey. I know of no better companion to travel with us to the year 2000 and beyond than the great thirteenth- and fourteenth-century poet Dante Alighieri. When I first read *The Divine Comedy* I couldn't help applying the cantos to the present day and to my own situation and experience. They were not only ways of interpreting the present but *"missiles for capturing the future."*[1] In spite of the centuries between us, Dante is a startling spiritual guide for contemporary human beings.

Since I came to Dante twenty years ago, *The Divine Comedy* has been a spiritual guide for me through many adventures of my soul. It has become a prism through which I have been able to interpret my own life and understand something of the world's social and political processes. The poem has taught me about my sinning and my hoping, about my mistakes and the possibility of forgiveness and new beginnings. It has also opened me up to see and experience others as means of grace. It has shown me the hell in which I sometimes choose to dwell. By the magic of its images I have seen just how easy it is to be lost in the dark wood of my own willfulness. I have toiled up the mountain of Purgation and experienced the freedom of someone whose willfulness has weighed him down and who now knows the power of new life. I have even caught a glimpse of heaven when God's breathtaking sanity has broken through the controlling madness of my plans and projects. Yet I would make no claim to have understood it. Rather, it has understood me.

The Divine Comedy asks fundamental questions about human decision making around our longings and desires. Dante's understanding of the gift and demands of love is strong and unsentimental. The beauty and wholeness of his vision can be found in the integration of the spiritual and psychological with the social and the political. He was a person of great spiritual courage with a passionate intelligence and strong will. He was unafraid to reveal his weaknesses as well as his strengths to his readers. He had the audacity to interpret the universe through the probing of his own experience of disappointment, betrayal, and exile, and to see it all as a cosmic love story. Dante's vision of the human journey from birth to death is relevant today because his own intellectual and spiritual history (not least his own apocalyptic adventures) gives us a clue to what might be universal in the human condition—a sense of exile and a longing for home. To appreciate his vision, we need to know three things about him: the political and social world in which he lived; his spiritual conviction that God's presence—in flesh and blood in Jesus—is played out in the drama of the cross and resurrection; and the impact that his encounter with Beatrice had on him. Without her, there would have been no poem.

DANTE'S WORLD

I find it difficult to sympathize with anyone who, on visiting Italy, does not fall immediately in love. Florence is one of the most beautiful cities in Italy, and its architecture and art give one a sense of Dante's world. There is also the everyday life of contemporary Florence—the smells from the restaurants and cafés, the crowded narrow streets, the crazy bustle of the open-air market, the strange feeling of intruding into Dante's world when walking across the Ponte Vecchio, the lazy part of the afternoon when there is nothing to do but sit in the open air and watch the world go by or have your wallet or purse stolen. Florence is still Dante's city and there are signs of his world everywhere.

Dante was born in Florence in 1265 and died in exile in Ravenna in 1321. His vision of who we are is based on the primacy of the will—the importance of choice in the ordering of our personal, social, and political lives. It follows that the depth and quality of relationships, both personal and civic, are central to his vision of radical mutuality. To be human is to be a member of a community—"a citizen of the Rome of which Christ is the Roman."[2] For that reason, Dante was intensely political. The work of the soul involved living in engagement with others. He was no lovesick poet on some private quest, pining on the margins of society—although he started out as a young man that way. Early on, he became deeply involved in the political intrigues of his day—involved enough for his rivals to exile him on pain of death in 1302 on trumped-up charges of corrupt practices, betraying the city, and plotting against the pope. He knew what it was to flee for his life—to miss the stabilizing and nurturing power of institutions and communities, to be deprived of friends and loved ones. The fact that he had to rely on the charity of others and live in places not his own stuck in his throat. He hated to have to climb another man's stairs and eat another man's bread.

DANTE'S SPIRITUAL VISION

To understand Dante's version of the soul's journey, the reader has to know something, not only about the politics of Dante's time, but also about the drama of God as it is played out in the passion of Jesus, through which Dante interpreted his experience. Dante's world is Catholic and Christian but accessible to those who are neither. Some critics are embarrassed by Dante's perspective and want to de-Christianize him altogether. This seems to me deeply wrongheaded, but it is equally inept to claim too much for Dante's Christianity, as if he could be used as a weapon for some kind of religious polemic. I believe he was a deeply committed Christian but equally disappointed and disillusioned with the institution of the church. The Christian revelation was, for him, the mythic vehicle that enabled him to explore the depths of what it means to be human. His Christ was cosmic and universal as well as personal and unique.

Dante, therefore, will not be co-opted by a particular group for propaganda purposes. He knows that all human systems are subject to error. He writes in a Catholic Christian context but is not owned by the church. In fact, he has bitingly sarcastic things to say about religion. He can be the companion of atheist and believer alike and is a means by which the two may walk together. Nowadays, Christians are challenged with the question, "Is it legitimate to talk about Christianity in the singular? Should we not talk about Christianities?"[3] It is also true that there is no single atheism. Some modern atheists make it a point of honor to embrace a "chilling and impersonal" worldview, bravely rejecting religious belief yet admitting that they are puzzled by people who treat the absence of God and of God's heaven as unimportant. I have a friend who describes himself as a radical atheist, and yet we find that his serious unbelief and my serious belief often meet in a companionable way as we both struggle with life's problems. We're not locked in an intellectual battle. We know that no one can win the debate, but we acknowledge that we need each other. We both experience life as a gift and stand together in our love and concern for the planet—this lovely earth. We also honor the power of friendship and our need to listen to many versions of the human story. Atheists and believers alike, we all need to walk side by side. United by a revolutionary doctrine of human significance, we are all challenged by the possibility of alternative futures. We are all convinced that how we behave and what we do make a difference.

The Divine Comedy looks at the story of the soul's journey through the prism of the Christian revelation (apocalypse). It begins in Holy Week 1300 (some prefer 1301). Holy Week is the week of weeks in the Christian drama of passion, death, and resurrection. Imagine the sphere of the earth and that you are traveling from one pole to the other by going through the center. Dante enters the dark wood on the evening of Maundy Thursday (the night on which Christ had his last meal with his friends) and is led into Hell on the evening of Good Friday, the day of betrayal and passion. He journeys deeper and deeper until he reaches the center of the earth on Saturday evening. When he enters the new hemisphere of Purgatory on the opposite side of the earth, time goes back twelve hours. He spends Saturday climbing to the surface in time to be at the foot of Mount Purgatory on Easter Day, just before dawn. On the Wednesday morning of Easter Week he reaches the Earthly Paradise, where he spends six hours (the same amount of time Adam tells him that he spent in Eden before his expulsion).[4] His final vision, a vision of the great white rose of heaven, occurs on Thursday, the *eighth* day of the journey—the symbol of the New Creation. Love has been the engine of the itinerary, and Dante's terrible and hopeful message throughout the poem is, There is no escape from love! Not even in hell.

BEATRICE, THE KEY TO DANTE'S STORY

Christian revelation (let alone the politics and intrigue of his time) doesn't fully explain Dante's great inner pilgrimage, which led him into a world of enormous complexity and generosity that he was able to render in story form. We know that his unique journey was erotic and occasioned by a deep attachment to a particular person. Dante's great lifelong attachment was Beatrice. She was his inspiration. In 1274, when he was a small boy, Dante had an encounter with a little girl, Beatrice—a real person of flesh and blood—who changed his life. He looked at her and saw the glory of God. This is no exaggeration. Dante had gasped with astonishment at the sight of the nine-year-old Beatrice. He tells us that she wore "the most noble of colors, humble and crimson."[5] (Crimson is Beatrice's color. She appears to Dante in *Purgatorio* 30 wearing *color di fiamma*.) But he had little or no idea of the significance of this first childhood encounter. He had to go to hell because he failed to see the true meaning of his longing for Beatrice. In his ignorance he betrayed both Beatrice and his truest self, yet in her was the extraordinary epiphany of Presence that changed and determined his life. His new life began with an actual, unique historical experience that changed the way he interpreted the world.

Dante saw Beatrice only one more time—nine years later walking near the Ponte Vecchio when they were both eighteen. She soon married but died at the age of twenty-four—within a few days of Dante's twenty-fifth birthday, June 8, 1290. Meanwhile, Dante had married Gemma Donati, by whom he had four children. His wife is never mentioned in his writings, and he never saw her again after he was exiled. Beatrice, however, was always with him.

We read about Dante's early "falling in love" in his first work, *La Vita Nuova* (1292–94). It was written when he was about twenty-eight, after Beatrice was dead. The memory of her had begun to fade. Ambition—the desire to "get on"—made him forgetful. There were, after all, other women. Maybe Beatrice wasn't the *one*. He knew that something profound was going on inside him and that it had been occasioned by his encounter with the real woman Beatrice, but this flesh-and-blood person was also related to "someone" inside him who knew him better than he knew himself. But what could it mean? What was the relationship between his vocation to be a poet and his attraction to the Creator through a creature? What was the relationship between his literary and mystical agendas? What was the relationship between the storytelling and the real world, between the map and the actual terrain? How are words related to truth? How is longing made bearable and even glorious through storytelling? He knew that *praise* was the inner vocation of poetry. Poets praised heroes, athletes, statesmen, ladies, and the homeland and enabled them to be *remembered*. Poets are the keepers of memory. They guard the stories of human experience. Dante also sensed that, not only are our lives capable of being *told as* a story, but, more profoundly, our lives *are* a story. This is no mere literary discovery. It is spiritual because if we are a story, then the meaning of our lives is discovered in terms of their end and not their beginning. The past can be retold because we are defined in terms of our future rather than our past. Our stories do come to an end—like time itself—but their end is God who has no ending. The task of poetry is to allow the transcendent to shine through the particular, to become the means by which we catch a glimpse of and experience something of the End right now. The experience has various names—joy, bliss, beauty.

For Dante, true beauty is always *embodied* and is naturally attractive. It is adorable. It can be appreciated only through the senses. That is why his inspiration has to be a real person of flesh and blood. Saint Thomas Aquinas wrote that there are three conditions of beauty: *integritas, consonantia,* and *claritas*—integrity, harmony, and radiance.[6] Integrity is the perfection of actual beings. Harmony signifies the way all the parts fit together. Radiance suggests an intelligent luminosity. Dante's language about Beatrice (and heaven) is full of light. She radiates the healing beauty of the divine. When we enjoy something or someone beautiful in this sense, our longing and aching hearts can be at rest. According to Thomas Aquinas, what the beautiful brings to rest is the restless commotion of our appetites.[7] They are not only pleased but placated by beauty's light. Dante takes our desires and attachments so seriously that he understands our passions as palpable signs of God's presence. Beatrice was, for him, a revelation of the divine.

THE POEM AS REVELATION

Although each generation has to make its own way, we are not without resources. Our stories, cautionary tales, and myths are often about being lost (perdition), trials and tests of character (purgation), and homecoming (heaven). Dante's *Divine Comedy*, in following this classic threefold pattern, is part of a long tradition of a visionary voyage through the worlds of pain and bliss. We all have our own peculiar version of life's story with heroes and heroines; we even have a large role reserved for ourselves! We need to be clear that each of us is a suitable candidate for such a voyage. All traces of false modesty should be shed, because to be human is to be a pilgrim who is to be taken seriously because he or she is deeply loved and longed for. We need not worry about becoming inflated. There will be plenty of fellow pilgrims to act as deflators, and there will be many opportunities to fall flat on our faces. The basic erotic myth of desire binds us all together. If our desires are to be educated and we are to survive as a people, we will need to recover the symbolic life in which our longings are truly acknowledged and given place. No one can live for long without symbols of binding and holding.

In an age peculiarly anxious and unsure of itself, Dante's poem deals with themes of self-betrayal and self-destructiveness in such a way that we are not left in despair. The symbols of binding and holding come alive once more. On the one hand, the *Commedia* is relentlessly unsentimental; on the other, it is powerfully healing precisely because of its terrible truth telling. There are themes of hope that need resurrecting for our time: not least, themes concerning the nature of love. Dante rescues our romanticism from the merely private and makes it a grand gesture of mutuality. Romantic love ceases to be a slushy celebration of the projection of two trapped egos and becomes the affirmation of a love holding all things together in freedom. Dante called this the Love of the Holy and Undivided Trinity, which, for him, is the model of a community of love that binds us together, yet respects and enjoys our differences. We are invited into this community as free citizens. We were made for communion. This is the poem's revelation.

It should be clear by now that Dante's vision of the soul's journey is not merely an individualistic (that is, private) journey but a communal one as well. The fate of the planet will depend on those who are willing to undertake the inner work of transformation. Dante's "story" is inclusive yet personal, biting yet compassionate, visionary yet nontotalitarian. We are not sucked into an all-embracing explanation of everything. We are left to wonder. The story is incomplete. Above all, what makes him a suitable guide for us is his understanding of human frailty and his appreciation of human error. Winston Churchill supposedly said, "People will always do the right thing after they have exhausted all possible alternatives!" The spiritually mature know the importance of dead ends and the vitality hidden in personal failure.

Dante's style is sublime—it speaks to our highest aspirations—and it is also grounded and "vulgar"—it speaks to common human experiences and passions. His genius lies in the fact that although he was a brilliant diagnostician of the human condition (which would incline anyone toward pessimism), he was a man of hope.

The poem has been described as a celebration of our moving "from the hell of attachment to the heaven of consciousness."[8] That suggests a journey of heroic proportions—from being stuck in our identification with things and ideas to our being transparent to the divine Love and, therefore, fully alive. When we confuse our ideas and impressions with reality, there is hell to pay. In Jungian terms, we are to withdraw the projections, pull back from our narrow interpretation of the world, and work with the dark energy of our personality—the shadow. Jung wrote to E. L. Grant Watson, "Please don't mix me up with your unconscious, which projects itself into everything obscure and unreasonable. We must discover what belongs to oneself and what is objectively universal. If you don't discriminate enough I am on the best way to becoming a real Museum of Metaphysical Monsters." Jung realized that we are far from skilled at being able to discriminate in this way: "There are very few beings yet capable of making a difference between mental image and the thing itself. This primitivity is poisoning our human world and is so dense a mist that very few people have discovered its existence yet."[9] The journey is bound to include the largely undiscovered and unacknowledged territory of primordial violence infecting our world.

THE THREEFOLD PATTERN

Dante saw order and pattern everywhere, even as he acknowledged chaos and disorder. He took delight in numbers, especially the number three. Three is the celebration of love. Love requires not only the coming together of two in mutual attraction but also the promise of a third without which the lovers would only feed on each other. There is a threefold pattern in *The Divine Comedy:* three books in verse made up of stanzas of three lines each—the *terza rima*. Each book has thirty-three cantos. The three books together come to ninety-nine, making one hundred with the introductory canto. One hundred is ten times ten, the number of perfection. The Inferno is divided into nine narrowing circles where the damned are grouped under three capital vices (incontinence, violence, and fraud). Each of the three books ends with the word *stelle*—stars. The ultimate "threeness," of course, is that of the Holy and Undivided Trinity.

We find a long threefold tradition of separation, initiation, and return in the Old Testament: the threefold movement from Egypt into the wilderness and into the promised land—the Sinai myth. Egypt was the place of slavery, of unfreedom—hell. The wilderness of Sinai was the place of formation and renewal where the rabble that left Egypt were made into a people—purgatory. Heaven was glimpsed in the promised land of Canaan. In the Judeo-Christian tradition, the story begins in the Garden of Eden, the earthly paradise from which humanity is banished, and ends in the city of Jerusalem, the community into which all humanity is invited.

There are two visions of paradise: one of our origins, the other of our destination; a glimpse of our beginning and our end. Our life's pilgrimage is to move between the two. That is why the theme of the Exodus and Exile is so central to the journey of the soul. In the Middle Ages the journey was simply called the *Way.* By definition, a human being was *homo viator,* a voyager. Men and women were adventurers, people on a journey. Each hoped eventually to be *homo comprehensor:* the one who has arrived at the point where all desires are known and fulfilled. Heaven.

The number three, then, is primary. Stories (just like our lives) have a threefold shape of a beginning, a middle, and an end. It is the number of love. It is the number of art. The mind loves the three patterns that shape journeys and pilgrimages: the straight line, the spiral, and the circle. In all three we find both movement and stillness. We sometimes move in a straight line; at other times our progress is in the form of a spiral. Often, we go round in circles until (if ever) a particular lesson is learned.

Thus, for Dante, the soul's journey is circular, or better, spiral. We repeat things but at different levels. There are three spirals: hell, purgatory, heaven—three labyrinths of desire through which the soul must move. In Dante's time it was thought that the straight line, the spiral, and the circle were the three motions of the soul. The circle in its benign form represents the contemplative desire to be united with God, the Lovely and the Good. In its malignant form, it represents the hell of endless repetition—the vicious circle. Hell is a funnel, a descending and narrowing circle in which souls are fixed forever in the consequences of their false choices. Purgatory is a mountain up which the soul can slowly move out of the cold and rigid world of mistaken desires. Heaven is a great white rose where every soul has a place in perfect freedom.

Dante and his contemporaries did not separate the inner world from the outer as we tend to do. For them, the two were part of one inseparable reality. The microcosm and the macrocosm reflected each other. For example, theologians studied the properties of light not only for scientific but also for spiritual reasons. If you knew how light worked in the physical world, you could begin to understand it as a principle of your own inner life. Fire, flame, and light are primary images in the *Comedy* and are encountered as Dante makes a spiral motion toward his goal. While it is difficult to discern much of a pattern or an ordering of things in contemporary life, there are signs of our recovering this old holistic vision of unifying and revealing light.

Dante finds that he needs three guides through the labyrinthine intricacies of his soul, with its chaotic and disordered longings. His first guide is the Roman poet Virgil, whom he admired because of the former's tale of exile, wandering, and new birth—the *Aeneid*. Virgil represents reason, not in the modern sense of rationality, but as the ability to discriminate. Hell is for those who have lost "the good of intellect," the ability to tell one thing from another. For Dante, the intellect is the faculty of integration and intuition. Love cannot do without the intellect. Traditionally, love is blind but can move, and reason can see but cannot walk. Reason has to sit on the shoulders of love and give direction. One has the eyes to see the path ahead; the other has the legs to bring the soul to its destination.

Dante's second guide is his first love, Beatrice, who, while being a person of flesh and blood, represents revelation—a sign of the Creator's longing for us that no amount of reasoning could uncover. We find his third guide in Heaven—Saint Bernard of Clairvaux, the theologian of love, who shows Dante the longing that holds everything together.

This literary device may sound remote and old-fashioned to us. The point is that we are not alone in our journeying, although some aspects of what we are called to do may well be solitary. There are guides and companions all around us, if only we can recognize them. Dante assumes that we need discipline and training in the art of being truly human. Being human is like learning a craft. It is a kind of apprenticeship involving teachers and guides. Apprenticeship requires both submission to authority and a sense of continuity. Contemporary culture has little appreciation of either.

Life is all one journey with and into the heart of love. But our desiring, hungering hearts get off track and need, from time to time, to be redirected. The education of desire begins with the healing of the imagination by grounding it in tradition, that is, by placing it in the context of a story. Tradition has, of course, a bad reputation as something fixed and rigid. In fact, it is alive and supple, capable of passing on life, just like a good story.

Tradition is important in our search for pattern. Tradition addresses issues of scale and perspective. One theory of the universe, for example, insists that it has to be as vast as it is to allow for the evolution of human intelligence. There is no way we can live in the world without traditions. In fact, living traditions make the world possible. Without them there would be no world at all. A lively tradition is the prerequisite for the healthy life of a disciplined and focused imagination. What has happened to the life of the imagination today? For many people, it has become a means of an anesthetizing escape from the very inner life we long to embrace and explore: virtual reality as an alternative and antidote to the real thing.

We need to ask apocalyptic questions that will deanesthetize us. Where are we stuck? Where can we move? Where do we feel at home? These are the questions of hell, purgatory, and heaven. The life of the imagination is important because that is where our characters are forged. The philosophical maxim is: Consciousness precedes being; that is, what you *see* is what you get. Our imaginations (what we are awake to) shape our experience and place us in one or another of the three realms. Novelists write their stories, in part, to work their way through the hells, purgatories, and heavens of their imaginations. Great ones, like Charles Dickens, Leo Tolstoy, and George Eliot, show us the power of fiction to provide images of the soul's journey. They, like most of us, were often haunted by their past. What are we to do with the past? As we get older, there is more of it to regret. It cannot be undone, but it can be retold and reinterpreted. Peter Ackroyd suggests that Dickens could sometimes be "found wandering desolately inside one of his own fictions."[10] How can our past be reinterpreted, redeemed, healed? The only way out is down. We must go back to recover what was lost.

THE EDUCATION OF DESIRE

The defining metaphor of the *Comedy* is love—the deep longings of the human heart. The issue of *desire* is peculiarly applicable to a society whose longings are in disarray and are now well identified as crippling addictions of a deadly and mendacious eroticization. Dante's message is that our desires need educating and that they are best educated by a godly (that is, theological) and intelligent (that is, philosophical) vision of love. The poem begins with the famous words:

NEL MEZZO DEL CAMMIN DI NOSTRA VITA
MI RITROVAI PER UNA SELVA OSCURA,
CHE LA DIRITTA VIA ERA SMARRITA

> In the middle of our life's way
> I found myself in a dark wood
> Where the right way was lost.

Dante insists that it is our (*nostra*) life he's talking about, not just his. We are all brought to face the bankruptcy of our desires. We are often puzzled to discover that we are not happy, even when (especially when?) everything seems to be in place. It is frightening and sobering to find oneself caught in the sin and mess we have willingly if unwittingly chosen—in a pattern that began, perhaps, years ago. I once saw a message scrawled on a New York City subway station: "Sex—a blast from the past." The disordered desires acted on in the past can still send us reeling in the present. If the past cannot be undone, why bother to have a change of heart in the present?

The issue for the spiritual pilgrim is not only to have what he or she wants, but also to know what it is that is *worthy* of desire. Desire, then, is a problem. We are not clear about what we really want, yet we are not happy if we do not have what we want. But to have what we *think* we want doesn't necessarily make us happy. I used to think that my devouring longings would come to an end if I reached certain goals or possessed objects of desire. I have the objects in hand and the goals have been reached, but the longings do not go away and I have been left holding nothing but ashes.

My attraction to Dante had to do with his acknowledging that desire never comes to an end, except in God who has no end. After years of moving through life half-asleep, Dante becomes once again conscious of himself. His life slaps him in the face, demanding his attention and presenting him with a parody of his desires. He spirals into the depths of hell on that secret path of resentment that leads first to hatred of others and then to hatred of oneself. The lover of self is pitched against others fully occupied with loving their own selves. Exhausted, the soul finally turns in against itself. At the center of hell is Satan, once so beautiful and now the threefold parody of God, frozen in the ice of impotent desire.

To be human is to possess a heart not at home with itself. Many of us feel that we have lost or mislaid something, but we don't know what it is. I see that vague and undefined desire in the eyes of the people I encounter every day and in the hearts of those who come to me for counsel. All of us look outside ourselves for causes of our distress. We cling to the role of victim because finding a cause inside ourselves would be unbearable. We find ourselves in hell *now*, not always because of something specific. Often it is because of something we cannot put a name to. Hell is the constricting funnel where we *choose* to be frozen in misery, just as purgatory is the liberating mountain where we *choose* the possibility of freedom and conversion, and just as heaven is the place where we *choose* to enjoy God's love. Most of the time, I believe, we are in purgatory—the place of movement and conversion. This doesn't mean that hell isn't the dominant reality for some or that others may not have more than a mere glimpse at paradise. But most of us most of the time are in the middle realm between heaven and hell.

The context of the poem, as we have seen, is the *Triduum* (the three great days of Good Friday, Holy Saturday, and the Day of Resurrection). These days correspond in some sense to the three realms through which Dante journeys. Most of us most of the time find ourselves in the second realm (of purgation)—the Saturday of the soul's waiting. This is where George Steiner locates us: "*But ours is the long day's journey of the Saturday. Between suffering, aloneness, unutterable waste on the one hand and the dream of liberation, of rebirth on the other.*"[11] Dante reaches the pit of Hell on Saturday evening, and, because time goes back twelve hours, he spends the rest of the day climbing down through the center of the earth until he reaches the foot of the mountain of Purgation where he can move and breathe and live in hope. This is our journey too. The secret is: the way up is the way down. It is now time for us to go down.

PART ONE

HELL

IMAGINE THAT WE ARE IN THE YEAR 1300 AND IT IS MAUNDY THURSDAY, the night of April 7. Tomorrow is Good Friday. We are the companions of the poet Dante, who is thirty-five years old (at the midpoint of his life). We are lost and find ourselves in the middle of a dark wood. We can see a path out by way of a mountain lit by the early morning sun, but a lion, a leopard, and a wolf bar our way and force us to go deeper into the wood to the entrance of a great funnel-shaped cavern—the wide part at the top and the narrow part far out of sight. We learn that the beasts represent the ways in which human beings lose their way, seduced by self-indulgence (narcissism), arrogance (inflation), and greed (which is a kind of rage).

We are terrified and feel helpless, but assistance, both human and divine, is at hand. The Roman poet Virgil—the author of the adventures of Aeneas (who also visited the underworld)—has been sent by Dante's first love, Beatrice, to help us find our way out of the narrowing funnel of Hell. Virgil is Dante's inspiration, a poet's poet. Virgil tells him that there is a way out but only by going through the depths of Hell and out the other side. From him we learn the first rule of the soul's journey: the way up is the way down. It will take twelve hours for us to go through the circles of Hell to make our escape. Dante is encouraged by thinking about two other adventurers of the Spirit: Aeneas and Saint Paul. Both of them claimed to have been given a glimpse of paradise. They represent two aspects of human life that Dante knows to be necessary to human flourishing: a stable and just human community (the empire) and an openness to communion with God (the church). We are not isolated individuals but social beings with temporal and spiritual needs. We need institutions to bind us together. We need companions on the soul's journey.

Fortunately for us, Dante is well-connected. Mary, the Mother of God, has taken pity on him by calling Saint Lucia who, in turn, has summoned Beatrice to help him. But Beatrice will appear only when Dante is ready, only when the distortions of his disordered longings have been healed by the discipline of the mountain and he can see clearly.

We first find ourselves in the vestibule of Hell, which is reserved for the indifferent who are stuck forever in their indecision and apathy. They are the lukewarm, those who in life were not one thing or the other. They were neither hot nor cold. They are not welcome even in Hell. Since they couldn't or wouldn't take sides, their punishment fits their state. Some rush about after a banner. The lazy are tormented by flies and wasps. We follow Virgil and Dante through the vestibule and come to the river Acheron. On its bank are the lost souls waiting to be ferried across into Hell proper. Once on the other side, we see the daunting inscription over Hell's gate: *Lasciate ogne speranza, voi ch'intrate* (Abandon all hope, ye who enter). But the gate is broken and permanently open after Christ rose from the dead and harried Hell (he scared the hell out of Hell).

The funnel of Hell is divided into three great areas of human error: incontinence, violence, and fraud. Incontinence describes human beings out of control—beside themselves—with longing and desire. There are the lustful, those lost in sexual desire; and the gluttonous, those with misdirected appetites and addictions. As we go deeper into Hell, hope to satisfy the longings of the body gives way to a different kind of consumption: the hoarding and the squandering of money. So we follow the two pilgrims down the first circle of Hell and into its ever-narrowing depths.

The second circle punishes the "warm sins" of sexual passion. Dante is sympathetic to those whose love gets out of hand and devours them. Dante knows how easily his pride and passion have brought him into hell. He shows his compassion especially when he hears the story of the lovers Paolo and Francesca, who were murdered by her husband, Paolo's brother, because of their illicit love. Their punishment fits their crime. They are doomed to drift together forever in a close embrace, caught in their futile longing for each other—a parody of passion.

The third terrace is for the gluttonous—those who stuffed themselves with this world's goods. It is full of slime and filth. Gluttony, when stripped of its glamour, is seen for what it is. The inhabitants of this circle become less and less recognizable as human beings. Greed of this kind makes us lose any sense of discrimination. We gorge ourselves and yet are always hungry. The consumer is consumed by his own consumption. We learn that hell is a downward regression. We move from the inordinate love of others to the disordered love of things that money can buy. We regress to the love of money for its own sake.

When it comes to money, Dante follows the ancient view that miserliness and wild spending are two sides of the same sin. People, either way, are possessed by their possessions. Love of money is a kind of lust, and the money lovers form the biggest crowd in Hell. The sign of avarice is the clenched fist. It is the worst sin of the incontinent and the besetting sin of the clergy. The pursuit and hoarding of wealth set us against one another and weaken the bonds of community. We can't see straight. In fact, imagining we own anything is a form of self-deception. God is the one who has the power to dispose of the world's goods. In this fourth circle of Hell Dante finds it hard to tell one person from another. The deeper we move into hell, the less we are truly ourselves. Individuality is beginning to be lost.

The third section of Hell is for the fraudulent, those who misuse language to mislead and deceive others—troublemakers, malicious gossips, liars, and traitors. The seventh circle is reserved for those beside themselves with rage. Their anger is directed not only at others but also at themselves and God. This suits Satan's purpose because the devil is the great divider. Sin has its own terrible logic of separation. Its reward is the hell of a terrible loneliness. Dante discovers, in this seventh circle with its three rings, the open rage of blind fury and the bubbling anger of the resentful and the vindictive. Here we find the worst of the sins of the flesh—"the sluggish, persistent bitterness of the souls which are so mastered by their resentments that they refuse the light of the sun, the goodness of God."[1] There is so much wasted, so much squandered of the glory of human life that we are understandably terrified.

We follow Dante and Virgil as they move from meeting those who commit sinful acts to those who have evil dispositions. Malice in the lower inferno is an indelible characteristic. Wickedness becomes a dark mystery from which we need rescue. What can we do when, in the end, our deceiving of others gives way to our deceiving ourselves? Dante's image of deceit or fraud is Geryon—a monster with an upright body and human face and the tail of a scorpion. He encounters ten types of fraudulent souls, ranging from those who betrayed women (either by procuring them for others or by seducing them) to those who used their position in the church for their own personal gain. The latter are called simonists after Simon Magus (Acts 8:9–24), who tried to buy the power of the Holy Spirit from the spirit-filled apostles. The simonists tried to buy and sell what is a sheer gift—the Holy Spirit received at baptism. They are punished in a parody of baptism by being immersed upside down in burning holes.

As we get deeper into Hell, the distortions of the bodily forms become more pronounced. The con artists and the swindlers are shady characters who are punished under the surface of a ditch filled with boiling pitch. The hypocrites, on the other hand, march in procession wearing cloaks that are gilded on the outside but are actually made of lead. They can barely walk because of the weight. And so we move into that part of the inferno where we find the thieves whose bodies change shape and the evil counselors "who applied their burning eloquence to the concealment of their real mind."[2] Everything is conspiring toward falsehood as we approach the great Father of Lies at the center. At last the pilgrims reach the ninth and narrowest circle—a vast plain of ice in the middle of which is Lucifer surrounded by his court. The proud and the envious are fixed in ice, impotent for eternity. The deepest part of Hell is reserved for the frozen and closed-hearted—the treacherous. Satan, parodying the Holy and Blessed Trinity, has three heads: a red one that loves evil for its own sake, a black one that represents ignorance, and a pale, sallow one that reflects sheer impotence. The three mouths crush three traitors: Judas, who betrayed Christ, and Brutus and Cassius, who betrayed Caesar. The church and the empire, the two things that hold life together and make human life human, are betrayed and the traitors suffer the everlasting torments of the damned.

We, with Dante, wonder how we will escape. Virgil tells Dante to hang on to him as he grabs onto the hairy loins of the devil and begins the climb downward to the very center of Hell. We make the leap, too, but are confused. This can hardly be the way out. But when we pass the center of the earth, "down," of course, becomes "up" as we make our way to the opposite pole. To our amazement, the downward path turns into the way up out of Hell. And so we find ourselves on the other side at the foot of the mountain of Purgation where the air is breathable and there's enough light to find our way.

THREE

FINDING ONESELF IN HELL: THE LOSS OF THE SENSE OF SELF

Being human is not a private trip. We need one another in order to be fully alive. I cannot live outside of society and, over the years, I have found my soul broken in pieces and stuck back together with the glue left by the confrontation between my private longings and public expectations. The rules for public life keep changing and my own desires seem to have no foundations. We are caught in the cross fire of conflicting reports about what is acceptable and what it not. I have never been a smoker, but I grew up in a world where smoking in public was not only acceptable but even considered chic. In movies up to a few years ago, people smoked a lot. In California, where I live, smokers are made to feel as if they are moral cripples. The narrative about what is acceptable no longer contains stories of people who smoke. Nor is this the only area in which the ethical climate (or fashion) has changed. Only the very brazen would wear animal skins in some circles, and most of us are nervous about the delicate and treacherous choreography of sexual relations. What new rule might we be breaking? What recently identified line might we have crossed?

Human beings are animals whose defining characteristic is the freedom to choose, and Dante's poem is "the drama of the soul's choice."[1] Dante lived in an intellectual and spiritual world that emphasized the disciplined life of the will and its struggle to choose the good and refuse the evil. He believed that we are able to choose rightly because the universe is intelligible. Because we are made in the image of God, we are illumined by the light of the divine intelligence.

Of all the places in hell, the vestibule itself is one of the worst. Here we see the anguish of the opportunists—the fence-sitters, the "well-adjusted," those who refused to choose. The question the vestibule of hell poses is, Do you see the human condition as essentially both romantic and tragic—

fraught with significance and challenged all the time by the drama of choice? Great literature affirms the tragic view that life is a struggle. In Dante, Sophocles, Shakespeare, there is no sentimental or superficial idea of human perfection. We mess up and we mess up royally.

Hell is reserved for those who have lost or turned away from the light that makes the universe intelligible. Those who find themselves in the inferno can neither see straight nor feel with any integrity. For Dante, the coming of Christ was precisely to heal this terrible double wound to our intelligence and emotions, to our minds and hearts. Sin blinds us with regard to our true nature and hampers us in all our actions. Christ became one of us and, consequently, in our flesh enters the depths of human experience—including its hells and purgatories. Hell has to exist if human beings are to be truly free. Human freedom requires the possibility of damnation because we must be free to turn our backs even on what truly gives us life. We must be allowed to go to hell.

At first sight, the plan of the *Comedy* seems excruciatingly boring and too well ordered for an age suspicious of hierarchy. Hell is made up of three sets of ever-narrowing concentric rings—each much like the others. Dante and Virgil have to go down and around every one of the forty-four rings and encounter the damned in their torment. Purgatory consists of ten more circles around a mountain up which the pilgrims must toil and meet more souls moving through various forms of pain and suffering. Heaven, too, is made up of ten rings where people are—at last—enjoying some form of bliss. Yet Dante is such a superb storyteller that he is able to take this unattractive scheme and make of it a banquet for the imagination—delighting and terrifying at the same time. The feast of the poem will not be pleasing to everyone's palate because it requires people willing to be educated in tasting things they thought were completely outside their experience. How did I acquire my taste for red wine, let alone unsweetened dark-roast coffee? Our imaginations need as much education as our taste buds. Dante requires his dinner guests to be open to new experiences and to be ready for an exercise in disciplined attention. Like the stories of the Bible, Dante's visions are not all readily accessible. The poem needs to be read, marked, and inwardly digested—often in small doses. This is very demanding in an age unaccustomed to paying attention to texts and entering into conversation with them as a means of understanding our longings and dissatisfactions.

Dante's intellectual world collided with his experience of the outer world of politics and social life. His world was a frightening and wretched place. People died suddenly and violently. In the prevailing worldview, life was cheap and religion was characterized by the spirit of *contemptus mundi:* contempt for the world. Dante brought hope to his world by inviting it to reimagine itself. He brought order out of chaos and helped heal the wounded imaginations of his contemporaries. There's a story that illustrates the terrified state of the popular imagination. The spirit of a holy monk appeared to a bishop in a dream. The monk, who had died at the same time as Bernard of Clairvaux, told the bishop that of the thirty thousand souls who had died in that short period, only he and Saint Bernard had made it to heaven, three had gone to purgatory, and the rest were in hell, in "everlasting torture."[2] It was this imagination that Dante transformed. In the light of this we may ask, What about our own day and the images in which we are imprisoned? What informs and deforms our imagination? Our world, too, is a terrible place for millions of people. What will it take to reimagine Bosnia and Rwanda in the decades ahead?

There's an old map of Dorset and Devon, printed about 1740, that shows the county town of Exeter but doesn't name it that. Exeter is called Exoriensis or Isca Dumnoniorum. Some of our spiritual maps are like that. The places are there but the names are different. If we're using an old map, we shouldn't be surprised that people are confused when we ask directions. A local inhabitant of Devon might say, "If you wanted to go to Exeter, why didn't you say so in the first place?" If the maps we are using are confusing, perhaps we should think about getting a new one.[3]

Much of religious language is like that found on an old map. The places are still there, but we call them all by different names. Idolatry is now called addiction. Sin is called neurosis or pathology. Salvation is called liberation or individuation. Dante's "map" would have named what we call mechanisms for rationalizing our neuroses and pathologies "dispositions to sin." But the reality is largely the same.

Dante's is but one map of the inner journey, and he gives names to certain places that will seem strange to those who are ignorant of or who react against the Catholic Christian tradition. Readers have to be their own translators. If the word *sin* is off-putting, try *brokenness* or *alienation*. If the words *church* and *empire* drive you crazy, find other words that speak of community and communion. If you are from a religious tradition other than Christianity, translate. Perhaps the hardest idea for us to translate is the affirmation that life has meaning and that each of us is desirable.

It is difficult to claim that life makes sense without sounding sentimental or stupid. Yet not to do so is to give in to cynicism and despair. It is dangerous to look for pattern and order when one is in desperate straits. Meaning can be a kind of spiritual mirage in the desert. Perhaps that's why I have always found, with regard to meaning and purpose, that maps in novels and poetry are more helpful and accurate than those in creeds and dogmas. People are often too tied to results and goals. They mistake the maps for the journey itself. Hope is a disposition of the heart, not a commitment to a certain outcome. Hope is no guarantee that things will turn out well but a conviction that pattern and purpose prevail no matter what the outcome.

Hell, then, is the map of the terrible loss of choice. To understand Dante's hell, however, one has to have some idea of his heaven. It is against the vision of heaven that all our choices are judged. Dante believed that the will of God cannot be irrational and can, therefore, be trusted. There is a purpose to life and it is good. Our life's journey, therefore, is a moral one. The soul is destined to shine with integrity and wholeness. We are to ask ourselves, Does what I am about to do lead toward or away from integration and harmony? Dante also believed that the heart has to surrender itself in love. There has to be a sense of "abandon"—a lack of anxiety and the risk of letting be. Our experiences of betrayal and exile teach us that providence (the inner meaning of things) works in a mysterious way with flexibility of purpose and not with the rigid following of a predetermined plan.

Being stuck in hell and journeying through it are not the same thing. The soul moving through hell needs a sustaining vision to prevent its getting stuck—a faith vision of integration and harmony. The soul needs a spiritual discipline that unifies, balances, and simplifies, that lets be. The soul armed with such gifts can dare make the journey downward. Is Dante's vision of integration and harmony possible for us today?

Aren't we creatures who "naturally" desire autonomy to the point of screaming isolation? We in the West are, after all, part of a history that beheaded kings and threw off authoritarian forms of religion and politics so that we could be free of constraints. But do we have to be a law unto ourselves in order to be free? Perhaps that's why hell is more interesting than heaven. It gives the illusion of autonomy. It's the place with which we are most familiar. Perhaps one person's heaven would be another's hell. According to our guide, Dante, hell is the place of the isolated and unrelated self. Have we wandered so far that for some of our contemporaries this would be a description of heaven? From Dante's perspective, there is no such thing as the sovereign individual. Freedom is found in surrender to the One whose service is perfect freedom.[4]

We have to "go to hell" because of a false diagnosis about who we essentially are. Our society has got it wrong about what it takes to be human. Why don't we belong to ourselves? Why aren't we self-sufficient? Because we are essentially relational beings. We have no real substance on our own. There is no private soul. We are the products of church and state, religion and government, spiritualities and sociologies. We are who we are—to some extent—because our parents were who they were. So we are in a bind. How far are we truly free? How far are we determined by external realities? How are we bound by the past? What hope is there for rebinding in a new way?

Religion is that which binds and rebinds things together into a coherent whole. It comes from the same root as the word *ligament*. Religion is about binding the strands of life together into one volume.[5] There are other related words like *obligation* and *negligence*. In our negligence we failed to see how the world is bound together by love and justice. Hell is the reward of our negligence. We look back and can remember those occasions when we missed the point or were ignorant of the significance of an event or relationship. We failed to see God working in our lives. We lost sight of our obligations. Our memories and regrets provide occasions for a new orientation in the present. Our scattered lives are thus collected together and rebound by the love of God. Nothing is wasted, and hell is the place where the repressed must be remembered and acknowledged if there is to be a true rebinding. Who we are is revealed in the ligaments of story. Thus hell is facing the consequences of our negligence, and purgatory is finding opportunities for rebinding.

What was liberating for Dante was that the past, while it cannot be altered, is not fixed with regard to its significance. Its meaning can change as the story unfolds. "Ah, that's why I behaved in that way. It was wrong, I see that now. I am no longer held hostage by the past. I am free to change." The story isn't over yet. It is always unfolding. The past is always being reinterpreted.

Going to hell is a way of testing the boundaries of our freedom and dis-covering what it is to be truly free. We want to see how far we can go in one direction or another. It is our way of trying to reach rock bottom in both senses of the term: on the one hand, to find bedrock—a place on which to stand; and, on the other, to come to the end of our rope in an encounter with the unspeakable. Perhaps hell in one aspect represents our attraction to and repulsion of the primitive—the formless and the chaotic. In this re-spect it is like the sacred. We have a nostalgia for the primitive because, in one aspect, it represents a simple and uncomplicated life—like Tarzan and Jane living with and like the animals. We like to think that there could be, somewhere on earth, a tribe of "noble savages" unspoiled by the corrup-tions of civilization. But there's another side to the primitive. It can also mean violence, savagery, and horror. Perhaps that's why we're fascinated by it. It attracts and repels at the same time. We see in it the promise of free-dom. We back away when we catch sight of the violence beneath the sur-face. Hell has the fascination of the primitive, and we all need to go there to be cured of its attractiveness and find out the meaning of our longing.

As the soul moves downward into its weakness, it realizes that it has lost a vital connection within itself that affects all its relationships. Hell is the revelation of that loss. The dark mystery of human freedom is that God allows us to construct unrealities as if they were real. Virtual reality is no news to the soul. It has known about it for centuries. Hell is a sign of a double failure of love and intelligence to tell the difference between the real and the spurious, and we are condemned to live in the unreal world we have constructed for ourselves. Even love is deceptive because love places us in a position of peculiar vulnerability that can enslave us in a relationship of immature dependency, lock us up inside ourselves, and distort our view of the world. And when the intellect (the faculty of discrimination) sleeps, monsters run wild. We are haunted by our past and plagued with regret in a tribunal of the present that judges us as worthy of damnation.

Hell, while being the place for those who have lost or abandoned the power to discriminate, has a special place for those who are overly intellec-tual—those who are besotted by their own cleverness, in love with their own ideas. Dante knew this temptation firsthand. He placed his old teacher, Brunetto Latini (who taught him how to win eternal fame through writing poetry), in Hell—in the circle of sexual perversion—signifying symbolically those who use language to unfruitful ends, those who are intoxicated with words rather than with meanings. Ostensibly, Brunetto is in hell for the sin of sodomy (*Inferno* 15), which can be interpreted as a metaphor for the unnatural act of indulging in sterile actions that have no real creative outcome.[6] The sins of those who fall in love with language are those of a promiscuous but uncreative imagination. They have been my sins, too. A wise friend and priest once prayed over me this prayer: "O, Holy Spirit, descend on Alan and help him tell the difference between what is essential and what is merely interesting!" When ideas are pursued without discrimination and discretion, they become dangerous. They are turned into a kind of lying. When everything is thrown into the jaws of a devouring and controlling consciousness, clarity and order are lost.

Our tendency is to fall in love with the images themselves and be indifferent to or culpably unaware of the tenuous relationship between metaphor and truth. We blur the distinction between our representations of reality and the reality itself. When my oldest daughter was in eighth grade, she bought herself a T-shirt bearing the legend "Sex, Drugs, and Rock and Roll!" I wasn't pleased. She pointed out that (*a*) she'd bought it with her own money and (*b*) they were only words. That's when I blew up. *They were only words!* We had a long family discussion about words and their meanings. Could we ever say words were only words? To me it was like saying something was *only* significant. I felt uneasy, too, because I tend to prefer the *sound* of some words over their meanings (I like the Spanish for garbage—*basura*—and the French for twilight—*crépuscule*). The joke in the family was that the words I really objected to were *rock and roll!* I reimbursed my daughter for the shirt and put it in the bottom of a drawer. I wonder what happened to it. The conversation still goes on in the family. What is the status of words? Words count for something. That's why I find the justification for the offensive words of rap (that they merely reflect the situation on the street) sleazy. Words mean something. That is why I resist an interpretation of life using only the words of psychotherapy or science. Such words narrow the narrative possibilities of a person's life and render him or her a mere case history in the great file of human error.

Brunetto Latini's sin was his failure to make the distinction between truth and its representations. This failure meant his own confusion and damnation. He is so in love with his words that, even in hell, he mentions one of his own works (his *Tesoretto*). He is so caught up in his own text that he doesn't know where he really is. The beautiful lie has become a damnable one. He is trapped in his mental constructs and blind to his real state. There is a hilarious irony here: on the one hand Dante sees the real fate of his old teacher in hell, and on the other Brunetto Latini is so captivated by the vision of a life transformed by literature that he doesn't know how pathetic his situation is.

What we need is a radical sense of exile—separation, distance—if we are to be saved from the illusion that we are at the center of reality. We need poets of separation, distance, and exile who know that language is a trap. It is not accidental that Dante reserves a special and revolting place in hell for those who misuse language. The flatterers (those who debased language) walk around covered in human excrement, scratching at themselves. The wily Ulysses is a symbol of the seductiveness of words. He is the craftsman of persuasion and, ironically, is enchanted by his own song. He was spellbound by the song of the sirens. He reminds Dante of the easy treachery of his own language and the insecurity of his own journey.[7] The purpose of poetry is to *disenchant:* to break us of linguistic bad habits. It is a difficult art because it uses language but always with an awareness that a wedge often separates language from the truth. We must never lose sight of the discrepancy between actual and imagined life. That is the peculiar sin of intellectuals who are in love with ideas, concepts, and constructs. Intellectuals are, more often than not, in love with their own ideas and damned by their own cleverness. Dante's arrogance because of his superior intelligence was tempered by exile. He suffered the humiliation of banishment. He was saved from illusion by the pain of his being turned out of hearth and home. This was a lesson only the experience of exile could teach him.

We easily are imprisoned by our own images—by our little picture of the world. I notice, for example, that some people are more alive in their journals than in their actual lives. The rich material of their interior life gets trapped between the pages of a book. Like Brunetto, we confuse our own reality and the images of a text, particularly when the text or script is our own lives. Then something wakes us up and we wonder where we are. It's as if the apparently well-built structures we were relying on to shelter us as we got older have collapsed. There is something truly terrifying when someone else has control of the story and we become a mere incident in his or her "growth" or an explanation of his or her pain and struggle—

or, worse, an occasion for his or her revenge and vindictiveness. This is a pattern we often find between parents and children.

The world I thought would be waiting for me when I turned fifty simply wasn't there. Am I simply growing older or is MTV really as bad as I think it is? Is my complaint only the perennial one of those moving into the second half of life, or is the world falling apart in a sense that it never has before?

Can anything be done to help us "feel good about ourselves"? One way is to feed the addictions that mask our self-hate and to sustain the illusions that enable us to justify our self-seeking. But can someone who despises herself really love her neighbor? Can a man who cannot stand himself bear to be with others? Doesn't self-hate lead to hatred of others? Doesn't the fear of not getting enough make one greedy and suspicious? Don't hatred, suspicion, and resentment lead to the loss of the self? We talk of people being beside themselves with hurt or rage. People can also so lose touch with themselves that they are virtually unreachable.

To those who are bent on "feeling good" without giving up their illusions, Dante's diagnosis of and cure for our ills will seem draconian. His vision of hell shows that the human will is so atrophied by addiction that the soul is stuck forever with the consequences of its false choices. *There is no time.* The clock has stopped. In hell there is no *where* or *when.* There is only the dead time of the passing hours. It is a salutary place of nowhere and nothing. But entry into the infernal regions is described by the author of the fourteenth-century *Cloud of Unknowing* as something that the soul needs to do. We are called to "leave aside this *everywhere* and this *everything,* in exchange for this *nowhere* and this *nothing.*"[8] To come to nothing in nowhere is a profound if harrowing spiritual experience. Its name is hell, but it's a hell that we need. Hope requires time. We, however, tend to see time as the enemy. Time is redeemed by the painful work of memory and the energy of the will pushing us into the future. Hell shows us what life is like without time.

Hell, which is where our obsessions and addictions live, is where both the will and the imagination have ceased to change. There is no time to change. We find it hard even to think about change because we don't know what we really want. The maddening thing about addiction is that it never delivers what it promises. The desire of the addicted person gets lost in hellish obscurity. We don't know what we want but we want it now! Such

frustration points to the fact that we are already familiar with the constricting atmosphere of hell and know some of its damning circles. There is a
slippery slope into addiction. We move from choice to habit to disposition,
until we are possessed by inner compulsion. We confuse our compulsive
state with the whole of reality. We think that nothing can change because
that's "just the way things are." We become trapped in the web of our own
choices and build our world out of the bits and pieces of our wounded
imaginations.

Sometimes the only form of spiritual education is to follow our mistakes
right down to their bitter conclusion. The maxim is: To be conscious is to
be sad. It is the experience of *Zerrissenheit*, which William James translated as "torn-to-pieces-hood": the feeling of being divided and pulled in all
directions.

There are three things we can expect to find out in hell's *Zerrissenheit:*
first, our misery is the consequence of false choices; second, our false
choices make us lose our bearings and further alienate us from the relationships that sustain us; and third, sin is its own reward. There is no punishment in hell as such, only consequences. We are not punished by a
vindictive God but are so loved that we are allowed to live through the consequences of our choices, which, in hell, are resentment (frozen anger—a
sullen lazy smoke in the heart), malice, and hatred.

One of the ways in which my soul is fed is by reading novels. I identify
with the various characters and I am able to follow them into my imagination for a while. They help me experience the world in a new way. Frederick
Buechner's St. Brendan is one such character. He is in an interior hell that I
can understand. "For long days after, I think, Brendan's only voyaging was
away inside himself. Such wonders and Hells as he may have seen there he
never spoke to a soul. . . . He was sailing the seas inside himself. His
prayers was his craft. Rue and shame were the winds that drove him."[9] I
find such descriptions not only suggestive but healing when some inner
and unbidden chaos or pain rises up to consciousness. A wandering memory or a sudden sick feeling in the stomach makes us feel that our life, at its
center, is a catastrophe.

How is it that we get lost—disoriented with regard to our own selves—
and yet come through it and recognize the current that we dare call our
lives? How is it that we find ourselves on the road to some hell or other?
What is it about the lostness of the so-called midlife crisis that captures our

imagination? How is it that there is grace even in hell? The poet Edwin Muir writes about waking up in "a dark wood" of moral confusion where he had lost his way. He was, like Dante, thirty-five years old. The vision of hell (getting one's true bearings) is the first step on the road out of hell. Once Muir had seen how he had wasted his life, the blood began to flow and he found himself alive in a new way. He came to understand that he had to live over again the years that he had lived wrongly. I was particularly struck by his insisting that everyone should live his life twice, for the first attempt is always thrashing around in the dark.[10]

Poets bear witness to the power of the awakened and liberated imagination. What happens when the imagination is truly liberated? One realizes that one is not alone but is part of a deep system of interconnection and possibility. What is humiliating is that when we wake up, we become aware of two things: that we are not as much in control of our lives as we thought, and that we do not belong to ourselves. From the perspective of faith, the coming to such a realization is a sign of spiritual maturity. Whether they know it or not, communities as well as individuals are on spiritual journeys for the enlarging of the heart. To know that is to find oneself in what seems to be a hell of powerlessness. We think the way out of this particular hell is through the kind of knowledge that is power. We are driven by a longing to be in control, but the desire for control cripples the imagination. It is literally damnable when people experience a fissure in their lives in a world divided into those who are staunch individualists, motivated solely by self-interest, and those who see life as a communion with families, spouses, friends, lovers, neighborhoods, cities.

The exiled suffer from wounded desire that gets out of control. Sometimes our perception is deeply divided by a sense of exile and we don't know where to turn for the truth. What is the remedy? Is language, even at its shadowy best, always menaced by duplicity? Is love possible? Is loving someone always a form of interference? Is sexual love, as some extreme feminists would have us believe, always a form of tyranny if not actual rape? Are human sexual relations nothing but a power play? Dante's way through for the exiled heart is to insist on an eschatology (the study of the end of all things) even for metaphors. Meanings do not merge in their fullness until the "end." It is in the silent space at the end, when the struggle to put into words the sense of a text, a life, and a history is over, that meaning begins to emerge. To put it another way, the journey of the soul turns our usual understanding upside down. We are not, after all, defined in terms of our past. We are defined in terms of our future. That is why we can dare enter the dark labyrinth of the self with confidence and hope, guided and protected as we are by Virgil and Beatrice—by reason (the power to discriminate) and by love (the lure that guides us home).

This brings us back to our theme of exile, to the imagery of exodus and desert wandering. Like Abraham and Sarah (who were "as good as dead"), we are called to go out into the wilderness of untried things. Doing so means revisiting questions that once seemed utterly settled. It means realizing over again that one is capable of infidelity and betrayal. It means facing the disturbing truth that one's memory is faulty and even treacherous. It means living with the fact that events may have several meanings and the meanings may contradict one another. We must always be "alert that every garden hides a snake, every definitive answer may be a mirage. One must be a restless nomad like the poet, till the end comes."[11] Dante invites us to enter a free space where exiles and pilgrims can live in hope even while they are in the thick of things.

The road through hell is important because it puts the soul in touch with its awesome weakness, and, en route, we recover lost parts of ourselves that, if left unnoticed, cause havoc in the world. We need to make a ritual of the journey of the soul. Rituals provide the container (the safe space) for the repressed material to be uncovered. It is not accidental that Dante places his journey in the context of the liturgical drama of Holy Week. The story needs to be acted out as well as heard and read.

Aldous Huxley writes of "the partial damnation of everyday life." Even the most fortunate in society experience, on occasion, "a deep-rooted horror of their own selfhood, a passionate yearning to get free of the repulsive little identity to which their very perfection of their 'adjustment to life' has condemned them."[12]

To find our origins, we must travel downward and backward and endure this partial damnation. This going back and down is inevitable. Sigmund Freud went back to the old myths of Oedipus, Hermes, and Pan and exploded the illusion that we can be disinterested observers of our inner selves and of human events. Objectivity is a chimera, and any promise that partiality and prejudice can be avoided is a lie. Hell shows up the futility of our tendency to colonize everything—including ideas—and put them under our control.

We may ask, Doesn't this view of life fit too neatly with the prevailing mood of the times—ambiguity divinized? It may seem naive to point out that Dante believed in God—and not in god-as-an-idea but in God, separate and sovereign, independent of Dante's subjectivity. Belief in God, at the very least, will save us from the illusion of believing in ourselves as monuments to eternity.

We need to learn, as we travel through our own particular Comedy, to say yes and no to the journey at the same time. We say yes to the enlivening images. We say no to their tendency to devour and exhaust the reality they represent. All the figures in the *Comedy* can be understood as representing the cast of characters present in Dante's own soul as well as actual people. I do not think he would have presumed to assign any actual person to hell for all eternity. In fact, in the *Paradiso* he insists on his ignorance. He was able to see himself in others. Perhaps that's why he puts some of his friends in hell as well as his enemies. He focuses on error as the means of hope because he finds that walking the straight path is itself erroneous. It is often (always?) our mistakes that get us going on the spiritual journey. Error is turned into pilgrimage. The errant knight becomes the questing knight.

I find it unnerving that I meet aspects of myself in others. I see my own lostness in the eyes of a man who catches my eye at a busy intersection. Sometimes I hate what I see. On other occasions, I am moved by the sight of a noble aspect of myself—long hidden—that I see reflected in the eyes of another. This may seem rather narcissistic, but I too am a mirror for others. We go through life reflecting back the world to one another. The exchange isn't always simple. Sometimes I see something to admire in someone I would otherwise despise. Occasionally I am dismayed when I catch a glimpse of the despicable in the eyes of someone I love. We have to endure truth and half-truths coming from the mouths of those we do not and cannot admire. How far can we blame people for what they do? How far should we hold them responsible? I see a well-dressed drunk out late one night wandering the streets, perhaps searching for some sexual encounter, for some form of temporary connection. How should I judge him? Are some of us too drunk with pain or power to know or to care where we are? What is it like to think it's too late to worry about consequences? What about my own capacity for evil? How far am I implicated in what is going on in the world? I know I'm not responsible for the carnage in Bosnia, but am I not connected to it in some way?

This is hell. When the drunk sobers up, he has to face his futility and emptiness. He reaches for another drink unless something within him or the intervention of family and friends sets him on the road to recovery. When the sex addict wakes up after a one-night stand, perhaps he admits for a moment that falling in love seems to be a great imaginative act quite beyond him. When our imagination is promiscuous and undisciplined, when there is no overriding principle or pattern, when it has no points of reference, no indicators as to where we might be found on a spiritual map, we can be pretty sure we are in hell. Absurdity and profundity go hand-in-hand. Think of the way profundity of thought and outbursts of childish behavior go together. I have often seen grown men who run successful businesses lapse into petty and infantile actions when they are thwarted or disappointed. Suddenly this sixty-year-old clutching his scotch in one hand and his cigar in the other is back in the nursery.

I am appalled by the way my own struggles can be reduced to my longing for mother—not necessarily my birth mother but a comforting mother figure of my own imaginings. What I find humiliating is having to admit that, somewhere deep down inside me, I still want my mother. There—I've admitted it and played right into the hands of my unbelieving friends, let alone into those of the mocking atheist and skeptical agnostic. But the mother is a dominant figure in everyone's psyche. The primordial desire for comfort has caused me to project all sorts of unreal expectations onto real women. I search for the real or imagined security of my beginnings. One way of withdrawing these damaging projections is to allow them to explode inside the soul and wait for them to run their course—a bit like a fever. Another way is to move from one addiction or idol to a less destructive one in some sort of spiritual progression. At its worst, this strategy is one of repression; at its best, it is sublimation. History is full of examples of men and women who sublimated their desire into lives of service and heroism. All our acts—however noble—are tinged with neurosis. This isn't something to be feared or despised. It is simply what it is to be human. We are inevitably neurotic sometimes, but our neuroses don't define us. The struggle with the inner energies of the psyche (often called, as we shall see, shadow work) yields much fruit.

The work on my search for mother has driven me to acknowledge (with joy and relief) the feminine aspect of the divine. I am unashamed to admit to a devotion to the Blessed Virgin Mary, and I have come to embrace the darkest and most wonderful mystery of all—marriage as spiritual path, as the supreme way of living day by day in relation to the other as other, with a woman who steadfastly refuses to be anything or anyone but herself. Slowly I have come to know the mother who is already there in my own depths as a nurturing and challenging energy. But the inner work isn't over because of my tendency to idolatry; or, to put it psychologically, anything (even "God") can become a project of the ego to protect itself.

Then there are the tedious demands from the therapeutic community for me to "get in touch with my inner child." Perhaps there are more of us out there who wouldn't dare admit that we are just marking time until mommy returns. Perhaps there are other "childish" admissions that need to come to the surface. Perhaps "growing up" in this kind of society does irreparable damage to our souls. Children have a rich fantasy life and do not doubt it until an adult undermines their confidence. We call the process of disillusionment growing up. How wonderful, if painful, to resist taking as one's own some secondhand vision of the world doled out to us by others. If we refuse to live in our own vision, we will find ourselves acting in someone else's play.

Early fantasies are important for feeding the imagination, but there comes the moment when we enter the dark wood of self-knowledge, of knowing with a chilling but bracing clarity and certainty that we have to live our own lives and not somebody else's. We face the fact that there is no going back to an idealized past. In our despair we may go too far and think that old wounds can never be healed, that there can be no wiping away of tears from our eyes. At one time I came to the conclusion that everything was an illusion: I would never get what I really wanted, never find what mother represented.

I am afraid of power and afraid of not having it. I fear the one-way ego trip to nowhere, but power is difficult to renounce. It clings to those who have tasted it. Sometimes I feel as if I have gone on a long journey that surely has brought me to the far reaches of the universe. Having traveled for years, I stop, footsore and weary, to check where I am and find that I have only moved to the end of the street where I was born. All my striving has only brought me to the edge of the city I seek. If happiness and joy elude us, we at least want our lives to appear grand and tragic rather than as hell shows them to be—silly, repetitive, and trivial.

Why is it important to go to hell? The process of transformation requires our being broken open. An availability, a vulnerability is necessary for the making of the soul. There is a great deal of risk in the dark wood. Many of us stumble into this drama of longing and risk. There is always the danger of falling into either despair (as a way of ending desire) or lust for power (as a means of fulfilling it). I get to a point where nothing and no one can reassure me. My longing to be satisfied—to come to the end of my desiring—gets confused with my lifelong search for acceptance and love (attachment). My hell is knowing that nothing could reassure me conclusively that all is well and that I have a place in the world. Having experienced repeated disappointments with every available pleasure, we are driven to look for a satisfaction that nothing could disappoint. The desire to come to the end of desire itself could be the first sign of the longing for an unconditional good that will never let us down. For some, maturity means giving up the quest as a childish illusion. For others, the quest is the bearer of hope.

The funnel of hell sucks the soul into a downward spiral of the loss of connection, of mutuality. We get lost and cut off from one another, first in forgetfulness (like the lovers Paolo and Francesca), then in betrayal and malice. From deceiving others we move easily into deceiving ourselves. We move through the sins of lust, gluttony, avarice and prodigality, anger, heresy—to those of violence, fraud, and treachery at hell's cold heart. Count Ugolino eternally bites the nape of the neck of Ruggiero, the archbishop of Pisa who had Ugolino, his two sons, and his grandsons nailed up in a tower to die. We end in the icescape of hell.

Our struggle to be human always occurs in a moral context. The infernal energies in us need some kind of container. We need a theater in which to act out our play. We need a dramatist to craft the script into something playable. We need a structure that will support us as we explore our part. The soul needs a moral context in which the work of transformation can take place. In modern terms, those who are awake psychologically know the difference between acting out and containing the explosion of passion and desire within the psyche and allowing inner transformation to take place. We have come to understand that repression and acting out are two sides of the same coin. There is a third way (Dante's way) of making the inner journey, the pilgrimage into a symbolic world of healing and transformation. It is a question of "living in" rather than "acting out." We need to "go to hell" in order to know just how far our loving can be contaminated and corrupted by the unacknowledged darknesses of the soul. We go there to face the consequences of love's disorders. We begin to understand the salutary role of conflict and guilt in the making of a soul. This journey for the sake of love is the most difficult of all because we have to go in two directions at once. We have to move inward, yet, because love (eros) is a reaching out to others and to the world, we have to move in the opposite direction as well. This inner work also requires a giving up of control, an openness that few dare embrace, not only because we fear it but because it is nonheroic. It is simple. It is humbling. It brings us into touch with our weakness.

Human joy and freedom require the possibility of perdition. Love has to involve risk and the possibility of loss, unless, of course, we want to live in a romantic theme park where the adventure is only simulated—hell. Dante shows us a way out. He shows us the plight of the lost self. But what of the consequences of that loss on our other relationships? The love story involves others in a banquet of communion, but the human family too has stumbled into the dark wood and lost its way. We must now turn to the wounded community.

FOUR

LOSING TOUCH WITH OTHERS: THE BROKEN COMMUNITY

The experience of hell has something to do with our illusion of being the center of the world, with humankind divided into two categories: oneself and everyone else. Yet I am merely one of billions and lack a privileged position. I am shocked that I am not in control and that my world is subject to recurring disruption. I need and fear others, and I find it impossible to believe that my attachments could be liberating. We see our need and fear of the other played out on every level of our lives, in marriages, in institutions, in communities.

Our descent into hell begins with a look at the warm sins of the flesh, which are nowhere near as serious as the malicious acts punished in the deeper regions. Hell's downward spiral starts with acts that cut us off from our deepest selves. As we go deeper, having lost touch with our selves, we go spinning off away from others. Intimacy and community feeling require a sense of sacred connection deep within ourselves. In short, we require the sacred as we require oxygen. When that is lost, we are in hell.

I learned early on how to lose touch with others and my deepest self through the warm sins of the body. I love food, the comforts and conveniences that money can buy, and the warm world of physical intimacy. There's nothing intrinsically wrong with these things. That's why I was puzzled that I sometimes felt isolated. "Am I alone, after all?" I asked myself. I have always felt out-of-tune with my times. I disliked the sixties with (what was to me) their self-righteous radical posturing and the promise of a sexual free ride. I see men of my own age living in a sixties time warp in my neighborhood in San Francisco near the corner of Haight and Ashbury. Their brains fried on drugs, they still think it's the Summer of Love. Hell. The beautiful city where I live has the capacity to fantasize about sex, money, and power.

Dante was a man of disobedient desire. He was not a priest or a monk for whom celibacy and "unworldliness" were ideals, even if unattainable. He was a man of the world who knew what betrayal and infidelity were. The promises of sex, money, and power—the three great seducers—were all around him as he was growing up in Florence. He succumbed to all three. In midlife, having failed with regard to both love and power, Dante didn't know where he was. He was displaced. His only way out was down and dark in the hell of isolation from others. His being was out of alignment. He didn't know his place.

Dante had lost touch with others. He had no center from which he could relate realistically to the world. He had ceased to be in communion, in community. His two great images of community—the church and the empire—were both necessary for human well-being, but he felt betrayed by both. Today we might say that humanity loses touch with itself when religion and politics degenerate into mere theater, when our hunger for transcendence is ignored or derided, and when concern for justice plays no genuine role in public life. The spiritual warfare between conscience and community, between the inner light of the individual and the demands of the pragmatic order, is made clear in the circles of hell.

It is a wonder that society holds together at all, given the tenuousness of civic discourse. There is an irony implicit in our aspiring to virtue and excellence in human relations. Dante reached for both and found himself mired in hubris and resentment, hating and despising the society that sent him into exile. Think of our capacity for self-deception, bitter rivalry, and narrow dogmatic assertiveness, which can reduce to ashes all hope for building a caring and compassionate community. When I arrived in Nicaragua recently, there was a transport strike over the price of gasoline. Five unions, not one, were in the negotiations. A Nicaraguan working with the poor told me that while the strikers may have a point, their winning means that many others will lose. "We all drink from one cup," he said, "and there is only a little water in it."

Think of how easy it is for us to be reduced to less, or transported to more, than the truly human by the simple choices we make. We either betray the best that is in us or overreach ourselves. Is there a way through the hell of our being less or grotesquely more than ourselves? What would it be like to be a true self? When we aspire to be more by trying—through sex, money, and power—to transcend the limits of time and space and overcome the constraints of the particular, we reveal our contempt for the truly human. When we settle for less, we betray the best that is in us. Either way, we are in hell. The challenge is one of discernment—how we look at things. The workings of the intellect, in Dante's sense, need to be restored so that we can see clearly the different orders and levels of reality.

The ability to discriminate with regard to how our loving is to be ordered, our desires educated, and our relationships nurtured is seriously threatened when we lose touch with or abandon the traditions and stories preserved for us in ancient texts and old maps of the spiritual journey. The old creeds with their mighty doctrines still haunt me with their strange language of promise and healing. Their liberal interpretations leave me cold. It's not that I want to believe in them literally or uncritically, but when the liberal and, to me, vain and iconoclastic spirit wants to update them or throw them away, I am overcome with a deep sadness that something precious has been lost. Our ancestors weren't all stupid. Human beings are reduced in the process of throwing out the old stories. There is an irreducible "impossibility" to life that cannot be explained away and that can be rendered only in story form. Many people still believe that they get to know things by *thinking*. But we don't know anything about the meaning of things and how they are connected by mere thought. Narratives connect. Stories help us see the ironic and disturbing relationship between the sentimental and the cynical, the trashy and the sublime, the absurd and the rational—all played out in our adventure with sex, money, and power. Stories help us sort out which is heaven and which is hell. A good narrative, while coming to some resolution, leaves us wondering about the possible futures of the protagonists. The danger is our getting lost in a text rather than being liberated by it into real life with real relationships.

We need to be fully in our bodies, and not trapped in a false sense of beauty and order (like the Nazis in the death camps who slaughtered by day and listened to Beethoven quartets by night, or the Russian noblewoman so caught up by the emotional impact of an operatic performance that she stayed transfixed in her box while her coachman froze to death waiting for her outside in the snow). Being properly earthed (aware of how all things are related) without being mired in it is required of those who would be truly human. Intimacy requires bodies to be present to each other. I remember seeing a performance of Wagner's *Tristan and Isolde* once. The lovers never touched each other. They sang their narcissistic love duet on either side of the darkened stage, lit only by two spotlights on their faces. Disembodied love is not love at all. To be a lover, one has to have a sense of place and be able to enjoy and endure the limits of time and space.

In spite of the recent (perhaps decisive) demise of Marxist-Leninist ideology, Karl Marx forced us to think about the social meaning of things, to take into account all the labor that went into making our breakfast. He still challenges us with questions about our place in the social order, and shows us the wickedness of making politics merely a matter of aesthetics, cosmetics, and convenience. Everyone has to occupy a space. Where are we to stand? How much do we need? How are we going to get it? Sex, money, and power. We are losing a sense of historical continuity, yet "tradition" is very marketable. We love package tours specializing in nostalgia. There's profit in manufacturing an illusory past, but it is not inhabited by people of flesh and blood. We don't like it when people mess with our cherished images, even if those images are artificial.

I remember the controversy in England over Dennis Potter's TV play *The Son of Man,* in which Jesus is played as a stocky and argumentative man half-crazed by what is going on inside his head. When asked whether it is lawful to give tribute to Caesar, Jesus impatiently demands a coin from his questioner: "Here, gimme a coin, gimme a coin! Whose head and inscription is that?" When his questioner timidly replies, "Caesar's," Jesus shouts at him, "Then give to Caesar the things that are Caesar's, and to God the things that are God's. Now, shut up!" The play caused quite a stir at the time. I'm not saying that Potter's Jesus is the "real" one, but I live with a sense that the very subject matter of the Christian myth is too hard for us to bear and has to be trivialized. Yet the narrative seems to be calling us to grand/grandiose visions of ourselves and our place in the universe. Why do we choose one story over another, one person over another to make connections and patterns? Why do we seek comfort in the particular? Why do we put up with the pain? I suppose because to be human is to be so earthed, to be bounded by the particulars of time and space. Hell shows us what it is to throw off these limitations and be frozen in a place where time is just one damned thing after another.

The seven deadly sins are deadly precisely because they are escape routes from the burden and delight of being embodied human beings. Perhaps one of the deadliest is gluttony—insatiable consumerism, to which sex, money, and power are related. Avarice and greed have no natural limits and can never know ultimate satisfaction. There will never be a point at which we think we have enough and "the other lot can have the leftovers for free."[1] Communism may have been discredited and capitalism and competition may have triumphed, but human life goes on being diminished by whoever is in charge. In the West, religion has withered away into strategies for private salvation. Is there no longer any place for self-sacrifice, dedication, brotherly love, compassion, community? Aren't we at the limit of what we can consume?

There can be no connection with others without a sense of place. Losing one's settled place in a settled world is a devastating experience. This is why going to hell is a golden opportunity to recover a true sense of place. It provides the unsettling we need. It is a refining journey separating the dross from the gold. It asks disturbing questions about our connections to others. How controlling and manipulative are we? How far are these connections based on fear? Are they really only held together by the narcosis of habit?

In our isolation, we fail to imagine the radical otherness of others. Our addictions blind us to it. In fact, the inability to imagine the other as other is a good description of some forms of mental illness. When we hate others, when we manipulate and hurt them, when we envy their good fortune, we demonstrate a failure of imagination. Do you confirm or undermine my presence in the world? Does everyone diminish someone? We turn to hatred when we come to believe that nothing can change, that we are stuck forever in a particular hell. Our contemporary hell forces us to relate to one another "primarily as givers and deniers of approval."[2] When does our refusal to believe that things could be otherwise degenerate into vacuity—into dangerous stupidity? In hell there is no possibility of a movement toward risk and reconciliation—no new way of being.

What distressed Dante and what he found in hell was the loss of all right relations to people and things. People were treated like things and things like people. Their passions were confused and their loving disordered. At such times, rights and obligations become unbalanced and distorted. When we are afraid, we easily take offense and mobilize our resentments. We are litigious and assume that others have gone *farther* astray than we. At my worst, I take comfort in the fact that there are people morally inferior to me: terrorists, drug dealers, white supremacists. My comfort is short-lived when I am made to realize that we are all connected by both guilt and hope.

We talk a great deal about entitlements. To what are we entitled as human beings and why? When it comes to personal relations, our sense of entitlement can become destructive. If love eludes us, we can at least demand what we are owed. It is a kind of open account for revenge. Hell. Our longing for love functions like an entitlement or a right—something one has earned or deserved, especially through suffering, real or imagined. For example, because I felt neglected as a child and exploited by a class-conscious society, I have every right to be angry, suspicious, and resentful. I have the right to seek reparation in any way I can. I am even entitled to revenge. I am *owed*. I have every ethical right to mobilize my resentments and make sure society pays. Perhaps you have a genetic illness. It's unjust. Why me? Perhaps your father was an alcoholic or your mother abandoned you when you were little. At any rate, you were hurt by events and someone is responsible. Right? This is the logic of terrorism. My suffering—real or imagined—justifies any vengeful and violent act. We think we have the right to take our pain out on someone and continue the cycle of injustice— all in the name of justice.

Such a view of entitlement destroys relationships and undermines societies. It leads to the inferno, and there are a lot of us there, looking for scapegoats. "What looks like evil or stupidity—endless tribal or ethnic warring—is much better explained by destructive entitlement." But "feeling entitled and being entitled are not the same thing." Dante would call it misplaced or disordered love and would have agreed that "the motivation for revenge is actually driven by a deep sense of justice and a deep loyalty to those who loved but injured us."[3] Following Augustine, Dante believed that everything we do is driven by love but we must take care what we love and to what degree. The root of our problems is disordered desire. Hell is where our "inordinate affections" and our raging disappointment with them bring us.

Historically, societies swing between puritanism and permissiveness with regard to the passions. Each generation tries to compensate for the excesses of its immediate forebears. The things we tolerate in the name of freedom and the things we won't tolerate in the name of rights don't fit together.

Let us look at hell through the prism of politics, money, and sex: our ways of relating to each other.

POLITICS

What is the real condition of our lives and our relations with others? An old definition of politics is "the art of holding everyone together in a just *polis,* a city or community." Dante believed that there can be no distinction between the personal and the political. All relationships are both. A marriage is, in one sense, a political entity and every nation is a kind of family. The personal informs the political and the political the personal. Each needs sacrifice and forgiveness for the human experiment to stay truly human. Our real situation is that the human race is one community living in one home. Every age wants simple solutions to complex problems. In Dante's time, there were those who sought stability in a strong political entity—the empire. Others preferred to side with the papacy as ground for human community. We see the need for stability finding fulfillment in vindictive forms of religion across the world. We see it in the battles between the politically and the patriotically correct. Great danger exists when one group gains power and makes universal totalitarian claims. The French and Russian revolutions started out with a rallying cry to the highest of human ideals— to throw off the yoke of oppression and form a new society of citizens and comrades. The resulting human degradation became hell on earth.

As confusing as they are, it is important to understand something of Florentine politics if we are to appreciate Dante's vision. Italy in the late thirteenth century was a marvel. Marco Polo returned to Venice from his travels in the East in 1294, the same year that the Florentines began to build both the church of Santa Croce and the cathedral. In 1298 the Palazzo Vecchio was begun. During this time, Dante was a public figure—a representative of the state—who went on important missions, and in the year of Jubilee (1300) he was one of the priors of the Republic. It is not hard to see parallels in the complex politics of our own time. Those in power in Florence were divided by different attitudes toward class and wealth. The Ghibellines followed the older tradition, which respected hierarchy and the feudal notion of service to a lord. The Guelfs were more individualistic and egalitarian, insisting that nobility was a matter of individual worth, not of birth or inherited wealth or position. These attitudes permeate the *Commedia.* For example, the worst crime is breaking one's oath. Disloyalty was a grave sin because it destabilized the social order. That is why we find the treacherous—Cassius, Brutus, and Judas—at the very center of hell being gnawed at by the devil himself.

By 1265, the year of Dante's birth, the principles that divided the parties were somewhat obscured and the parties were also divided among themselves. In fact, their history is as confusing as that of the Republicans and Democrats in our own day, or the Cavaliers and Roundheads in seventeenth-century England. The Guelfs were, more or less, for the pope and for freedom from imperial control. In our terms, they were middle class, with all the virtues and vices of that group—hardworking, moralistic, and intolerant. Their spirit was invoked by Savonarola.

In 1260 the Guelfs were severely beaten. They took such revenge that, from the year of Dante's birth, Florence became irrevocably Guelf, that is, supportive of the papacy and wary of imperial pretensions. The Guelfs soon split into two parties, the Blacks and the Whites. The city was controlled by the Guelf Council (rather like the Orange Lodge in Northern Ireland), with bitter rivalry between two families, the Cerchi (nouveau riche) and the older and less rich Donati. The Donati were the Blacks. They tended to be the snobs (as is often the case with the rich who have lost some of their wealth). They were unscrupulous and overbearing. The Whites were the Cerchi, the rich upstarts—liberal, vulgar, and showy. What started as a family feud blew into a serious rivalry. The Whites were more popular with the people, but the Blacks gained influence by intrigue. Dante belonged to the White faction and was on the list of those who were proscribed by the Blacks when they came to power. They banished him from Florence. In the end, he had as little time for his own party as he had for the Blacks. Dante never returned to his native city and ended his days in Ravenna. He would have enjoyed the final irony of his exile. When he died, Florence wanted his bones returned. The people of Ravenna refused the request.

Dante's political vision was that of a *citizen*—a humanist. I don't know whether there is much hope in our rescuing the word *humanism* from its contemporary atheistic overtones. He was passionately interested in what goes into making us citizens. He and his contemporaries often used the metaphor of the city, especially the city of Jerusalem. Besides being the

Palestinian location of Christ's crucifixion and resurrection, it was a symbol for the Christian community on earth and in heaven (the Church Militant and the Church Triumphant). Lastly, the city came to signify the individual soul.

The city is as important a symbol of human community as it ever was. Those of us who live in cities know the fragility of civic virtues. The medieval maxim was: *Stadtfuhl macht frei*—Our freedom lies in citizenship. Participation in a civic community was a form of liberty. Is this true now? We tend to live in life-style enclaves rather than in true neighborhoods. Politicians seek ways to herd, handle, and manage us. We see the city as Disneyland or Toontown, with shopping malls made to look like a Mediterranean village, a development to represent a movie location on the Maine coast, a public space to simulate the piazzas of Florence or Venice. American cities are the meeting place for fantasy and nightmare. Where my daughter lives in New York might as well be downtown Managua. Within one city there are now vast distances. It is easier for the wealthy to fly to Hawaii than to make the journey across town to see evidence of the so-called Third World on their doorstep: poverty, despair, and institutional collapse. The world has been likened to two groups of people, two kinds of nations: one group living on the streets in a slum; the other cruising through it, avoiding the potholes, in a locked, air-conditioned limousine. The new challenge (close to Dante's vision) is to see the world as a single community. Such a vision does not come cheaply, but the cost of failing to grow into a just and caring community is beyond our comprehension.

Dante wanted to know the roots of human society. Are there any enduring realities behind human community? A community must have a covenant at its heart as its moral foundation—as opposed to a mere contract. We like to fix things and feel good about ourselves while we're doing it. Can our approach be merely therapeutic? Politicians accuse each other of having a Band-Aid approach to society's ills, but it takes courage to undertake the surgery required to build a more just society. We opt for aspirin rather than radical surgery. Dante had a hard-won catholic vision of human solidarity and mutuality and was horrified by a divided and divisive society. He believed that to be able to say *I am* with any depth one must first learn to say *We are*. He knew that the root causes of our distortions and corruptions need a healing that is beyond human agency. It's not merely a question of keeping moral rules; the community must be a moral force.

Dante was a severe critic of the church and the empire. Their representatives are found in the depths of hell because of their faithlessness and apostasy with regard to communal values. But Dante could not conceive of human life without church and empire. Human beings need social, political, and mediating institutions in order to flourish. Without moral and spiritual foundations, institutions become corrupt and evil. There is no just society without just citizens, dedicated to delaying immediate gratification for the sake of a greater good. Christianity sees true citizenship as being willing to take up one's cross and follow Christ, which is hardly inviting, unless we see this way of the cross, this road to the hell of self-denial, leading to a joy next to which worldly success seems pathetic. Not many will be convinced, and those who are do not follow the path with consistent enthusiasm. The rewards of faith are skinny and frail next to the robust promise of immediate gratification. We don't, therefore, go on this journey willingly. Dante didn't. He had to have his life turned upside down and be thrown out of Florence. Exile made him take evil seriously. Dante also had a strong sense of irony and a nose for self-deception and humbug. He knew leaders in church and state who consciously or unconsciously promoted evil while claiming to fight it. There is a progression from an evil act casually committed to habits of mind that eventually become dispositions and ingrained attitudes. Politically we are very vulnerable. Slowly and casually, we become collaborators in prejudice.

Such was the case of the rise of Adolf Hitler in the 1930s. I grew up with the vision of him as the incarnation of evil. But until 1938 (when the beast of anti-Semitism was unleashed on Kristallnacht—the Night of the Broken Glass, when Jewish shops and synagogues were vandalized), he was the adored leader of his people. Moreover, up to that point, the world community regarded his anti-Semitism as regrettable but understandable. Some excesses were "forgivable" if Germany was to rise up out of the ashes of the past. He was, therefore, grudgingly admired by many world leaders for putting the country on its feet. Lloyd George, the prime minister of England who was in power during Germany's defeat in the First World War, was delighted to visit and praise Hitler not long before the outbreak of the Second World War. It is easy to be outraged after the event, but each of us should ask how we would have behaved if we were unemployed and depressed in Germany in 1935. I don't like to admit it but I would have almost certainly been part of the Hitler Youth movement if I'd been a teenager in Germany in the 1930s. There is the story of Reserve Police Battalion 101 and the killing of Jews in the Second World War. What is remarkable about this battalion is that it was made up of ordinary men with ordinary faces. They did not belong to the SS and they were too old to be drafted. Most were raw recruits from Hamburg (by reputation one of the least Nazified cities in Germany). Few were active members of the Nazi party. But early on the morning of July 13, 1942, they went to a Polish village (Józefów) while everyone was still asleep and rounded up three hundred able-bodied male Jews for deportation to work camps. They were told to shoot the remaining Jews (fifteen hundred women, children, and elderly men). Between July and November 1942 they killed thirty-eight thousand Jews and sent another forty-five thousand to the gas chambers of Treblinka. Such mass killing could not have occurred without mass collaboration.[4]

Why did they do it? There are lots of reasons—wartime brutalization, racism, and deference to authority. The overriding factor was conformity to the group. Most of us cannot live without a group identity. That is why lynchings are always possible. It is hard to break rank, to get out of line, to take personal responsibility for one's actions. It takes a special kind of courage to be a particular person. Hell is the loss of particularity. In politics, it is the abandonment of personal responsibility.

Do we need to create new ways of feeling and experiencing the world—a permanent spiritual revolution in our relationships with others? We see the destructiveness of the "casino economy," which has produced a malignant rather than a respectful appreciation of *otherness*. The *others* are the poor, the homeless, and the marginalized. Not to see them is to live in a world cluttered with illusion, fantasy, and pretense. There are warnings for us to watch out for "the bitter harvest of charismatic politics and ideological extremism" in a society whose "cultural forms are based on fashion, nostalgia, pastiche, and kitsch."[5] Postmodern cultural nihilism (even when it is fashionable and chic) leads straight to the dark wood. We live in a society that romanticizes schizophrenia. It edits out its terror, as if it were merely like a controlled LSD trip. What are we to make of the following statement by Alan Sugar, chairman of Amstrad Corporation? "If there was a market for mass-produced portable nuclear weapons then we'd market them too."[6] This brings us to the issue of money.

MONEY

Our society is adept at creating new needs and artificial appetites: "As commodity producers seeking money . . . we are dependent upon the needs and capacity of others to buy. Producers consequently have a permanent interest in cultivating 'excess and intemperance' in others, in feeding 'imaginary appetites' to the point where ideas of what constitutes social need are replaced by 'fantasy, caprice, and whim.'"[7] Yesterday's luxury easily becomes today's necessity. And why shouldn't people be given what they want? It's a free country. Why not allow the market to determine everything? After all, there is no way to adjudicate between different things. Mozart and Gangsta rap. One is as good as the other. Who has the right to say otherwise? There's nothing to differentiate the Las Vegas Strip and Disneyland from Chartres Cathedral and the Taj Mahal. The latter can be replicated by modern technology anyway.

Making money is the reason for the creation and manipulation of new appetites, and cash is the proper object of desire. Two realities seem to be at play in any human enterprise: the ideal and the so-called real. Our rhetoric is high-flying but the "real" agenda is "the bottom line"—money. Dennis Potter's novel *Blackeyes* (1987) portrays the selection of a model to advertise a new line of body lotion. The male organizer explains the purpose of the audition to the carefully selected women ("girls," of course): "The basic idea is that of a timeless space in a timeless nowhere and everywhere." Contrast this philosophical claptrap with the reality of the advertisement: "Let's get to the bottom line. Let's chew on the nitty-gritty. What we want here is a blonde with terrific tits who's got the sense to make love to the fucking bottle."[8]

The bottom line is money as the guide to our political arrangements. Who gets what and how much? is the question. It was said of London that it was never England's heart—always its brain and its moneybags. How far is that true of other great world cities? Ours is a passion for consumption. Greed is the engine of desire. We confuse "the good life" with the upward spiral of acquisition. The money-grubbers in hell had all but lost any recognizable sign of humanity. The only way to tell one from another was by the insignia on their moneybags. Their modern counterparts in the corporate and banking worlds are well known to us.

Money easily becomes a substitute for transcendence. Greed and the fear of not having enough break down the commonwealth. Conspicuous consumption is a threat to civic life because luxury undermines our common life by protecting us from having to enter into the messy business of relating to one another. Extreme wealth promises contentment and safety by enabling the crassly wealthy to treat people around them as mere suppliers of pleasure. I see boredom and loneliness in the eyes of the wealthy I meet in the course of my work. They mix only with one another, eat with one another, vacation with one another. They fly to the other side of the world only to sit down to dinner with their rich neighbor from down the street. But wealth can never be a substitute for personal relations or political responsibility.

Vesle Fenstermaker's poem "The Consumers" describes the soft hell of those who take their luxurious existence as an entitlement:

> Today I remember, see us as we were at Las Brisas.
> Soft pool water enters my suit. I push aside
> floating hibiscus and lift my chin
> to smile at the blue bay down the hill.
>
> Once more a small dark boy retrieves our tennis balls,
> wide margaritas arrive at the beach table,
> sandy backgammon stones, like fat pink and white cookies,
> slide into place. The para-sailors float
> down to the double raft.
>
> Our hands, warm in the sun of Mexico,
> touch across the table.
> Salt and lime pucker our smiles.
>
> Who are these people,
> yoked in luxury,
> eating the world?[9]

"Who are these people, yoked in luxury, eating the world?" They are those for whom money has no value in itself except as a defense against the world. Money has many ways to bring a soul into hell. I am shamed by the homeless on our streets. Sometimes I justify my not helping out with money for feeding or shelter programs by imagining that the homeless are all con artists. It's all a bit of a drag and some of the panhandlers have hatred in their eyes. They could find work if they tried. By such a pattern of reasoning I can hang on to my money, but at the great expense of diminishing myself.

SEX

Lust separates us from the real world of relationship by placing us in an isolating bubble of desire. Lust is not necessarily ugly. Its object is often beautiful and genuinely desirable. It is to be pitied because it is always a revelation of distorted love. Paolo and Francesca in the fifth canto of the *Inferno* were caught up in a moment of passion that destroyed them both because they did not take history and context seriously. They thought they were in a timeless moment. On this earth, there are no timeless moments. The lovers are caught in *la bufera infernal*—the infernal whirlwind.[10] Francesca da Rimini loved her husband's brother. Her story is all the more poignant because she goes on loving Paolo even after she is placed in the midst of hell's torments. Love as overwhelming desire is irresistible. "Amor, ch'a nullo amato amar perdona mi prese del constui piacer sì forte"—Love, which exempts no loved one from loving in return, seized me for his charms with such might. She is in hell for love. We may wonder at Dante's apparent moralism, but we should note that he puts her in one of the higher circles of hell while her husband and murderer is placed in one of the lowest. George Steiner calls such loving "apocalyptic eroticism," which "is not a homecoming of and to the self, but a kind of final dispersal, a dissemination of the ego—however compacted the act of love, however unitary—to the *bufera*, the whirlwind in which Dante encloses lovers."[11]

If I had to choose one modern novel that meticulously chronicles the disorder of sexual desire it would be Josephine Hart's *Damage*. It is one of the best contemporary documentaries of a self-destructive apocalyptic eroticism of Dantean proportions. The dark mysteries of damnation and salvation are woven together with great economy and skill. Hell is a perfect parody of heaven. Perhaps they are not so far apart as we imagined. We look for mercy for having lived, and fear judgment for refusing life. The novel shows us that self-recognition can be a horror, self-knowledge a torment. There is a map all right. There is a story but it is damnable, and to find one's lover is to feel "the agony as the twisted iron in our souls unlocks itself and we slip at last into place."[12]

As a modern Paolo and Francesca, Hart's lovers recognized each other. The recognition is made all the more horrendous because of its sheer beauty. Imagine what it is like to feel the electricity of meeting someone with whom one feels utterly at home and in whom one finds the lost half of oneself. The soul rushes toward the other and the recognition is so clear that the coming together must be the will of God; it must be the conspiracy of the universe. Surely, there can be nothing wrong. Hart's hero confesses, "It is in that essential misreading that many lives stumble. In the utterly wrong idea that we are in control. That we can choose to go, or stay, without agony."[13]

In a terrible parody of Dante's encounter with Beatrice, our hero reflects on his encounter with Anna. "She was the split-second experience that changes everything, the car smash, the letter we shouldn't have opened, the lump in the breast or groin, the blinding flash. On my well-ordered stage set the lights were up, and maybe at last I was waiting in the wings."[14] It was as if he had come across a hidden treasure in a secret cave but its price would be the collapse of his well-crafted life, and the betrayal of all that he had hitherto loved—his wife, his children, and his home.

The irony is painful. "I had recognized her. And in her, had recognized myself."[15] What could be more wonderful? This is the miracle love, the elixir of transformation. Heaven. The beloved enables one to savor the experience of seeing everything as if for the first time. This is Beatrice's gift to Dante. Yet, it is twisted, because in the blindness of conversion, the lover cannot make the distinction between the creature and the Creator. The hero can see nothing but the beloved.

I have often expected people who love me to do for me what I cannot do for myself—to tell me who I am. I sometimes feel that I have had constantly to invent myself and my history. Others come with theirs ready-made, with aunts and uncles, parents and grandparents, all bound up in a story beginning in some faraway country, the collective memory of which holds the family together. I envy people who can return to the village where their great-grandmother was born or visit the farm where their father grew up. I feel sad that there is nothing much I want to show my children of the England of my past. I tried, for a while, to make history begin with me and to become my own god. When that failed, I tried to appropriate someone else's history and demand that someone else play god for me. Many such petty and failed divinities litter my past. Eventually, such strategies fail because it is not only exhausting but futile to ask others to play the role of divinity for us. The blindness of love drives us mad. The laws binding ordinary mortals do not apply to us.

Not all lovers' torments are the same. Some are merely worried about scandal; others are locked in a passion against which the threat of scandal is powerless. How could anyone be anxious about something so paltry as a scandal next to the cosmic dimensions of their happiness? The justification is as simple as it is naive. We say things like: Everyone does such things nowadays. There's no such thing as a scandal. We owe it to ourselves to live with the truth of our emotions. A love like this is self-justifying. It is such a view of human love that drives many of our actions and causes many of our hurts and disappointments.

What, then, are we going to do with the modern myth of sexuality—with its romantic longings, unreasonable expectations, restrictive fantasies, cruel exploitations and delusions? It promises so much. It promises what is real, true, and eternal, but no age has ever got sex quite right. We either trivialize sex or beat it down with moralism. Is human sexuality merely a battleground for power? In our day, it is a matter of endless and tedious negotiation. Every gesture has to be agreed upon beforehand.

John Updike, perhaps more than any other American novelist, has documented the middle-class white male's fascination and struggle with sexuality, and tries to write about sex in a way that is both bawdy and reverential. Although he is a novelist I enjoy reading, he leaves a nagging question in the mind about the truth of his vision. His vision is carnal (some would say it's just plain dirty), with pretensions to romanticism and theology. Updike links sex inextricably with our "stumbling pursuit of God."[16] Did Dante in his first adolescent experience sense the wonder of the Creator in the creature, or did he only realize that every girl has a center of pleasure—an organ of delight put there for his pleasure? Updike loves to describe in detail the female genitalia. There is wonder in it. An interviewer in one of Updike's short stories asks a woman: "How can you bear to be the constant carrier of such splendor?" Updike's fixation on the woman's genital area—its color and texture—teeters on the brink between woman-as-bearer-of-divinity and woman-as-object-to-be-exploited. Yet the woman's reply in the story is direct and poetic: "My pussy is the color of earth, of fire, of air, shuddering on the vein of a rock by the side of a stream, of fine metals spun to a curly tumult. . . ."[17]

No matter how offensive or boring one might find Updike's sexual descriptions, they come from a genuine religious consciousness. Many forms of religion have been repelled by female flesh, which is seen as that which perpetuates our earthly and sinful existence. Perhaps men and women are at war because we are the carriers for each other of an unbearable splendor. Updike loves the wonderful physical presence of the female body. He loves all its smells. He adores the taste and feel of it. In short, he loves the flesh as manifested in women as a gift from God, a sign of the loveliness of God's creation that one can touch and actually enter. This is a territory dotted with land mines. There are as many signs to hell as there are to heaven. Is a woman merely the occasion of man's pleasure—a delicious route to God? I am not confident that Updike's childish and narcissistic men ever see women as anything other than the objects of desire. Many of my women friends dislike Updike for this very reason.

Dante would have placed Updike's adulterous couples in the upper circles of hell. Still, I am left with a nasty taste in my mouth after reading many of Updike's descriptions of lovemaking because of the lingering offense of depersonalization. Updike's most famous and notorious novel, *Couples*, was published in 1968. This "sexy" book "is not about sex really, but about the emptiness of sex when it denies creation's goodness."[18] Where are we now? In a period of new restraint and puritanism—the age of AIDS and sexual harassment. Permissiveness has given way again to fear and constraint. So the pendulum swings. What was tolerated in one era is condemned in the next. Whatever we do, we and our bodies are one. In Dante, over and over again, the issue is faithfulness—in both romantic love and marriage. These are the theaters in which erotic love has to be played out.

At the end of *Gaudy Night*, Lord Peter Wimsey proposes to Harriet Vane. Dorothy L. Sayers beautifully exploits a musical image to describe the growing love between them. Wimsey cannot quite fathom how love is possible. Won't it mean the acceptance of irretrievable loss? They are listening to a Bach concerto for two violins. During the music Peter finds the courage to propose. What convinced him that love was possible? It was "the whole intricate pattern, every part separately and simultaneously, each independent and equal, separate but inseparable, moving over and under and through, ravishing heart and mind together."[19] Heaven.

What would modern feminism make of Updike's fantasies, Sayers's idealism, and Dante's projections onto the Feminine? Two main strands of feminism exist in our culture: one that rejects complementarity—a sort of sexual apartheid; the other, a vision of a cohumanity as male and female—cooperative and complementary. Only the latter would want to be in conversation with Dante. The former is a tragic response to ancient patriarchal distortions and injustices—a denial that we need each other.

Marriage has traditionally been an important metaphor of spiritual complementarity. It is a great loss that this metaphor is rejected by many today, because there is much in it that applies to the unmarried and the married alike. Marriage is a metaphor of our loving each other so much that the other is always respected. Marriage is not only a metaphor for friendship but also one that tells us something about the nature of the world. The world is a wedding—a marriage of all things in one communion. The lover knows that intimacy requires honoring the other's need for solitude. Relating to the other as other is a vital discipline of Dante's world. In Sayers's novel, Peter says to Harriet that "anybody can have the harmony if they will leave us the counterpoint." I see love like that—two distinct tunes (sometimes the same, sometimes different) weaving together in counterpoint. The glory of human love is trusting oneself to someone who is not finally predictable or fathomable. Love is not the other holding up a mirror to the lover, but a risky journey into the unknown. The spiritual task of being and staying in love is for the sake of healing the hurts of our isolating individualism by inviting us to pay attention to someone who is utterly different and who will not be controlled or manipulated.

What is it about love as lust that demands punishment? It is, after all, an expression of longing. But lust seeks to circumvent the tedious and day-to-day aspect of our intimate relations. It breaks up the community by undermining our willingness to do the endless ordinary things that keep life going—emptying the garbage, fixing a dripping faucet, taking the cat to the vet. If we are unwilling to endure little sacrifices, we won't be able to sustain a community for very long. Lust confuses our view of others by putting them through the blender of our desires and depersonalizing intimate sexual encounters. When we deny the originality of others, our vision of society is flattened out and made less interesting. Hell is the vision of a society in which true distinctions are defaced and we flounder in relationships that can go nowhere. Their fate is endless repetition.

Real human relations are infinitely wonderful because history is not repeatable and people are not interchangeable. Those who surrender themselves to "the lusts of the flesh" make the error of thinking that the same experience can be had over and over again. In hell, we get what we've chosen over and over again, until we are sick of it.

Maybe sex, money, and power are closer to religion than we would have anticipated. A. N. Wilson's *Daughters of Albion,* set in the early 1960s, begins in the back room of a seedy pub. A small group is talking about the Profumo affair (a notorious sex scandal in British politics) and the apparent agnosticism of an Anglican bishop. One character says of the sex scandal, "It isn't buying people . . . it's buying a fuck. Most of the girls do quite well out of it, better than if they were waitresses, or barmaids." Another disagrees. Quoting William Blake's "The Whore & Gambler, by the State / Licenc'd, build that Nation's Fate," he says, "A fuck, as you call it, my friend, unites us to the Sacred Fire. It's not that it shouldn't be paid for, so much as it can't be paid for. . . . It can't be paid for any more than you could pay for Holy Communion or buy a ray of the sun."[20] The reader is left wondering if the sex scandal and the doubting bishop are connected in some way. Are they mystically linked? Is it absurd to imagine that they are? Are sex, money, and power the sacraments of human life? There are, for Dante, alarming connections and mutualities among people and things—the ancient connection between *eros* (longing) and *thanatos* (death) being one of the most profound.

In counseling those who are convinced that love is not for them, I have noticed that the conviction becomes a self-fulfilling prophecy. They steel themselves against it. It is too painful. They tell me that for them it is too late. They point to their failures and say, "See, I told you so." Life is a party to which they have not been invited. Often I don't know what to say because they seem to be right. But I can hope that a Beatrice might send a Virgil to them to guide them down and out of the hell into which they have wandered.

Our use of sex, money, and power to find out and express who we are is but the sign of a much deeper longing for meaning and connection. I often wonder what has *actually* happened in my life and to my generation. I had little or no relation to my parents. My father died when I was twelve and my mother slipped into a kind of fatalistic passivity from which I escaped as soon as I could. I've spent a great deal of time in my adult years trying to understand what they bequeathed to me, what they "did" to me. It was one of my ways into hell, into a cycle of speculation and blame. My brother and sister, who are quite a bit older than I, point out that they didn't experience our parents in this way. That's precisely the point. I make no claims to objective truth, simply to my having to move into and out of hell in my own way. The journey wasn't a waste of time. I learned to acknowledge, even honor, my parents and to let them go.

Over a meal a few years ago, my son and I had one of those theological conversations that a father treasures. It was just the two of us. Edward was fourteen and had left home for the first time to go away to school. He had "religion" up to his ears and was beginning to think for himself. "It's all in your head, Dad," he said, with a certain amount of amused exasperation. I agreed with him, thinking how different a view of my parents I had "in my head" from that of my brother and sister. Edward and I got into a discussion of exactly what is going on in our heads and how whatever is in them gets in and out. I had no answer for him except to say that it was all in his head, too, and that the way we could sort some of it out was to pay attention to our hearts and sift through the stories we tell one another. Edward was looking, as was appropriate, to the future. I, on the other hand, was more interested in the past (I hope not stuck in it) because, as a friend of mine puts it, "The present is what the past is doing now." Such musings were appropriate for a father who was old enough to be both shamed by and grateful for his past. Was I, I wondered, becoming an old fart—one of the great army of aging adults who begrudge the young the future? What began to intrigue me that evening was the way in which the past *changes* and shifts, and how we perceive it by the working of the imagination. Life is a continual readjustment. I am brought back to the roving pain inside me—a pain highlighted by my struggle with sex, money, and power. It's a pain I need, a pain that calls me back to a life that cannot be controlled or manipulated. It calls me into the life of faith. It calls me from my depths. The mystics would say that it is the Holy Spirit calling me to herself. The fully human life requires our response to the Spirit, to the vision of God, and we shall now turn to this as we move down the circles of hell.

FIVE

LOSING TOUCH WITH GOD:
LOVE REJECTED AND BETRAYED

Great artists redefine the past and point to a previously unimagined future. That is why they are often viewed as dangerous and subversive. Dante takes the story of the passion of God and tells it anew, leading us through it in a new way into a future we could not have imagined on our own. The context of *The Divine Comedy* is a liturgical drama in the form of a love story played out in the human soul. Its setting is the *Triduum*—the three great days of Good Friday, Holy Saturday, and Easter Day—and the entire action takes place over these three familiar days. The story has always been the basic stuff of Christian consciousness, but familiarity breeds contempt. Dante reforges the stock Christian story that his contemporaries took for granted.

No one is forced to take part in the drama. It is a matter of freely choosing, and, as we have seen, Dante's poem is the drama of the soul's choice. The *Comedy* documents the mystery of human freedom as it is played out in the passions. We are even free to choose futility and live with the consequences of that choice. We are also free to choose an edited and sentimental view of life and live with the consequences of that. Today we live in a world where many people think that one choice is as good as another. A meaningless tale told by an idiot is just as valid as the story of God's passion for us. Perhaps there is no tale to tell—not even by an idiot. Perhaps we're just making it all up.

Dante's journey ends with the vision of God—that vision in which the poet sees the divine nature and himself through God's eyes. Which is closer to the truth as a reflection of human experience: the mind of an idiot or the mind of God? Both have something to teach us. Dante's poem suggests that we had better explore the former before too easily affirming the latter. It takes poetic imagination and a reasonable faith for us to affirm that life is not a tale told by an idiot, even if it sometimes appears to be.

The fully human life is the vision of God (so runs a maxim of the early Christians). But the vision of God seen by a hardened heart comes as a message of damnation. The damned are in an eternal fix. That's why they dare, in their despair, to be rebellious and insolent. Who gives a shit? Nothing they do can possibly make a difference. They "do not have to suck up in a pointless attempt at influencing divine intolerance."[1] The point is that we have the freedom to choose between the mind of an idiot and the mind of God. Even our despair is a kind of choice.

Hell, then, is forgetfulness of our primal relationship to God and a homelessness with regard to ourselves. It is the abandonment of hope. In Stanley Elkin's short story "The Conventional Wisdom," the hopelessness of hell is starkly described. The hero, Ellerbee, who has lived a good life according to the conventional wisdom, is killed while his liquor store is being robbed. He finds himself in heaven. It's no surprise. After all, he deserves it. Paradise turns out to be just as the old stories said it would be—with pearly gates, Saint Peter, and saints with halos. It's wonderful. He knows that he will be very happy. It is at this point that Saint Peter "beatifically" says, "Go to Hell!" Hell is also as the conventional wisdom would have it—a place of unremitting pain and punishment. Ellerbee finds it unfair and unendurable. He doesn't deserve it. He eventually takes the advice written over the gates of hell, "Abandon hope, all ye who enter here." Being a conventional person, Ellerbee did as he was told and abandoned hope. Along with it, he gave up "memory, pity, pride, his projects, the sense he had of injustice—for a little while driving off, along with his sense of identity, even his broken recollection of glory."[2]

It is a harrowing picture. There is no redemption, except of a dark and terrible sort, born out of the virtually impossible task of being able to recognize oneself reflected in the blisters and wounds of one's fellow sufferers. Elkin's tale is deliberately but accurately offensive and darkly in tune with Dante's vision. Ellerbee dares to ask God for an *explanation!* "For openers," God roars, "I made the heavens and the earth! Where were you when I laid the foundations of the firmament? When I . . . . " Ellerbee presumes to interrupt God's speech and rages:

> *An explanation . . . an explanation!* None of this what-was-I-doing-
> when-You-pissed-the-ocean-stuff. . . . I wasn't there when You
> shaped shit and fashioned cancer. Were *You* there when I loved my

neighbor as myself? When I never stole or bore false witness? . . .
Where were You when I picked up checks and popped for drinks all
round? So no Job job . . . an explanation.

The divine pettiness and intolerance permeate the universe. God throws
at Ellerbee every trivial transgression he has ever committed: his staying
open on the Sabbath, his taking God's name in vain, his routine lusts. There
is then a scene of hideous sexual coupling worthy of Dante. It is Ellerbee's
effort to connect and to see himself reflected in the blisters of another, after
which he prays to God to kill them, "to end Hell, to close the camp."

> Then God cursed and abused Ellerbee, and Ellerbee wouldn't have it
> any other way. . . . He would seek out . . . his murderer's accom-
> plice. . . . They would get close. And one day, he wouldn't look for
> himself in [the other's] glowing blisters.

HELL IS WHERE THE SHADOW OF GOD LIVES AND
WE MUST GO THERE TO FACE IT

For Dante, good and evil spring from the same source. Virgil tells him
that "love is the seed in you of every virtue and of all acts deserving punishment."[3] We cannot help but love, but we should take care what we love.
Our every action—even the most perverse—springs from the longing of
love. That is why our desires need educating. Our hungering will need
focus and direction because love requires an appropriate object.

We wonder what to do with the ache of desire that leads us to do things
we later regret. What would be considered the most vile thing you could do
and be? What would be the greatest betrayal you could imagine? What are
the characteristics of your peculiar woundedness? In what places is your
shadow the most potent? Where do you need to recognize and own your
darkness, and face your own weakness? We meet our shadow in our
dreams, where we are reminded of acts long past, events of betrayal breed-
ing resentment and fear and lurking in wait to be brought to consciousness.
Eventually, like Prospero at the end of *The Tempest*, we must embrace our
Caliban (our rejected self) and say, "This thing of darkness, I acknowledge
mine." The journey to hell and back is for the sake of retrieving the lost and
rejected self hiding in the shadows.

The spiritual journey isn't so much about conventional goodness as
about wholeness, and wholeness cannot be received by those who are

unable to admit to and work with their dark side, the shadow. Working with the shadow is Dante's concern. He knew that he was born with an aching desire for God and that that desire was unruly and unintegrated. He spent his life to prepare himself for the gift of wholeness.

We need to go to hell by entering that place where our longings and desires are trapped. What particular hell do we need to confront? What or who in us is lost and crying out for help? James Hillman implies that going to hell is vital for the soul because "the cure of the shadow is a problem of love. How far can our love extend to the broken and ruined parts of ourselves, the disgusting and perverse? How much charity and compassion have we for our own weakness and sickness?"[4] What can help me take on the spiritual task of confronting my deep sense of shame? Is it possible really to love oneself? What about those unworthy and unacceptable parts? Must we love them too? It is hard to love the shadow but it, too, is worthy of our attention and care. Our desires are untidy. Our longings are messy and incoherent. They can bring us to horrible and harrowing places, but where would we be, who would we be, without the engine of desire? Our desire for God and God's desire for us are at the heart of this story.

Denial has always been a human reaction to psychological and spiritual pain. A trip into an idealized past can anesthetize us for a while. I think of an America depicted in Frank Capra's classic movie *It's a Wonderful Life*. Jimmy Stewart is great in it. In many ways, it's a silly and sentimental film, but it never fails to get me choked up—in the same way that I get teary when "Jesus loves me, this I know, for the Bible tells me so" is sung. There is a truth somewhere in old movies and revivalist hymns, but they can also be shallow and manipulative. *It's a Wonderful Life* feeds our narcotic attraction to happy endings. Life doesn't always have a heartwarming twist at the end. There is also horror and terror, about which we cannot easily comment hopefully without sounding shallow. It has been said that Capra had no capacity or personality for self-examination. He feared self-knowledge and showed no patience for working cooperatively with others. It could be argued that these are current personality traits of Western society. They are traits resistant to the revelations of the apocalyptic, traits that render us unavailable to Dante's breathtaking and healing vision that redefines the past and opens up the future.

Is there a way out of the contemporary wasteland? For the past few years I have been trying, in vain, to get the hang of postmodern consciousness, with its visions of heaven and hell. On the one hand, the anything-goes, one-story-is-as-good-as-another attitude promises freedom from dogma; on the other, though, it makes us slaves to the dogma of a self too shallow to mean very much. Trying to comprehend contemporary attitudes is a futile exercise, in a sense, because whatever they are, they are already busy at work inside me. I try to develop strategies to prevent the unknown and uncontrollable from getting the upper hand. It's as futile as trying to stop the future from happening. It's as if our minds are like computers into which someone has placed a spiritual virus. The virus running rampant in my heart and mind places a question mark beside all my conclusions and decisions. It's like stumbling into a game and not knowing the rules, or wandering onto a stage and neither knowing one's line in the play nor having much clue about the plot. Hell is like that—a place of shadows and stale air.

Shadow work is vital because the good is easily corrupted. We know of evil perpetrated in the name of a high ideal. One of the most insidious expressions is, "I'm only doing this for your own good!" Perhaps that is why religious people are often thought to be capable of the greatest evil. Invoke the name of God and you can get away with murder. As human beings we are messy bundles of undifferentiated desire who have to find ways to plumb the depths of our longing. To try to do that utterly alone leads either to despair or to confusing God's will with one's own. The latter is a dangerous soul sickness (the greatest spiritual pathology I know) easily discerned not only in the fanatically religious but also in the cloyingly pious. There is something pathetically funny about people becoming competitively religious. Our love for one another is easily eroded by our struggle for moral superiority.

Pitching one's tent on the moral high ground can be very addictive; we will grab at anything that helps us feel superior to others. There is a story in our family about two maiden aunts who lived in perfect enmity with one another. One would deliberately test the patience of the other. One evening at dinner, one so provoked the other that the latter threw a glass of water in her sister's face. The injured party (having succeeded in goading her sister into a rage) silently got up, went over to the piano, and played "Jesus loves me, this I know," singing at the top of her voice. There's also a story of a pious couple who tried to outdo each other in religious practices. Their life together had degenerated into a "competitive

martyrdom: competitive fasting, competitive holiness, competitive forti-
tude and self-denial, a dreadful uncomplaining cheerfulness."[5] It was a
battle to the death. The wife spent all her allowance on paying for prayers
and masses for her husband's spiritual welfare. There are religious people
who are so afraid of sinning that they are afraid of life. They repress life
and let it out only a little bit at a time when they think that nobody's
watching—like "a bake-bean fart at a Baptist cookout," to use Frederick
Buechner's hilariously accurate image. We need to dare to live, and daring
to live means risking making a mistake.

Dante believed that our relationship with God is primary, the source of
our identity. We are linked to God and to one another by rejection or acceptance: damnation or salvation, hell or heaven. God has made us so that we
are free to reject this primary relationship, to abandon our true selves for
something shriveling and diminishing. There's a cartoon of a smiling
demon welcoming a new contingent of souls to hell with the words,
"There's no right or wrong here. It's just what works for you!" This is a
perfect description of the infernal regions. There you do your own thing
and do it forever. The past cannot be changed and the future is only repeti-
tious—one damned thing after another.

LEARNING TO PLAY SERIOUSLY WITH LANGUAGE IN TALKING ABOUT GOD

One of the most common misconceptions about sin is that it's fun. Religion is thought to be the enemy of joy, the wet blanket at the party, the killer
of honest pleasure. The spiritual life, however, is about being conscious,
staying awake—*playfully* as well as seriously. To be conscious is to be sad
at times, but it is also to be alive to our basic orientation to life and to what
brings true liveliness. To be conscious in a world full of suffering is to be
open to its pain. The things that pass for fun in contemporary culture are
often devices to prevent our being fully awake. In our society almost everything that goes by the name of pleasure tends to be a more or less successful attempt to destroy consciousness. There are the sadomasochistic
entertainments that hold the mind in chains. There is sexual fantasy with
its promise of covert or in-your-face violence. We are bombarded and managed by the image industry. Packaging is becoming more important than
content. In fact, a graphic-designer friend of mine designs containers and
then challenges manufacturers to come up with something to put in them.

Many of our pleasures (not all of them) make the hell in which we live habitable. The devil is the great deceiver and the master of disguise. He can make death look like life. No wonder we cannot always see clearly. To see through the destructive devices of the demonic, not only must we be watchful but we must also develop a sense of humor. Without an appreciation of the absurd, religious people easily become moralistic and paranoid.

Over twenty years ago I wrote my doctoral thesis on an extraordinary man called Herbert Kelly (1860–1950), an Anglican monk who founded the Society of the Sacred Mission in England. HK, as he was called, had a certain attitude to life and approach to theology that, through his writings and the reminiscences of his community brothers, he passed on to me. I was, above all, attracted by his playfulness and his irritability. As a sign of the community's approach to life, the members once read *Alice in Wonderland* in the refectory instead of books on prayer or the lives of the saints. *Alice* seemed perfectly apt for the human situation. Religion should be taken with a pinch of salt—with a sense of hilarity. Religion needs to be broken open if it is to be life-bearing. As Father Hilary, S.S.M., puts it, "The first element in our theological tradition can be summarized as: Down with religion and up with God."[6]

Religion—unfairly—has a bad name. Someone or something is to blame for our chronic distress and disappointment. Hence the tendency of the unthinking to lay all the world's ills at the feet of religion. There's a grain of truth in this but at the same time little appreciation of the way religion shelters even those who reject or are indifferent to it. Many people who fancy that they are spiritual have a parasitical relationship to religious traditions and institutions. Belief in God is considered foolish at best and dangerous at worst among many intellectuals.

There is also the war between the literalists and those who invoke the "merely" symbolic. But the two positions are not necessarily incompatible. What is hard for the intellectual is to come to the *second naïveté*, a childlikeness on the other side of doubt and skepticism. The life of faith does not equate to the surrender of intelligence. Nikos Katzantzakis's Saint Francis asks one of his would-be followers: "Can your intellect bear our certainty?" This is a pivotal question because much depends on the way "certainty" is invoked. The mindless literalist stands as a stumbling block to faith for the person of probing intelligence. This brings me to the second element in the Kelly tradition: the insistence that the opposite of faith isn't doubt. *The opposite of faith is certainty.* It should not be thought that a sense of humor and a lack of certainty mean that we are all floundering in the dark. There are things to hold on to—good things, like friendship, honor, truth telling. All we have to remember is that these thing are not God. That's all? That's everything. Science and general common sense cannot tell us anything we really want to know about who we are and where we are going.

It should be noted that the uncertainty invoked by *The Divine Comedy* is of a special kind. It is not the divinizing of ambiguity (summed up in the inane comment, "Everything is relative") but the placing of humility as the center of all our attempts to capture meanings in language. At the heart of the spiritual journey is our commitment to truth telling and promise keeping. We mustn't lie about the vicissitudes of our human lot. Religion worth anything is not a problem-solving device. It is the presentation of a saving narrative. We need to teach one another how to live and be there for one another when we die. Kelly reveled in the paradox of faith. We don't like paradoxes. That is why religious traditions often try to neutralize them, to resolve them with dogmatic statements. Father Hilary's summary of Herbert Kelly's principles could well serve as a basis for our approach to the journey through hell and purgatory at the end of the twentieth century: "a reverent agnosticism in all things, including human morals; a tendency to teach and meditate with paradoxes; and (the ultimate paradox) a slightly flippant attitude to human religion, eclipsed by a loving trust in the God of paradox."[7]

Dante's vehicle of truth was *una bella menzogna*—a beautiful lie, not literal fact. His poem is a device to express deeper levels of truth, and his *bella menzogna* appeals to me because it speaks as much to my need to disbelieve as to my need to believe. My need to disbelieve isn't some perverse drive to put down or destroy. Still less is it advocating mendacity. It is, for me, part of what it is to be a person of faith. Disbelief helps set up protocols against idolatry. That is why an appreciation of metaphor and allegory is important. They give us the means of saying important things that we couldn't say adequately or appropriately in the language, say, of science. Dante was at home with allegory as a vehicle of truth. Today many are still infected by the myth of science, which has spawned new forms of fundamentalism and literal-mindedness. We need a way of dancing round those truths that cannot be spoken. That's why Dante wrote a *poem*. It was his way of taking into account the distortions of his own peculiar point of view. Such a work relies on "the science of error"—the awareness that the mirror at the poet's disposal is cracked and flawed. Moreover, it includes the notion that our lives are constructed around a central secret, a skeleton in the closet. Most of the time the actual secret or scandal is irrelevant. What is interesting is how it functions in the person's life. Dante had a lot of secrets, disappointments, and betrayals. These soul secrets drove him to make sense of them in poetry. Poetry was a biographical alchemical quest for transformation. It enabled Dante to draw the map of hell.

The writing of poetry relies on revelation—often through dreaming, daydreaming, or sudden flashes of insight. But one must be capable of receiving the gift of revelation. It involves not only waiting on the images but preparing for their coming. As Dante himself explains it,[8] just as a signet ring (no matter how beautiful) will not make a clear image on the wax if it is of poor quality or if the temperature is not just right, so the untutored and unprepared imagination is incapable of receiving clear and accurate images. Many people have been damaged by the spiritually and psychologically illiterate—those who, because of lack of preparation, received distorted and distorting imprints of what they took to be the great images of salvation. Dante had to spend a long time in preparation before he was ready to give utterance to his experience of Beatrice as a revelation of God's glory.

Getting started on a spiritual path can mean coming to several dead ends before one actually moves forward. It can be as funny as it is painful. We will fall flat on our faces more often than usual. I have spent a great deal of my life dressing up in vestments and walking in processions that don't actually go anywhere. Solemnity requires a pratfall. Balloons were meant to be popped. Preachers have nightmares about not wearing the right clothes, not showing up at the right place, not having anything to say. A friend traveling in Indonesia was the guest at a funeral (a week-long ritual) at which he was seated among the family members. As he watched a procession of exquisitely veiled young women from his seat in one of the pavilions, he shifted his weight and the legs of his chair slipped through cracks in the makeshift floor with a crash. Down he went into the pig-fouled mud. All the guests without exception broke into riotous laughter. His interruption of this solemn occasion "seemed almost welcome, as if fabled ritual needed the unanticipated to season it. Pretense was acceptable if it could be brought low by a pratfall from the unexpected."[9]

Not all breaking of expected norms is benign, of course. It is one thing to somersault into the mud and quite another to be on the run in fear of one's life—as Dante was when he overreached himself. As a young poet, intoxicated by language and seduced by literary forms, he fancied himself a man of letters. As a politician, he thought himself secure on the winning side. He needed something to hurl him into the mud. He needed to make the trip to hell. Humility didn't come easily to him. Like some of our experiences with a little psychoanalysis or a first spiritual awakening, Dante's first taste of poetry made him a little "drunk." Language can make us tipsy. A wise therapist once reacted to a sermon by a young priest: "That young man knows more than he can bear. One day he will break down." I have often felt open to knowing things that my soul was too unformed to bear, or been seduced by a good idea or a healing image because I was unable to see that a great deal of inner work needed to be done before I could make proper use of it. In fact, I had to learn to allow the ideas and images to make use of me before I could use them with the proper grace. Much of modern spirituality is like virtual reality; it needs to be grounded if it is to be real. A trip to hell grounds us.

We can become mesmerized by an image or metaphor that promises us a means of seeing pattern and order and thereby controlling our world. A newfound interpretative image swallows up everything and makes no room for its opposite—no room for contradiction. Hence the necessity of the grace of detachment—the need to deny as well as affirm, the need to risk the descent into hell.

Dante keeps himself aware of error by having three points of reference. He puts himself in three places at once. He is Dante the poet. He is Dante the hero of his own poem. He is also Dante the man who is able to distance himself from both and watch himself as he voyages into the unknown. The trick in the spiritual life is to be utterly involved in it and yet detached at the same time. We all need to acquire that skill in our efforts at self-awareness. Whatever or whoever our inspiration is, there has to be a threefold juggling act of involvement, articulation, and detachment. We have to let ourselves go, find some means of expression, and yet struggle to maintain a certain distance.

Dante set himself an enormous task in telling the story of his encounter with Beatrice and the journey of the soul that it inspired. He prepared himself for the journey downward into a peculiar kind of weakness by practicing various poetic forms and by playing with the emerging Italian language. In a sense, he had to invent it—mint it fresh for his poetic purpose. His struggle with poetry gave him a way of understanding his vocation. Writing poetry is a kind of training for going into the depths. It is a craft for forging fresh images of the human. Dante's visions, dreams, and flights of imagination caused him to identify with his heroes. He saw himself in a great tradition stretching back into antiquity. Maybe he was a second Aeneas or a second Saint Paul. This isn't necessarily inflated. We all need heroes. Before we can embark on a voyage of self-discovery, we have to find ways of experimenting and finding our own voice—our distinctive language. I need to find ways of interpreting my experiences to myself. Dante, along with many other writers, provides me with images of self-recognition. Texts are sometimes dangerous and often magical because they are agents of experience. They make things happen in the soul that wouldn't happen otherwise. For Dante, there was no distinction between poetry and life. He really experienced the things he wrote about in his great poem.

Dante's world is full of certainties, but they are all understood in the context of the unknown and inexhaustible God whose love and justice are the architects of hell as well as heaven. Dante had a sense of the supernatural—a sense that we lack, a sense that is often scoffed at by those who, climbing on the back of either Karl Marx or Walt Disney, reduce the supernatural to either "pie in the sky when you die" or a fantasy theme park. What I mean by supernatural isn't something spooky or weird but the transcendent and immanent reality of God permeating all of life. We are experiencing the fallout from our loss of this sense of the supernatural. Some think that because we cannot know everything we cannot know anything for sure; all we can do is agree to disagree because there is no common good. Dante would have insisted that there is a great Good and we are accountable to it.

Christianity is a romance that allows our lives to be interpreted, not by the worst that human beings can do to one another, but by the best we can be for one another. To be human is meant to be a delight. To be human is to be godly. This is Dante's view, and one can appreciate his horror at the thought of the fate of those who had lost touch with their own loveliness and godliness. Hell.

I wish there were an easy way through—a way of avoiding the hell of self-will altogether. Surely there must be a painless way to wake up, a quick route to consciousness. The promotional material for Maharishi Veda Land (a fourteen-hundred-acre enlightenment theme park in Canada, costing $1.5 billion) claims to "combine enlightenment, knowledge, and entertainment." It is the brainchild of Doug Henning—a magician. "Each of the park's attractions will expand visitors' appreciation of their own infinite potential. They will experience reality and illusion, immortality and change, unity in diversity, infinity within a point, and the universe within the self." The thirty-three rides include "Seven steps to enlightenment— Feel enlightened as you visit seven wondrous pavilions radiating out like the spokes of a wheel. Your path has been carefully designed to lead you, in an entertaining way, step by step to enlightenment."

I suppose some moments of waking up can be entertaining. The evidence is that when we see anything clearly, we are invited to change. We see and live with the political and social consequences of our not seeing clearly how things are related to one another. For example, I am puzzled by the extremely rich who think that they have simply *earned* their wealth in honest labor. They do not discern that their good fortune relies on a whole matrix of social relations without which their wealth could not have been accumulated. Still less do they appreciate that the rewards of human labor are often disproportionate and unjust. Some people are just plain lucky. Some strike oil and some don't. We are set in opposition to one another because we do not perceive how we are to relate to one another and the world. Hell is the place where the self becomes its own god—a pathetic deity that eats itself up and is never satisfied. As failed divinities, we fall into the abyss of the passions that Dante knew well. The lust to dominate, our fascination with know-how, and our desire to have power over things and over people conceived as things, bring us to ruin. The lust to feel intensely pushes us to do unspeakable things in the name of human freedom. Scientific materialism thought there was a place where we could rest at last "beyond good and evil," "beyond freedom and dignity," and beyond truth and falsehood. Such idiocies bring us to the dead end of human frailty. The world is left prey to the terrible beasts we let loose—the beasts of greed, chaos, and violence. This is not to embrace a shallow view of the Good. The discerning know how beautiful Lucifer is, how evil can be made to look like good. That's why training and discipline are necessary for the formation of free souls.

The most repellent aspect, from the modern point of view, of Dante's worldview is that it is absolute and uncompromising. It contains no mitigating relativism, no hint of our "doing our own thing." There are laws that are irrevocable. One of them is that without God, humanity cannot be true to itself. We were made to be in relation with the divine. That has the force of law. Hell is the vision of the fate of those who choose to break the law of right relations. It isn't the realm of punishment so much as the kingdom of cause and effect. We are not "punished" when we put our hand in the fire. We are burned. In hell we meet those who have chosen (perhaps by way of a progression of little choices) to go there. It fascinates us because it is the realm of the one who, in his pride, rebelled against the divine "intolerance" and said no to God. Lucifer cried, "Non serviam"—I will not serve. Left on our own, we often experience the taste of self either as bitter or as flat and bland. Psychotherapy bears witness to the corrosive power of self-hate and to the horror of being left only with a sour sense of self. When I have tried to live with myself as my only point of reference, I have been left with a bitter taste in my mouth. We are left in hell with the sickening taste of self: the self rejecting its true self in God; the sweating self all the more damned because it parodies the image of the One who loves but will not compel love in return.

The Christian mystical tradition affirms that to be fully human is to be like God because we are made in God's image and likeness—even the damned. We are invited to *share* in the divine nature. When we refuse, we parody the relationship. God loves us and wants us to *be*. God, as revealed in Dante's *Paradiso*, invites the soul to share in the divine splendor and shine back and simply say, "I am." Hell is for those who try to say "I am" with no reference to God and become no one. To be in hell is to have lost that sense of primal identity. We try to be our own god, to be our own agent of transcendence. We cannot stand the limitations of our frail flesh. We lose touch with God and with one another by forgetting what it is to live within the boundaries of time and space. Dante's God was subject to both in Christ. His God was enfleshed—a God who emptied himself. His God knows what it is to be human—bounded by time and space. Hell is the place where souls rage at these limitations and try uselessly to transcend them.

Boundlessness is seductive. Why clutter up one's life and limit one's freedom with a belief in God? But which is more liberating: to understand oneself as defined and related to the Unknown and Incomprehensible, or to be confined within the boundary of one's limited imagination? It has been suggested that when people stop believing in God, they do not believe in nothing. They believe in anything, which includes belief in a God unrelated to anything else—a mere device brought in at the end of the play to explain what happened. A basic question for us is this: Is God simply an idea in the human mind, or is God a separate reality—transcendent and in some sense objective? Are we defined in reference to something or someone above and beyond ourselves? The journey of the soul is about choosing God over the diminished self. Our moving through the circles of hell reveals the consequences of believing our ultimate reference is the unanchored, self-validating, and self-absorbed human mind that has nothing but itself to look at.

Are not there things about which we should be rightly terrified? I fear the ravenous human soul looking for ways to satisfy itself, hunting for a place where its longing can come to an end, where desire dies. I see this soul roaming our streets and infecting our politics. I see the ravenous hunger dominating international relations. The poet—like the good psychiatrist—renders "the unspeakable speakable," and makes us hear what we would prefer not to hear. Dante knew that our terrors are trying to tell us something about the choice between good and evil—with the human heart as the battleground.

STRUGGLING WITH THE GRAND NARRATIVE: THE VISION OF GOD

Much has been written about how our family of origin affects our subsequent development. Members of societies of the affluent West spend a great deal of time and money in therapy to get the record straight, to write their history and tell their story so that life becomes bearable. The family is the crucible of our becoming who we are. It is a much-maligned metaphor, yet one to which we return again and again. We all want to find our way "home." Is the family a necessary evil we leave behind when we grow up? We know that we are supposed to work hard to separate from our parents—especially our mothers. But maybe we need to recover the mother as an image of our being at home in ourselves. We casually disobey the primordial commandment to honor our fathers and mothers. We mistakenly think that if we blame our parents we will come out on top. Even as we scream at them, "Look what you did to me! It's all your fault!" we hear the same words echoing down the years from one generation to another and so right back to those first parents who got us into this mess. The victims of violence in its various forms become perpetrators, and the cycle of vengeance rolls on.

There are master storytellers who have the ability not only to spin a yarn but to work a certain benign magic on their readers or listeners. I love a great novel—a good narrative—but I am also a bit suspicious of story-tellers. I find myself becoming uneasy when they move out of the strict realm of recognizable fiction and into the world of actual relationships. It is here that I find their ability to tell stories, weave spells, and create myths a danger to themselves and to others. Some storytellers cannot help them-selves. They are constantly at work reinterpreting and sometimes reinvent-ing their own lives—trying to make sense of them, trying to understand their fear and pain by assigning blame. Imagine what it would be like to have one's life revealed to the world through the distorting vision of some-one else's prejudice and pain. On a larger scale, this is what the powerful have always done to the weak. The rich (those who control the stories and the images) interpret the lives of the poor—as indolent or deserving, trou-blesome or pitiable, or, worse, as of no significance at all.

Storytelling raises the important question of the relationship between myth and reality. How are myths tested and regulated? How do we under-mine destructive and harmful myths? How do we choose between conflict-ing stories? We are all in the business of mythologizing our lives. We cannot help it. But our mythologies need challenging and correcting from time to time in the light of a great myth or story that has been tested over time.

Because postmodernists assume that there are no foundations, they are most repelled by the dramatic coherence of the spiritual journey. It is im-portant to them that there isn't a story. We'd better grow up and make the best of it. It could be argued that at least postmodernism is an improve-ment on modernism, whose adherents believed that we have grown out of the childish errors of our ancestors and now know better. But postmod-ernism-as-know-nothing has its own peculiar arrogance in proclaiming the relativizing gospel of a world in which everything is up for grabs.

There's a joke about postmodernism: Ask yourself if you know what's going on. If your answer is no, you're postmodern! But postmodernism can be used as a buzzword to bypass thought. In Huston Smith's phrase, it can be "ambiguity elevated to the level of apotheosis."[10] Intellectual endeavor tends to spread suspicion rather than further knowledge. We will do any-thing to rationalize our failures and cut others down to size. I am reminded

of the Australian expression about cutting off the heads of tall poppies, referring to a spiteful egalitarianism that pulls everyone down to the same
low level.

That apotheosis is best seen in the arguments over modern art. This is
one area of contemporary life that acts as a laboratory in which we can see
the apocalyptic character of our times, often in its funniest and phoniest
form. The confusion, creativity, and pretensions of modern art are expressions of the soul as it tries to find its way through the hells, purgatories,
and heavens of our experience. When everything is relative, who gets to decide what's what? The media? The advertising manipulators? The political
handlers?

A December 1992 exhibition of the work of Jeff Koons at the San Francisco Museum of Modern Art revealed the intellectual sleaziness of what
passes for postmodernist thought. The exhibition was breathtakingly shallow, which meant it was a success. Jeff Koons is very good at being shallow. Among many other things, there were vacuum cleaners boxed in glass
and garish, larger-than-life cartoonlike figures. His depictions of sexual activity would fit well in a seedy waxwork museum. His work is derivative
and lifeless, the celebration of dead sex rather than lively eroticism. A picture of hell on earth. Museums of modern art would be embarrassed to be
thought of as primarily institutions with social and moral responsibilities.
The one in San Francisco often does a good job of showing us just how far
we have fallen from grace.

It is interesting that Jack Lane, the director of the museum, used a religious metaphor in his introduction to the catalog of the Koons exhibit:

> Picture holding an Advent calendar whose closed windows, rather
> than imprinted with dates counting down to Christmas, bear labels
> naming most of the difficult and contentious issues in American cul-
> ture today: class, race, money, sex, obscenity, beauty, power, desire.
> Slide your fingernail under the paper shutters, open the windows
> and see what is revealed. Instead of wise men, shepherds, manger
> animals, the Virgin Mary, and Baby Jesus, you behold the works of
> art by Jeff Koons, each emblematic of matters both troubling and
> unresolved.

This exhibition and others like it reveal that we have no vocabulary, no
way of talking about things that matter. If something is shocking and de-

grading, it must be art. The comfortable classes need to be shocked and outraged from time to time, but the controversial isn't automatically art. Matthew Barney's exhibit in the same museum (December 1991–January 1992) used the body as a vehicle of art. One of the two video monitors read, "MILE HIGH *Threshold:* FLIGHT *with the* ANAL SADISTIC WARRIOR." The catalog tells us that "Barney's fluid substances . . . become metaphorical devotions to sex and penetration."[11] It is a vision of technological horror of Dantean proportions: man and machine are indistinguishable; sex, sport, life itself are all mechanized. Dante would have recognized it as a truly infernal way of degrading human physical activity. We, however, merely exhibit. The crassly wealthy heavily subsidize depictions of hell—but a hell safely distanced by well-lit galleries and the "sanitizing" explanations of curators. Hell, as we have seen, is all about confusion and loss of identity. It's no wonder that we want to escape into a world of hard facts that can be known and controlled. The way to control our horror is to take it and exhibit it. Put a price tag on it. Make people pay the price of admission.

It is not only the artworks themselves but the pretentious words used to describe them that show how far we have fallen. Language is in a state of deterioration, yet there is a strange new moralism and puritanism abroad that is unnerving. The thought police are out in force to tell us what to think and feel. We live in a hellish world in which *everything is permitted, yet nothing is forgiven.* Hence our horror of moral judgments. Are there things unambiguously immoral—simply wrong? No matter how hard we try to live in a world in which everything is relative, we almost always manage to smuggle a few unannounced universal values through the back door. We struggle to be open to other cultures, yet we're not very happy about the status of women in many parts of the world. We are not thrilled by the widespread practice of female circumcision or the systematic murder of baby girls in India. We don't babble on about tolerating different life-styles when we read of the slaughter of black youth in our inner cities. We hesitate to judge when we should, and are wildly and often cruelly judgmental when we should remain silent.

We persist in thinking that facts will save us. That is why we labor to amass them, even though we don't know what to *make* of them when we've got them. We don't know how to mythologize in a conscious and responsible way. As depth psychology tells us, we are not satisfied with the world of bare fact alone. Piles of data contribute not one whit to meaning.

Mere information, as useful as it is, brings us little more than manipulative power. Facts and events have no significance until the imagination works on them and incorporates them into a story or a picture. If we don't use our imaginations, we become subject to other image makers. We even doubt our own reality unless it is reflected back to us in "the movie version." We live in a strange world that needs constant reassurance and validation. Whenever something significant, strange, or heroic happens, there is always someone who wants to glamorize it, replay it, and record it so that it can be repeated and made more "real." I wonder who should play me in the movie version of my life—John Wayne, Jeremy Irons, Groucho Marx, Robin Williams, David Letterman?

It's easy to see why many people seem to be only half-alive. It's because reality for them is something that has to be manufactured. Our lives aren't real until they're seen on TV. The images show you how you're *supposed* to be—how to make love, how to fall apart, how to die. Our lives need a script and what better place to find one than in the media? For me, one definition of hell is to be on the road from Alan Jones to "Alan Jones"—a specially made two-hour TV special. Take out the ads and all I am can be reduced to an hour and a half's playing time.

How far should we believe the assertion that things are really falling apart? Are we living in a historical moment in which all beliefs are suspended? Does the church (and institutions like it) merely represent a last gasp of the past, with its bossy little precepts and its claim to know who we really are? Has life so lost its imaginative and narrative shape that it is merely episodic, like a soap opera? Can any part be replaced by an equivalent that will do just as well? And is the attachment of people who try to live by faith, people who are attached to particulars—to husbands, wives, and lovers, to projects and ambitions, to sacred places and imagined communities—faintly comic, especially in playback?[12] The soap-opera approach seems to suit some of us. Nostalgia and escapism provide a barrier to protect us from apocalyptic truths. If things go wrong, we can rewind the tape and begin again. Hell.

The issue always is relationship. There are many reasons we don't connect. Religion or ideology can be a good disconnector. I remember a doctor in our community when I was growing up who had four children, all of them friends of mine. The doctor was a pillar of the church and a strict disciplinarian. The mother kept the family grounded and human, but it shocked me to see a family in which the father was dreaded and despised. Some parents sacrifice everything, including their family, on the altar of their spirituality. The children suffer, either by reacting against what their father stands for or by trying to please and appease his arrogant spirit. As a family man with two daughters, I was struck by the patriarch in A. S. Byatt's *The Game* who also has two daughters. The novel made me wonder what kind of father I've been. I must have seemed a hypocrite—saying one thing and doing another.

One daughter in the novel feels betrayed by the idealism of her Quaker father. Being brought up in a religious household has its drawbacks if the spirit is rigid. Imagine living in a religious world in which everyone spoke about "the inner light" and you didn't know what they were talking about. Imagine being brought up in a tradition that demanded that you have nice feelings at all times. What would you do with your rage? Imagine being told that you would feel the presence of God when you said your prayers or partook of the sacrament. What would you do with your disappointment, let alone guilt, when the feelings weren't there? For the daughter of the Quaker in the novel, the policy of nonviolence simply didn't work. Passive resistance did not always convert violence into love. Turning the other cheek could get you hurt or even killed. She looked at the world and saw a different one from that of her father. Yet she desperately wanted to place on the world her own religious interpretation. The world is more than unfair. It's cruel and arbitrary. People who think that they have some inner light are not only fooling themselves; they are a menace to others. "There *will always be* people who will slash open the other cheek when it is turned to them. In this life love will *not* overcome, it *will not*, it will go to waste and it is no good to preach anything else."[13]

The other daughter also found her father's "simplicity" sorely at odds with the world of her experience. His view of life was nonsense. But she reacted differently than her sister, preferring the complexity of the real world to the naive simplicity of a religious community. In the actual world there were "people who really cared more for their motor-cars than for anything else, people who spent *most of their time* thinking about who had snubbed whom at whose party in what dress." These people went on living and didn't seem to be bothered by the big issues that obsessed her father.

When I read this, I couldn't help but think of my own daughters. How much of their growing up did I miss because I was too busy? When a child finally grasps the sheer human frailty of a parent, she begins to get in touch with her own. Underneath the two daughters' reaction to their father is an unspoken longing for connection. There is something incomplete, unfulfilled in the relationship. The clue to their longing has to do with their connection with their father, who (like many religious people) had left them with a sense of being unloved in the midst of all his "loving." They were both anxious to get on with the business of rewriting the script. One of their mother's favorite sayings was, "Our children cannot doubt that they are loved." That was the trouble. There was no foothold for doubt. "It was only that she had to share his love with so much else: prisoners, a model village, refugees, lepers, delinquents, prostitutes. . . ."[14]

How many of us resent having to share our parents' love with too many other things—with others, with causes, with communities? How many of us feel guilty for feeling the resentment? We find ourselves caught between the two.

Whenever people speak with passion, one often has to work very hard to discern what is really going on. Often a family argument is not about the subject in hand but about who loves whom and how much. In such a situation it is hard to see straight. Dante couldn't see his vices for what they were. He couldn't see the seven deadly sins as deadly. The two daughters in the story weren't so much concerned with Quaker theology or with how ordinary people behave as with their primal connection with their father. This lack of connection had serious, practical, everyday implications. It put a strain on everything. It created continuous tension. "We just *behave* like a normal family. We know a—a hell of a lot about it, but we've no time left to spend *being* it."[15]

We know a hell of a lot about a lot of things but we don't know how to *be*. The terrible icescape of hell was made by the wisdom, power, and love of God to show us how to be. The funnel of hell has done its terrible work. It has sucked the soul into a downward spiral of lost connection and mutuality. We get lost and cut off from one another, first in forgetfulness (like the lovers Paolo and Francesca), then in betrayal and malice (like Count Ugolino eternally biting the neck of Ruggiero, archbishop of Pisa). From deceiving others we move easily into deceiving ourselves. We move through the sins of lust, gluttony, avarice and prodigality, anger, heresy— to those of violence, fraud, and treachery at hell's cold heart. We end stuck in the ice.

Is there any way out? Are we going someplace? Dante cannot get to where he wants to go in a straight line. In the dark wood he could see where he needed to go, but he could not proceed directly to the *dilettoso monte*. When he and Virgil reach the foot of Mount Purgatory, the same thing is true. They cannot climb straight up the mountain but must ascend in a spiral motion. As they climb the mountain, they pass the same spot but at a different level. It is thus that we acquire a little wisdom. As we have seen, what is damnable about hell is that souls there cannot move up or down on the spiral. Even the demons are unable to run after Dante and Virgil outside the circle of torment to which they have been assigned. This signifies a terrible psychological truth about "the infatuation, addiction and hatred of the damned." Hell is the vision of souls whose development ceased at a certain point. The sinners in purgatory, on the other hand, continue to grow spiritually. No matter how long they have to wait on each cornice of the mountain, they know that in time they will move up the mountain. To be human is to be free to move. To be in heaven is to experience uninhibited movement. "This the highest form of motion—what is in Hell for the sinners a vicious circle—becomes finally for Dante a circle of perfection in which his soul moves as one with God."[16]

At the center of the inferno, Satan stands towering over the ice. He has three faces. On the right the face is sallow (a yellowish white), and on the left it is black. The central face is red. Each mouth gnaws at a traitor: Judas Iscariot in the center, Brutus on the left, and Cassius on the right. Virgil tells Dante to grab him by the neck, and the Roman poet grasps the hair on Satan's body and begins to climb down till he gets to the thigh and then begins to turn around. Dante thinks that they are returning to hell but they have gone right through the center of the earth. They struggle up a winding road without rest—until, once again, Dante sees the stars. He experiences huge relief. The air is freer than the thick choking atmosphere of the inferno. He is no longer stuck in himself. He can move.

PART TWO

PURGATORY

O PPOSITE AND CORRESPONDING TO THE GREAT CAVITY OF HELL IS THE island of Purgatory—a mountain on top of which is the Earthly Paradise. Before we can get into Purgatory proper, we have to pass through Ante-Purgatory, where the souls of those who were too busy or too lazy to repent have to wait on a cliff before they can proceed up the mountain. Those who delayed "waking up" until the end of life must wait at least as long as they delayed before they can make the ascent. Such is the discipline of the mountain.

Purgatory has seven flat, narrow terraces or cornices up which the repentant sinners toil to regain the freedom lost by their willfulness. On each shelf are souls working through the consequences of their vices—those dispositions that are the source of human wickedness (they are worth repeating): *pride, envy, anger, sloth, avarice, gluttony, and lust*—in the reverse order in which we found them in Hell. Purgatory is a breath of fresh air after the stifling atmosphere of the inferno. Here, at last, is a place of hope and change. The good news is that we are not as stuck as we thought we were. There is great rejoicing in the progression of the soul on its journey. Dante has seven Ps (for the seven deadly sins—*peccati*) marked on his forehead, and as he moves up the mountain the Ps are removed one by one.

Dante spends three nights on the mountain beginning on Easter Day (April 10, 1300). As we journey with him, we find that we can climb up the mount only in the daytime. At night, the souls in purgatory have to rest. It is an opportunity to reflect, dream, and see visions. We reach the Earthly Paradise on Wednesday, and at noon on that day we are shot like an arrow into Heaven.

What is the purpose of purgatory? It is for the liberation of the imprisoned will, for the ordering of desire, and for the enlarging of the heart. For Dante and his contemporaries, the key to human personality is the will. We naturally long for the good, but we go wrong because we easily mistake something bad for something good. The terrible thing is that we get into bad habits that eventually become so engrafted that our disposition changes. What starts off in a moment of passion can become, by a series of repeated acts, an actual malicious trait. Sins of impulse are one thing, but premeditated sins are quite another. Our sinning has two aspects: one juridical (we've broken the divine law), which calls for forgiveness; the other therapeutic (we're wounded in our souls), which requires healing. Sin is both a "crime" that requires judgment and grace and a "wound" that needs a cure. We also know that the coldly judgmental does great harm and the shallowly therapeutic effects no lasting healing. We need both mercy and forgiveness. One aspect speaks to our willed acts for which we are legitimately responsible; the other speaks to the inner woundedness that our repeated acts (and the actions of others) have inflicted on us. We are both ruined and wounded by the seven deadly sins. Sin makes us unfree, and the point of purgation is to gain freedom from its terrible enslavement.

The order of the seven deadly sins is important. They consist of two sets of three separated by sloth. In hell the order is reversed with lust at the top, but here pride begins the list. The first set are the "cold" sins of a malicious disposition. The second are the "warm" sins of particular acts. Sloth separates the two sets, and we easily and almost imperceptibly slip from one set to the other. Such is the insidious work of sloth. In hell we began with lust and were led down the narrowing spiral into the cold heart of pride. In purgatory we begin with pride and its deadening weight and move up the mountain to have our loving set on the right path.

Purgation is the road to freedom. Traditionally, it consists of three steps: contrition, confession, and satisfaction. This process is called repentance. We wake up to the situation and acknowledge our lostness. We tell the truth. We are willing to make reparation where we can. Dante, with Beatrice's help, completes the process of repentance when he reaches the top of the mountain.

The punishments are fitting. On the first terrace the proud are bent over with heavy burdens—a sign of the putting down of pride. Everyone has to spend time on this terrace. There are three types of the proud: those who think they are better than others by reason of birth, those who believe they are superior to others because of their artistic or intellectual gifts, and those who lord it over others by means of naked power.

The second shelf is reserved for the envious, and because they could not bear to see the good of others, their eyes are now shut—sown up with iron wire. They sit, huddled up like beggars. The third circle is full of blinding and suffocating smoke—a fitting punishment for those consumed by anger. As Dante progresses up the mountain, he and Virgil discuss the meaning of love and the significance of possessions on the cornice of Sloth. What is wonderful about love, unlike worldly goods, is that love is *increased*, not *diminished*, by sharing. "God's love is poured out in proportion to the readiness of the soul to accept it, and upon everyone of the blessed is lavished all the love that it is capable of receiving."[1] The wonder of paradise is that love increases and multiplies. God loves us and we also receive love from one another. We were born for joy but, because of ignorance and inexperience, we cannot tell false delights from true ones. The point is that love is the "seed" of all our actions—both the good and the bad. Love comes in two kinds: instinctive (like plants and animals—plants "love" the sun) and freely chosen. We have power to choose the objects of our love and we can easily go astray. We can get off course by being cool toward what we should love and hot in pursuit of what we shouldn't.

We can't help being lovers, and we go astray in our loving in three ways: by loving the wrong things, by not loving the right things enough, and by loving certain things too much. We mistake the objects of our love and get things all out of proportion—like the man who came home to see his house on fire and cried, "Oh! My books! My books!" with no thought for his wife and children, let alone his dog. Our loving needs ordering. Our desiring needs educating. Both love and desire can easily go off in the wrong direction and be turned into hate.

The greatest enemy for some of us is sloth—*acedia* or *accidie*. It is a tiredness and listlessness of soul as strong as any passion. Considered a vice in the Middle Ages, sloth might usefully be thought of this way again. It is a sign of a deficiency in loving—a spiritual sluggishness. The slothful on the fourth terrace have to run around as fast as they can. The fifth cornice is reserved for the avaricious and the prodigal (the hoarders and the squanderers), who are punished by inactivity. "Those whose eyes were fixed on vile earthly goods must lie with their faces in the dust; those who eschewed useful activity are now tight bound and motionless."[2]

On the sixth terrace we find the gluttonous. They are reduced to skin and bones and subject to the rule of rigid abstinence. Finally Dante reaches the cornice of the lustful, who circle through the fire in two bands. The repentant Dante is ready to enter the Earthly Paradise. It is the morning of Wednesday, April 13, 1300—the sixth day of his journey. And, at last, Beatrice appears. The imagery of the Mass—the Holy Communion—is very important at this point. It signifies the coming together of spirit and matter in sanctified flesh. Being truly human *is* holy communion, and the path to this communion is forgiveness.

The full admission of who and what we are and have done—the offering of a contrite heart—is breathtakingly liberating. We lose our way through pride, ambition, and willfulness. Acknowledgment is reinforced and healing made possible by saying out loud what we have done to somebody else. We have to be willing to make reparation wherever possible (it's no use confessing one has stolen a million dollars and then expecting to keep the loot). Dante falls into a deep sleep after he has seen the reconciliation of church and state, of love and justice, in the perfect City of God. He is ready for the freedom of heaven.

SIX

CONVERSION: RECOVERING THE PATH TO ONE'S TRUE SELF

Part of the reason I disliked the 1960s was that the radicals had no sense of irony, no appreciation of their own sin. They projected all the ills of society onto "the system." We have to look at systemic problems but not at the expense of individual responsibility. I found myself in purgatory one evening in 1969 in the English city of Lincoln. I was a young, idealistic priest who had returned to England to teach. I had joined the Labour party and the local Labour club. One evening I went down to the club to have a drink and was shocked by the talk about the niggers and the Pakis (Pakistanis) taking jobs from decent white folks. My youthful naïveté about the socialist vision and the solidarity of the human race was exploded over a pint of bitter. My mind and heart went on a purging spree that I suppose is common for people in their late twenties. I became a man in transition. I joined the army of the disillusioned and found myself moving down into the pit of cynicism. As a result, I became very confused in my political thinking but also found that I could move a little more freely intellectually and spiritually. And now? I hope I haven't lost my liberal heart, but I am a lot more cautious about my political commitments, and I regard the political rhetoric of both the left and the right with skepticism. Politically, I am in purgatory most of the time. It is a place of transition where one can move, even if the going is hard.

Purgatory is a *good* place to be. It clears the mind and opens the heart. It is the realm of movement through a significant passage of one's life. In the popular imagination, Purgatory suggests an outlandish and cruel place to which the Roman Catholic church consigns its adherents who don't toe the line. The truth is that it is a *present* reality in anyone who is spiritually and psychologically awake.[1] Purgation will be an inevitable passage for anyone who chooses the way of consciousness. The popular idea of purgatory is less that of cleansing and testing than of revenge and punishment—even of vindictive punishment by a sadistic God. Purgatory is the passage into new possibilities. The circling here ceases to be vicious (as it was in hell). The old maxim is: The essence of purgation is self-simplification. We move from one passage to another: from remorse and resentment to repentance and acceptance. There is a genuine shift in the atmosphere when we reach purgatory. The spiritual climate is different. Unlike in hell, here there is genuine light. The air is sweeter. We have entered the second passage.

In purgatory hope is born simply because the soul can *move*. It feels itself alive in a new way when it can face the truth about itself without despair. We begin to live in hope when we realize that there is a love strong enough to sustain us so that we are able to remember everything we are and have done without lying, editing, or despairing. Our wills are liberated when the consequences of wrong choices are acknowledged. The discipline of the mountain is our continuing to work with the shadow—to work with all the unacceptable and rejected aspects of the soul, to be open to all that we have repressed and hidden.

When Dante and Virgil reach the shores of Purgatory, they cannot climb straight up the mountain. The journey continues on its spiraling way. They have, by the grace of God, to undo what hell has done to the soul. The spiral signifies a journey of inner evolution, and is the figure of the one who is not trapped by the ego.[2] In fact, anyone of goodwill who seeks to serve God strives to climb up the spiral, which frees the will to act in accord with its true inclinations. Thus, purgatory, like hell and heaven, is circular—a mountain up which the soul *joyfully* toils as it chooses to remember itself.

In the minds of Dante's contemporaries, purgatory was something to be feared. Dante's creative imagination was able to take the terrifying images of the afterlife and transform them into images of salvation and joy that spoke, not only to the future, but also to the present. His imagination forged metaphors that were able to take away the most terrible shame of all—the shame of being born. This deep sense of shame at being alive does not plague everyone, but there are those who, by simply existing, feel that they are in the wrong. This has been my struggle: the recurring nightmare of being in a courtroom and not knowing the crime but being found guilty before the trial begins. The myth of the Fall for them is not so much the story of how human beings fall into error as the drama of their "falling" into being itself, with all its limitations. It is sometimes referred to as the primal shame that precedes guilt. Dante does a great deal to heal the wounded imaginations of those who experience the terrible fallenness of being. Purgatory teaches us to be unafraid of the God-given process of being and becoming and the tension between them. We are meant to be on the move between the two.

Repentance reorients the soul toward its true end and thus begins the arduous process of liberating the will and enlarging the heart. The repentant sinners, however long their wait on each cornice of Mount Purgatory, know that in time they will move up the spiral way. In Paradise the wills of the blessed are so free that they can move about as they please, to revolve and gyrate by themselves, because they have found out who they truly are. The highest form of motion is to move freely in the place where one is, at last, at home. Dante now knows where he is heading. He knows who he is meant to be—a free, conscious being of delight.

As we shall see, when Dante reaches heaven he is amazed at his new-found capacity to bear intense light. He is able to gaze directly at the sun. What is in hell for the sinners a vicious circle (the parody of heaven) becomes finally for Dante a circle of perfection in which his soul moves as one with God. The grim pattern of hell's frozen dead-center mocks our human longing for freedom. You get what you pay for. Yet all, in the end, is gift. Tears of repentance get us moving once again up the mountain of Purgation. Our tears moisten and make supple a soul dried and hardened by its wrong choices and willful resentments. They help restore us to our original shape as the "image of God."

It is often claimed that everything we've ever done flashes before our eyes at the moment of death. Imagine what it would be like to review not only our own lives but also the lives of all those who have gone before us—people who have made us the distinct persons we are. What moments there would be of laughter and regret, of hilarity and guilt, of love and hate. Robertson Davies's novel *Murther and Walking Spirits* is about the life of a forty-four-year-old journalist (Gil Gilmartin) who is murdered at the beginning of the story by his wife's lover. His spirit has to review the lives of his ancestors in a sort of purgatorial film festival. He watches his soul's history. At one point during the movies, he remembers a picture called *Dégrès des Ages* that hung in the office of a friend, Hugh McWearie. It was a print from about 1830 that depicted the journey of life to its final dissolution. There was a curved bridge over which march a man and a woman representing the human race. We see them at various stages of their journey. At the bottom of the bridge they are two infants in a cradle, smiling in carefree innocence.

> Up the curve of the bridge marches Childhood, Youth, Maturity and then—as the curve begins its descent—the marching couples portray Decay, Old Age, and at last arrive at a couple lying in bed in their hundredth year, again like infants, but now hideously wrinkled and toothless, labelled *Age d'imbecilité*.[3]

The couple have been brought right back to their beginning. But there is no journey ahead to give them hope.

We don't like to think about such things as destinies and destinations. Our ancestors were often obsessed by stern themes of right and wrong, good and evil, heaven and hell. I used to own a print called *The Gate of Death*. It hung over the fireplace in my study in England in the late sixties. Dated 1911, it showed a group of people in a state of undress being ushered by a unisex angel through a narrow stone doorway. There were a scientist and a cardinal, a child, a woman of the streets, and a man who had been called to meet his maker in the middle of a cricket match. He was in full sports gear with his bat under his arm. It was funny and arresting at the same time. Death is waiting for everyone. So what? What follows? How should we act?

A friend of mine has a brass-rubbing of a tombstone. A skeleton addresses the onlooker: "What you are, I was. What I am, you will be." My print of *The Gate of Death*, the brass-rubbing of the skeleton, and the French picture of the man and woman walking over the bridge of life are part of a long tradition that with only partial success tries, not only to warn people of the life to come, but also to wake people up to present opportunities, obligations, and possibilities. These pictures were saying: "Hey, you! Wake up! You don't know how much time you have left. Given the fragility of life and the reality of your mortality, how are you going to live out your days?" In Davies's novel, McWearie had tried to warn his friend about the dangers of not taking the spiritual journey seriously. He accuses Gilmartin of being a "dangerous class of fool, a trivializer." He points out that nothing that runs in our blood or hits us in the gut is trivial. Each of us is living out a hero's tale and we need to wake up to it.

What a fuss about the Oedipus Complex—the fella who wants to possess his Mum! What about the Hercules Complex—the fella that must grapple with his twelve labors while his wife and kids go by the board? What about the Apollo Complex—the fella who thinks you can have all light and no releasing darkness? And women—our towns and villages are jammed with Medeas and Persephones and Antigones, pushing their wire carts in the supermarkets unrecognized by anyone but themselves, and then probably only in their dreams. All engaged in the Hero Struggle!

Gilmartin suggests that these men and women acting out the great myths are largely unaware of what they are doing. McWearie points out that they don't have to understand intellectually what's going on inside them.

They just have to *live* it, and endure it so far as they can bear. You suppose you're a thinker, Gilmartin, and what you are is a trivializer because your thinking isn't fuelled by any strong feeling. Wake up, man! Come alive! Feel before you think![4]

I can imagine such a scene in Dante's life. His experience of Beatrice and his downfall because of his arrogant regard for his poetic gifts and political pretensions pushed him into the realm of feeling. I think of my own soul history. What was being played out in me that began years, even centuries, ago with someone else's unkind act or loving gesture? How could I begin to *feel* what was going on inside me? We make jokes about getting in touch with our feelings; the phrase has become part of the therapeutic jargon. But I had to acknowledge that for most of my life I had no idea what my feelings really were. I knew what I *thought* about them, but I couldn't really feel them. It had something to do with the separation I felt from my body. I was like James Joyce's Mr. Duffy, who "lived a short distance from his body."

It has been a long journey back into my feelings and into my body. I woke up one day and realized that even my most intensely personal utterances were *derivative*. I received all I am and all I know from others. It jolted me to realize that I am part of a long tradition. Every time one says, "I love you," it is a quotation! Even our most intimate and personal utterances were said by somebody else first. We are intimately linked through time and space. Our bodies and sensations are the link. I think of those who were treated meanly and who now ladle out meanness to others with relish. Many a wounded child becomes a wounding parent. I began to think that much of what was going on inside me may have been initiated decades, even centuries, ago by an act of kindness or of cruelty that had been passed on down the generations. The effects of human actions go on and on. They fan out like the ripples of a stone thrown into a still pond. What, I wondered, am I passing on to those who come after me? What have I done to my children, my friends, my enemies? What have they done to me?

Years ago, an eccentric and holy friend confided in me that he believed that his inner distress was the spirit of his dead mother working something out through him. At the time, I thought he was crazy. Now I'm not so sure. I have come to believe more and more in a web of life binding us all together through time and space. My "crazy" friend also told me a powerful story of purgation in which the distorted souls of the Nazis are in a spiritual sanitarium and are being nursed back to health by their victims. Crazy? I don't think so. Dante believed in the existence of such mutuality. Purgatory teaches us that we belong to one another, not only now but in the past and the future. In a cultural center called the Ben Linder House in Managua, Nicaragua, are several murals, among them a representation of some ancient petroglyphs found in the mountains. I was told, "This is how our ancestors honor us." If we see ourselves in a great continuous chain of being, it isn't so odd to think of our forebears honoring us. The concept of the chain of being challenges us with how we plan to honor our descendants.

Gilmartin's film festival took him only as far back as the connections he had with his ancestors in the eighteenth century, but it was far enough for him to realize how deeply connected he was to everyone. Life is a festival and a nightmare of mutuality and reciprocity. Gilmartin discovered compassion for those who had made him who he was. When he thought of their "courage and resource, loyalty even to the point of self-destruction, crankiness and meanness, despair and endurance," he felt not only admiration and pity, but love.[5]

Dante's images help me get a little distance to take a look at my crisis. I hesitate to use the word *crisis* because it sounds too dramatic and there's a part of me that loves self-dramatization—a neat way the ego has of centering itself, nesting, and making itself at home in its own self-pity. But crisis it is. There are lots of reasons and many layers, most of them beyond me. I have, at long last, located an old pain inside me—a pain I seek to understand rather than suppress, a pain that I need, a pain that holds a secret, a pain about love and power, about love and fear. A friend of mine spoke of the pain we feel when we sense that we are growing. Maybe that's what it is—growing pains? I don't think of it as a midlife crisis. My crisis began when I was about eleven years old, when I realized for the first time that my life was not my own. It is definitely a spiritual issue rather than a psychological one, although the psyche provides fertile ground for the spirit. The strange thing is that it isn't merely a *private* pain. It's one that I see everywhere. Stranger still, it isn't a pessimistic pain. It is the pain of *life* demanding attention. Above all, it is the pain of choice. It is the pain of purgation.

It has been suggested that there is no point in searching for the missing link between apes and true humanity. We are the missing link! Because of our primal stupidity, we're capable of genocide through hunger and holocaust. We're not yet truly human.[6] I think this is what Dante sensed. He raged at the fact that human beings fail to take their own splendor seriously. He was disappointed by his and their unwillingness to make the journey to a humanity radiant with a mutuality that celebrates the uniqueness of each person in communion. For Dante, humanity found its home in the triune God—the God who is unity in diversity—a communion of persons distinct yet related in loving mutuality.

There used to be a theory that ignorance is the seedbed of religion and that *Urdummheit,* or primal stupidity, was its potting soil.[7] Given some of the historical manifestations of religion, the old theory has some validity. Our primal stupidity has to find some place to rest. Why not in a religious tradition? Why not in a scientific fundamentalism? Why not in a purified ethnic group? The possible playgrounds for our *Urdummheit* are endless. Religion is not the only place our primal stupidity is manifest. If you think religion is stupid, take a hard look at secularism. It simply hasn't delivered the goods—either materially or spiritually—that it promised. Our primal stupidity appears to be caused by a spiritual tone deafness that tunes out certain key elements of our lives. We often accuse the Victorians of having been sexually repressed. We are now coming to see just how spiritually repressed we have been. Spirituality is about the life of the will—the freedom to choose. The secular utopia has multiplied our choices, but given us little worth choosing. When I watch television I often get irritated because, in spite of the growing number of channels, there is less and less worth watching. The violence is gratuitous. The sex has no subtlety to it. It is a relief to find a program with characters who are occasionally wracked by political and moral anxiety instead of merely responding to some itch or other.

It's as if we've been going round in circles—seeing everything and learning nothing. Is life one damned thing after another—hell—or is there hope that the genuinely new can break in? Can the vicious circle be broken? Over and over again, Dante finds that he cannot get to where he wants to in a straight line. His actual path twists and turns in the same way that his life and character have been twisted and bent out of shape by wrong turns, infidelities, and betrayals. All the vices distort us and twist us away from the true path. Dante's message is that by climbing up and circling the mountain we, whom the world has made crooked, are made straight.[8] It is a turning from false ways to true ones. It is a winding route of reorientation—a turning from stumbling around in the dark running after the phony and artificial substitutes of substantial goodness, to an often-winding journey for the right goal, in the light of which previous paths seem chaotic and futile.

Memory plays an important part in the journey of purgation. Dante remembered what he was at his best. At first, the only road open to him, under Virgil's guidance, was the spiral one downward. Having gone to the depths, he is able to make his way upward. The only journey open to him was one into the realization of the consequences of human error and sin. And all for what? For the process of finding the fulfillment for which he longed beyond what he knew of himself; for learning the secret of the freedom of the human will as it circles and plays within its divine purpose: "E'n la sua voluntade è nostra pace"—In his will is perfected our peace. We are going somewhere. God is leading us to a city based on a love that must be freely given. God longs to bring us to a community where each citizen is truly himself or herself and says yes to the others.

Sin has a deceptively ponderous complexity about it—a great weight that slows us down and blinds us with regard to our true nature as a movement in and toward God. But once the soul has awakened, purgatory is the place it longs to reach. It's where we want to be because it speaks of the possibility of movement and change. The frozen will is thawed, the intellect begins to get its bearings, and desire begins to move in us again toward objects worthy of our love. Hell's terrible secret is that nothing gives us peace. Perdition may hold some perverse attraction because it, at least, locates us in the funnel of the damned, but there is no rest for the wicked.

Dante climbs the mountain to remove the weight of sin. As he climbs, his load is lightened as the seven Ps are removed from his brow. Here is a place, then, of painful realizations and recognitions. The soul begins to move by way of confession, contrition, and absolution. It is a time for shedding tears for all the wrong turns, wasted moments, and willful mistakes; a time of going back and retrieving all the lost bits and pieces of ourselves. We act as if what we do doesn't matter and what we say doesn't count. In purgatory we learn that there are no insignificant words or actions. Recently I met someone I knew over thirty years ago. There we were—in our fifties—staring at each other like the teenagers we once were. Fortunately, we looked at each other with love because the memories were good. Sometimes such encounters only give us pain. Nothing can undo the past. The unkind word cannot be unsaid, the unworthy act undone. Time's arrow goes only in one direction.

Nearly every year, in preparation for Christmas, I read W. H. Auden's Advent poem *For the Time Being*. He writes, "Unless you exclaim, 'There must be some mistake'—you must be mistaken." Confession is truth-telling, and here, in purgatory, "Truth is knowing that we know we lie."[9] Contrition is heart-piercing in that the soul sees the consequences of its actions and weeps. Absolution is sheer grace and gift—the mystery of restoration and transformation. As the place of truth-telling, purgatory promises immense relief to the repentant soul because it is released from the burden of living a lie. Souls *want* to enter purgatory. We know of this mountain in our everyday experience. It is the place where our desires and longings are stretched and challenged, the place of a special kind of pain—not the useless and repetitive pain of hell, but the kind of pain that, deep down, we know we need in order to move and grow.

On the first cornice are the proud—weighed down by their arrogance. It is here that the first P is removed from Dante's forehead. There is an earthquake—this is what happens whenever a soul is released from purgatory. On the second circle, the envious sit in sackcloth, their eyes stitched together with iron wire because they could not bear to see the good of others. The angel of generosity wipes the second P from Dante's brow. The third cornice is full of choking smoke, which contains the souls of the angry. The fourth is that of the slothful. It is here that Dante learns more about love. He and Virgil pause at the fourth cornice because the law of the mountain forbids ascent during the night. After their rest, they meet the angel of zeal and move on to the fifth cornice, where the covetous are chained.

The angels sing *Gloria in Excelsis*, and the angel of liberality erases the sixth P. Then they move on to the cornice of gluttony. Although the gluttonous now need no food, they still grow thin as if they are starved. Gluttony, when it is seen for what it really is (like all the seven deadly sins), is disfiguring and coarsening. The P is erased by the angel of temperance. On the seventh cornice, with its sheets of flame, lovers are refined in their love. Dante enters the fires of passion. Virgil has done his work, and Dante's intellect has been restored: he can discriminate; he can tell how one thing is related to another. Virgil, his task completed, disappears as Dante enters the garden of the Earthly Paradise where Beatrice is waiting for him. But there is no fond embrace of the united lovers. (They weren't actual sexual lovers in life, but Beatrice, in sending Virgil to guide him down the funnel and up the mountain, shows great love for him.) Beatrice sternly confronts him with his need to complete the process of confession, contrition, and absolution. Only after that will he be ready for Paradise.

Why is purgatory good news? How is sin neutralized? Can the past be undone? The man who helped me most when I was in my twenties was a monk who was a romantic Christian. He insisted that God's love for us is "the brute *fact* of the universe." He had in mind W. H. Auden's affirmation that *Sin fractures the Vision, not the Fact*.[10] Sin alters not one whit God's intentions for us. Another religious man, a Franciscan who was for a while my confessor, once prayed over me: "Always, always you love us; when we are good with a love that makes you glad, when we are bad with a love that makes you sad, but always, always you love us." Is this a brute fact? There's something in me that bridles at the thought. My resistance to the journey is very strong. Auden's three wise men say, "This journey is too long . . . we want our dinners." There's a great deal that I want besides my dinner. I want money, success, power. I want to cheat time. I want to get to the point where I don't have to be in school to learn things. It's time I graduated. But brute fact keeps getting in my way. Some of us have to be careful not to dismiss the brute fact of God's love as romantic twaddle because our hearts incline toward cynicism and disbelief. We have to learn to allow ourselves to be loved, to experience ourselves as chosen. Purgatory is learning to choose the One who chooses us.

Auden has the shepherds and the wise men in dialogue about what is, in effect, the journey out of hell and up the mountain. Purgation begins when our arrogant longing to get life over with by dying or to escape its responsibilities by climbing back into the womb is denied us. We are creatures of time and space. To be human means to have a past and a future. In the middle of our struggle to avoid the burden of our humanity—without our knowing—"Love has used / Our weakness as a guard and guide. We bless / Our lives' impatience. Our lives' laziness. . . ."[11] *Without our knowing,* "Love has used our weakness as a guard and guide." This is what it means to know that we live under the mercy and grace of God.

Purgatory reveals that there is no punishment for sin. There is no need. Sin is its own punishment. Here we find out sin's secret: it does not and cannot deliver what it claims to promise. Sex, as lust, does not deliver the longed-for connection for which one achingly hopes. Even understood as an itch, the maddening desire of sex is only made worse when it is scratched. Gluttony, seen in its true light, leaves the body unsatisfied and the soul once more cheated of its true end. Sloth is not an easygoing, laid-back attitude to life but a disease of the soul that does not even have the energy to hate. The soul possessed by anger ceases to be itself. Even the sin of expecting life to pay off for good behavior brings its own peculiar rage and resentment (especially reserved for the moralistic). I remember hearing of a woman who referred to her mother's frustration and puzzlement at dying of cancer. Her mother had done all the "right" things with regard to maintaining a healthy diet: "She'd been good. It hadn't worked." In the end it is not a matter of being good or bad, of rewards and punishments. It is a matter of orientation, of transformation, of conversion.

Purgatory after hell is the place of surprise. What was insoluble in hell is now capable of transformation. Here we give up all pretense of neutrality and learn to take sides. There's enough light here for us to see that everyone believes in some god or other. As I get older, I find that I am not as interested as I once was in people's beliefs. I am interested in *them*, in what makes them tick, but their believing or disbelieving often acts as a way of preventing spiritual growth. To be dogmatic or antidogmatic is often simply a device to bypass feeling and thought. Discussions about whether one should believe or not are a waste of time because everyone believes. The issue is what they believe and value. I get irritated by people who think their view of reality is somehow more "objective" than mine. It is a real step forward when we give up our pretense of neutrality.

The mountain is the place where it dawns on us that we are in the same plight as everyone else. There, values are recovered. But that's a weak way of putting it. Values are, of course, important, but the word is overused (especially by politicians and clergy) and no longer suggests the power and energy of a reoriented life. Dante was interested in a radical conversion, not in values clarification. Conversion is the road to recovering the path to one's true self. To do that we have to uncover what it is that really *rules* our lives. It is a question of a controlling image by which we interpret our lives and our world. In the West we focus much of our attention on marketability and consumption. These two things are the prism through which we look to discover our own value. Am I marketable? Will anyone want to buy me? This is the way we look at the world. Seen through the lenses of marketability and consumption, human behavior degenerates into manipulation and aggression, human knowledge into quantification, observation, and measurement, and human loving into transitory commitments and mechanized sexuality.

Hell shows us the cost of finding our identity in possessions and performance. Will I sell? When a teenager disappoints her parents in getting a B instead of an A as a final grade, she commits suicide. When the body won't stay young and the years take their toll, there are those who rage against the coming darkness and try to stop time. Purgatory brings us back into time, space, and place, not as crippling limitations but as the occasions of grace.

Much of our lives is a performance. Caesar Augustus's dying words in A.D. 14 went something like this: "I've played my part well. Dismiss me with applause." Purgatory is about passion rather than performance— passion for life, not its replication in the safe theater of private or public fantasy. On one level, it's appropriate that we see our lives as part of a play in which we all have a part. A friend of mine helped me a great deal when I was feeling burdened by my job—too many people to please, too much money to raise. My friend laughed when I told him my troubles. "Enjoy the play!" he said. His laughter wasn't cruel or unkind. It was infectious. It took me out of a particular hell of worry and threw me into a freer place of movement and possibility. But there is a sense in which seeing life as a play is destructive and illusory. "The passion that transforms life, and art, did not seem to be mine. But in all its essentials, my life was a good performance." So speaks the protagonist of Josephine Hart's harrowing novel *Damage*. "I had obeyed the rules. I had been rewarded."[12] He was in hell.

The spiritual life is not a matter of obeying or breaking rules. It's about breaking into and being broken open by a way of transformation. It's not about acquiring certain items of information or knowledge. Intellectually clever people can sometimes be spiritual imbeciles. On the mountain of Purgatory there is no foothold for the old logic of a manipulative rationalism.

To discover how to be human becomes all the more urgent when the times are obviously apocalyptic. Unless we are willing to do our own spiritual inner work and toil up the mountain of Purgation, we will be ripe for various forms of psychological and political totalitarianism. We live in constant danger of new servitudes because we so ache for love that we will do almost anything to find it. We were born with the longing to be loved, and we are easily seduced by anything that will act as a surrogate or will deaden the ache. We often settle for less than love—for power or servitude.

Conversion is recovering the path to our true self as one whose birthright it is to be loved. As I understand them, the great religious traditions offer us a purgatorial way through the temptations to power and teach us the way of love. Apocalyptic times intensify the call to climb the mountain. They push us toward the fundamental choice between love and fear.

What still attracts me to Christianity is its romantic vision of the converted life. It is a love story. Dante fell in love and had to spend the rest of his life finding out what that falling meant. He combined romanticism with a probing intelligence. His love had political and social teeth. As I experience the life of faith, I find myself believing more and more in the solidarity of the human family and, at the same time, am encouraged to be radically skeptical about everything else. In this respect, I have been affected by postmodernism. I think we are coming to a crisis (perhaps we are already in the middle of it and the barbarians at the gate are us) in which our sense of self is disintegrating. I can no longer believe in my self as something independent of others. We are irrevocably caught up in one another's destiny. There's a part of me that is cautious about this. I don't want to end up in the middle of some communal Marxist utopia. I am hoping for Trinitarian communion.

I get scared because the affirmation of solidarity means that I am peculiarly defenseless. I sometimes feel confused and even betrayed by the "established" instabilities of politics-as-usual and religion-as-safety. In order to be human, I find that I have to be willing to collaborate and live with the worry that my identity is something I share with others. To be a person of faith is to live in the context of one's own demise, one's own apocalypse. There is something impressive about our willingness to go on even in the middle of our confusion, hurting, and silliness. I have become convinced that our pursuit and celebration of identity are largely mistaken. Integrity should come first. Pursue integrity and identity will follow.

In bringing up my children, I have never known how far to push and how far to relax with regard to issues of identity and integrity. I want them to be happy and content, but not without effort and discipline. I want them to know joy, but not to be so mellow and laid-back that they have no room for outrage and sorrow. I don't want them to be crushed when their hearts are broken (as they surely will be, if they are alive and aware) by an event, a word, or a betrayal. Very few of us want to think and make the effort to have a well-furnished mind. We resist it because hard thinking tends to allow the hard truths of apocalyptic realities to puncture and deflate our view of the world. The process of deflation is both disastrous and necessary because thinking is only one way of knowing. That is why we need the intuitive artist to pump the air back into tired and deflated imaginations so that we can navigate the future with hope. There is also a strange relationship between the sentimental and the cynical, the trashy and the sublime, the absurd and the rational. We need something to unsettle our thinking in order to set free the imagination. A poem can be a great unsettler. Dante makes me feel *and* think, not only about the state of my soul, but also about how I should vote.

We live in hope because in purgatory things move; history is malleable. Dante's whole life as reflected in his poem is the radical reinterpretation of his own history in the light of the revelation of God's love, which holds everything in being. We know that hell is not remedial—there can be no pursuit of lost alternatives—but the vision of hell is renewing and full of hope. Repentance as radical change is needed for survival. Dante found it

hard to love his fellow human beings. He was proud, ambitious, and political, and had to find out through pain and exile that humanity is one. He
had to rely on the kindness, patronage, and hospitality of foreigners and
strangers, and this reliance humanized him.

For Dante, to be a citizen in a just commonwealth was the highest form
of humanity. This is a point we are beginning to recover today, at least from
an ecological perspective. Many people recognize that we are living in one
planetary system, but we have yet to see the political and social implications of this viewpoint. Even at his most aristocratic, Dante insisted on the
responsibilities of church and empire to support and nurture all their citizens. He saw only too clearly the correlation of various parts of the body
politic. He was passionate about justice, and justice is what we owe one another as citizens. For him as for us, justice is the agent of liberation, not the
means of punishment. Dante had been on the receiving end of the abuse of
political power. He was appalled by the misuse of authority in both church
and state. Hell is peopled with those in authority who failed to live up to
their responsibilities.

We have seen how appallingly cruel Dante's world was. He did a great
deal to humanize it and heal its wounded and twisted imagination. His vision of the human person—radically unique and unrepeatable, yet finding
fulfillment in community—had far-reaching political and social implications, implications we have yet to see and implement. Our hope depends on
our seeing how deeply we belong to one another. When that belonging is
fully acknowledged, there are implications for social policy and political
action. The New Testament phrase for all this is "the reign of God." Daniel
Maguire writes:

> The reign of God is a symbol in two senses. The vibrant sense of
> possibility causes it to crash against the inadequate present and to
> struggle toward a fantastically different yet plausible future. In the
> present tense it calls for a totally new mind-set, for new "habits of
> the heart" and mind.[13]

Dante calls his readers to struggle toward a fantastically different yet plau-
sible future. He doesn't reinforce the status quo. He turns it upside down.
In effect, he tells his contemporaries that they have got the great adventure
of hell, purgatory, and heaven all wrong. God promises a different future
than the writhing of the damned.

A STORY OF THE REIGN OF GOD: THE RECOVERY OF
THE RIGHT PATH

Once upon a time a holy rabbi was granted a vision of the Last Judgment. He found himself in a courtroom. Before him on a table were the scales of justice. There were also two doors and both of them were open. Through one he could see the light of Paradise; through the other, the darkness of Hell. It was the Day of Judgment and the human race was on trial.

The defense counsel entered the courtroom carrying a little bundle of good deeds under his arm. It had not been a great year for good deeds. Next, the chief prosecutor came in with two assistants. Each of them carried an enormous sack of sins. They were bent over with the sheer weight of the sacks. Dropping them before the scales of justice, they took a deep breath and went back for more. "This isn't even a tenth of it," they said, as they dragged in more sacks. The defense counsel, whose tiny bundle of good deeds was beginning to look pathetic next to the great pile of sins sitting on the floor, buried his head in his hands and sighed.

Just outside the door to Paradise, someone was listening. It was Levi Yitzhak of blessed memory, the rabbi of Berditshev. When he was on earth he had sworn that not even in death would he forget the plight of struggling humanity. When he heard the sigh of the defense counsel, he decided to slip into the courtroom. Seeing the tiny bundle of good deeds next to the huge sacks of sins, he didn't take long to size up the situation. He decided on a plan of action and waited until there was a recess. Left alone in the courtroom, he began to drag the sacks of sins, one at a time, to the door leading to Hell. It took all his strength and a great deal of time to throw them in one by one. He was almost finished—in fact, he was holding the very last sack—when the prosecutors and the defense counsel returned. Rabbi Yitzhak was caught red-handed. He did not deny what he had done. How could he? He had thrown away the sins so that the good deeds would outweigh the bad.

Since the court was bound to uphold the law, the chief prosecutor demanded justice. "It is written that a thief shall be sold for his theft. Let Levi Yitzhak be sold at auction right now in this courtroom! Let's see if anyone will bid for him."

By now the demons from Hell and the angels from Heaven had heard the commotion in the courtroom, and they came to watch the two parties lined up beside the scales of justice. The bidding began. Abraham, Isaac, and Jacob threw their good deeds onto the scales and the matriarchs added theirs. In fact, all the righteous contributed what they could. But the dark forces were able to gather up unnumbered sins stored in the deep places of the earth. The scale on their side went down and down and down. Rabbi Yitzhak was doomed. His crime had been to throw away the sins of the world so that we could be forgiven. "I buy him!" said the chief prosecutor, and dragged him to the door leading to the great darkness.

Just then, above the courtroom, from the Throne of Glory itself, came a voice. "I buy him!" There was a great silence. And God spoke, "I buy him. Heaven and Earth are mine, and I give them all for Levi Yitzhak—Levi who would have me forgive my children."[14]

Forgiveness is the key to the mountain of Purgatory. It is the basis of right relations among human beings. It restores lost mutuality and brings us close to one another.

SEVEN

RECOVERING THE PATH TO MUTUALITY

The village of San Marcos is a bumpy forty miles from Managua, Nicaragua. Just outside the village is a farm for street boys from the infamous Eastern Market in the capital. The boys are known as "the glue sniffers." All of them come to the farm with some form of venereal disease as well as an addiction to the toxic fumes of certain kinds of glue. The farm was founded by an Italian, Zerlinda, who is possessed of a vision of mutuality that drives her to get the boys off the streets and into care. Her grandparents were gypsies and her father a trapeze artist in a circus. The gypsy and circus background helps her survive in Nicaragua. "Nicaragua makes you live in the moment. The present is very strong here, and you need to have your feet on the ground and your head in the clouds at all times if you're going to make it here. I want to found another project for girls in Managua. I don't know how I'm going to pull it off, but you have to live from day to day and learn to trust. If you believe in a just cause and what you do is not for yourself, then you have available to you limitless energy—power you didn't know you had. . . . When you have something to live for beyond yourself, there is also a force beyond the self working with you and through you." To survive and flourish in this world, we all could do with some gypsy and circus blood in our veins.

Living in the moment and trusting the present is not easy. We live either in the past or in the future but not in the present moment—"the eternal now," as the mystics called it. The discipline of the mountain of Purgation is to put the self in touch with the energy or Spirit available to it when the soul gets back on track. The Spirit opens us up to a self consumed neither with self-hate nor with contempt for others. The Spirit's work is to bring the soul back to life with a vision of cooperation and mutuality. The mountain is the place where the pilgrim is given the grace to remember and recover the past, reenter the body and accept the limitations of the flesh, and live in the here and now. In short, purgatory brings us back into a story so that we can endure and enjoy being human in the present moment. The movement into a proper sense of self is also one into right relations with others and with the world. Mutuality, reciprocity, and exchange are the marks of the fully human. In short, we are called to love and to be loved.

Are we asking too much of the world to love us? Was Mozart right to ask everybody, "Do you love me?" Can we be dependent on one another and, at the same time, be truly and freely ourselves? Can I love another and still be me? Won't something of me have to be surrendered or repressed? Such fears are understandable, but they also miss the point of what love is like. Logic tells us that complete unity with another cannot allow for complete self-possession. Something has to give way. One has to dominate the other. Love is, therefore, an impossible ideal. In its romantic form, it becomes even more unattainable, existing in an orbit outside the human because it has no place for boredom and routine. That is why romanticism, with its inflated vision of an all-encompassing grand passion, is dismissed as immature and naive. Such is the logic of those who see the self as free only when it is isolated and autonomous. But we are climbing up the mountain where such logic has no foothold. Dante is the poet of romantic love and claims that the true romance of life pushes into the really real and away from inflated and inflating fantasies. The mountain warns us that true love requires our seeing one another clearly as images and bearers of the divine. And, because we are embodied and bounded by time and space, we should expect what feels like boredom and dull routine to be, in large part, the context of our enrollment in the school of love. Boredom rather than loathing is the most common ruin of love. Love requires "moral intelligence" to go on choosing the other during periods of ordinariness and routine.[1] Every act of love requires an act of faith. Our loving demands intellectual, moral, and spiritual conversion, which gives us a sense of belonging to something bigger than we are. This isn't a reference to the old cliché of one lover saying to the other, "Darling, it's bigger than both of us." Rather, it is an insistence that the "something bigger," in the first instance, is social and political life with its attendant responsibilities. Love has civic as well as personal duties.

Dante called for a new vision of the church and the empire, of religion and politics in the context of his vision of love. We need strong religious and political institutions for the passing on of the truly human. The vehicles for passing on a living tradition are ritual and storytelling. As we have seen, big stories that try to include everything are suspect. Rituals are common but often ungrounded and trivial. In California, the therapeutic culture encourages private and idiosyncratic rituals for personal use. For the most part, they have an artificial flavor because the participants have little or no historical knowledge or imagination. Rituals are often a pastiche of bits and pieces of traditions—a bit of Zen, a pinch of Native American, a poem from high school, and personal mementos and artifacts. Instant sacraments and quick-frozen rituals for private use. We should not be surprised at this, nor should we despise such efforts to recover the sacred—the sacrament of the present. I am often touched by people's efforts to build a holy place from the debris of half-remembered traditions. But we are not deep enough on our own. We live in a commodity-consuming culture where packaging is more important than content. We can even package instant meaning and serious intimacy. There's a cartoon of a message scrawled on the wall of a public toilet: "Lola gives good commitment." Is there a way of breaking through the trivializing of love? Not without recovering the sense of our lives as a personal and communal story.

Tradition has it that Saint Peter was given the keys of the kingdom by Christ. There were two keys, one gold and the other silver. Dante saw in the gold and silver keys the two complements of the reign of God. The gold (like the light from the sun) represented the outer realities; the silver (like the more subtle light from the moon), the inner. True community requires both the outer authority of just laws justly administered and the inner authority of mature citizens committed to their responsibilities, all in the context of a love story or passion play with God as the protagonist. The human community, when true to itself, is a godly community. There can be no community without mutual trust, and, since we let one another down, there can be no genuine trust without the promise of forgiveness. Without trust, the passions go crazy. They cannot blossom. And without forgiveness, trust is destabilized and undermined. The recovery of trust is, therefore, a central theme of purgatory. It means that I have to learn to trust without any assurance that I won't be betrayed. Trust asks me to give up my demand for immediate gratification, satisfaction, and reciprocity. I find the challenge to trust very disturbing because I can hardly trust myself sometimes. Trusting another takes an act of courage. Can I trust you to stick with me through the disappointments and misunderstandings that are bound to occur in our dealings with each other? Can I rely on you not to push your claims on me to their fullest extent? Can I trust you to exercise some restraint? More important, can I count on you to be there for me when things really do fall apart? Am I asking too much? One of the defining features of relationships of trust is a refusal to insist on a tit-for-tat accounting of gains and losses. We live in a litigious, tit-for-tat society where everyone sees himself or herself as a victim who is owed something, and this me-first attitude cripples communal life.

Surely our trusting one another would be an act of primal stupidity? Not when one considers the alternative. Hell. As we climb up the mountain, we see how real and imagined wrongs poison our social life. Human relations exist in an environment of vulnerability where great harm is always a possibility. *Love has to be learned*. We need to go to school. Love is an act of grace in which there is no trace of bitterness, condescension, or resentment. It is the ultimate self-definition, the most precious and unique mode of being. It is, nevertheless, marred by disappointment and failure, by boring and selfish repetitions, and subject to arbitrary rules and regulations imposed by the fashions and resentments of the day. There are cases of men and women who were once lovers of a sort who are now locked in strategies of mutual persecution because their love turned sour. Someone *must* be to blame. Someone *must* pay. There is a way through our resentments, disappointments, and our desire to get even, but we need to go back to school to learn the craft of being human.

Love as passion is deceptive, and purgatory is where we are forced to slow down, take time, and learn about love. Dante's myth of life's journey presupposes that our very creation was occasioned by God's falling in love with us. It is God's love that requires the possibility of hell. It is love that pulls the soul up the mountain of Purgation. Stephen Mitchell's translation of the famous dissertation on love delivered by Dante's guide, Virgil, on the cornice of Sloth sums up Dante's understanding of how we are to be in the world:

> The Love of God, unutterable and perfect,
> Flows into a pure soul the way that light
> Rushes into a transparent object.
> The more love that it finds,
> The more it gives itself;

So that as we grow clear and open,
The more complete the joy of heaven is,
And the more souls who resonate together,
The greater the intensity of their love,
And, mirror-like, each soul reflects the other.[2]

Who would not want to respond to the divine longing for us? Yet our seeking to plunge into the abyss of desire gets us into trouble. An old debt is called in. An old sin, long forgotten, intrudes itself into the present. We find ourselves in one, two, or even three spirals or labyrinths of desire at the same time—one leads to misery, one to change, the third to hope; all are the result of the Love behind all things. At the heart of the universe are both freedom and mutuality. Love understands both. The chaos of love is to long for the other and, at the same time, to honor his or her difference, his or her otherness. To love is to be free, distinct, one's true self. To love is to be together, in community, in communion. Dante knew firsthand of the relationship of the imagination to desire. His theme is perennial: the spiritual journey, our rising and falling in the search for meaning and community. We are caught up in a love affair—in the ups and downs, the messes that our longings and desires get us into.

Our hungering and desiring bring us to horrible and harrowing places, but where would we be, who would we be, without them? The supreme metaphor of desire for Dante is that of the incarnation—God's deep longing to bring us home by means of identifying with us, so that we do not look upon one another as enemies but as those on whom God has imprinted the divine image and identity.

Hell is seeing every other human being as a rival—as someone against whom to define oneself. Purgatory is beginning to see them not only as allies but as essential to one's happiness. Envy—in its most hideous form as *Schadenfreude* (joy at the distress of another)—is the insidious enemy of trust. Oscar Wilde wrote, "Anyone can sympathize with the suffering of a friend, but it requires a fine nature . . . to sympathize with a friend's success." Wilde told the story of the Lucifer who, while crossing the Libyan desert, came upon a spot where a number of small fiends were tormenting a holy hermit. The inexperienced fiends were hopeless at tempting the man of God. Lucifer watched them flounder and fail and finally stepped forward to give them a lesson in temptation.

"What you do is too crude. . . . Permit me for one moment." With
that he whispered to the holy man, "Your brother has just been
made Bishop of Alexandria." A scowl of malignant jealousy at once
clouded the serene face of the hermit. "That," said the devil to his
imps, "is the sort of thing which I should recommend."[3]

One of the hardest lessons to learn is that we exist only in relationship
to one another and that we can experience joy in the success, talent, and
giftedness of others. Sometimes the lessons of love come too late. For Oscar
Wilde they did. He was a generous spirit but he seriously miscalculated the
consequences of flouting the conventions of his day. His body and to some
extent his spirit were broken by the rigors of Reading Gaol. There he was
stripped of the trappings of personality and reduced to the facelessness of
imprisonment, where he realized the dreadful aspect of human solidarity in
misery. In a poem reacting to the execution of a fellow prisoner, he wrote:

> And we were vain and ignorant nor knew
> That when we stabbed thy heart
> It was our own real hearts we slew.[4]

Countless messages from the tradition speak to this awesome solidarity.
Saint John Chrysostom insisted that the words *mine* and *thine* are "chilly
words that introduce innumerable wars into the world."[5] If we are not
watchful, there is malice lurking in property. We mistake one form of belonging (what belongs to us) for another (we belong to one another).
Covenants get confused with contracts.

We all have a need to belong and this makes us vulnerable to utopian
sects and snake-oil salesmen (both secular and religious). The discipline of
the mountain teaches us to avoid dangerous forms of belonging and false
solidarities, and to seek mature ones. It is all a matter of how we define and
locate the self in relation to others. Carl Jung and others make a distinction
between the ego and the self, and, in one sense, the spiritual life is concerned with the connection between the two. The self is not God but is the
"opening" to God—a kind of gravitational point of reference for both the
collective and the individual. For Fritz Kunkel, we consist of an actual self
(that is, all that's going on), an idealized self (which gets us into trouble),
and a real self (which is who we want to be and really are). The real self is

not "I" but "we." And not only the "we" of human solidarity but the "We" of the creativity of God. As creatures who are defined by our relationship to Spirit, immense resources are available to us. The ego has only its own puny resources to work with, and since the ego is going against the spontaneous movement of the real self, it is constantly beleaguered and always at war. Kunkel writes, "The collective powers are to be found on the side of the Self, while the strength available to the Ego is limited to shrewd cunning and sentimental excitement, cleverly used but not at all creative."[6] Zerlinda, with her gypsy and circus blood, in her work with the young glue sniffers of Nicaragua knew this simple truth: the energy of the ego is used up defending itself against everyone else. No one is to be trusted, because who knows who might be a competitor or exploiter? Then there are the inner dangers the ego has to watch out for: strong emotions, unruly desires, and wayward thoughts. Being an ego is a full-time occupation. So many things are out to get you that there is no time for spontaneity and creativity. Yet the deeper part of us knows that this is a dumb strategy leading nowhere. And what about our need for loyalty, love, devotion, passion? To be fully human means to be able to take responsibility for something and to serve it unconditionally. Who would want to risk being shaped and even transformed by an unknown power? Isn't this why we are afraid of life even as we long for it? We are frightened of being swept away. We ache for and yet are terrified of ecstasy. We wonder if there is a difference between destiny and fate, between purpose and chance. We are internally divided between the conflicting desires of surrender and control.[7]

We love to belong. Note the way people say, "*We* won. *They* lost!" Who is this "we"? There is the undifferentiated "we" of the baby and the tribe. In spite of the baby's obvious immaturity, she is onto something. In spite of the dangers of tribalism, our urge to be together in closely knit groups speaks to a deep need. Too many children grow up with not enough food, let alone an adequate sense of significance and belonging. We hurt others deeply when we undermine their sense of belonging. We push one another into the hell of a loneliness that breeds not only distrust but also cruelty and indifference. I have seen one person behave despicably to another because the former believed that nothing he could do, however mean, could have an effect on the other. Since he didn't matter, nothing that he did mattered. If life is meaningless, what does it matter what we do? If we feel that we don't belong or that there is nothing and no one to belong to, what's the point of love, sacrifice, or tenderness? The only reason to relate to others is for a prudential strategy of security. Everything—even and especially our religion, if we have any—is brought under the umbrella of that crafty strategy. God needs to be manipulated, neutralized, or appeased by the ego taking care of itself. The strategy doesn't work in the way we hope, but it does serve a useful purpose. It brings the soul into the hell of a deep anxiety; through it, the soul comes to be led to the foot of the mountain, which can change everything.

Suffering is inevitable. The transition from the child's sense of solidarity and safety to the adult's maturing appreciation of community and communion is painful because the child *has* to grow up and let go. He or she has to move into a period of independence. But there is the further step, a leap in the dark, away from independence to interdependence. At that point, we tend to regress into old loyalties of a comforting tribalism. We easily become overburdened with pitiful strategies of self-preservation. We look for ways of defending ourselves against one another. We look for a group of people who are just like us. The stranger becomes the enemy. Hatred of the other becomes a destructive strategy of immediate safety.

Purgatory teaches us that no one is his or her own rescuer. Home is other people. Spiritual maturity is moving away from "Hell is other people" to "Heaven is mutuality and sharing." But we are frightened by the messiness of actual relationships, by the bumbling corruptions of democracy, by the confusion that the "others" always bring with them. We long to be rid of complexity, and hope for the false simplicity of totalitarian solutions to our political and social problems. We opt for shallow resolutions to our moral dilemmas. It wouldn't take much to reform the world. If people would only shape up, stop sleeping around, stop taking drugs, get a little discipline, start going to church again, all would be well. If the politicians concentrated on safe streets, economic superiority, and military readiness, our country would be back on its feet in no time. This God-is-on-our-side-ism is very tempting in times of instability.

Like migratory birds, we need more than one climate in which to live and are never completely at home. Our restlessness is related to our spiritual poverty. In the affluent West, we tend to choose fear over love because of our "advanced poverty." This isn't to play down the horror of actual grinding poverty. Robert Bellah characterizes our advanced poverty as

Great riches and poverty of soul. Advanced poverty is close to what
Jesus meant by the rich, those who depend on themselves alone. The
key to biblical poverty is reliance on the grace of God, not reliance
on ourselves, not reliance on the things we have, on what we have recently bought.[8]

Such sentiments, however noble and true, do not sell well on the street. It is
no accident, then, that the truly spiritual in the world's religions have understood the emptiness of the advanced poverty of the materially rich. But
how many of us really believe the ancient wisdom?

Albert Borgmann suggests that our culture is marred by two unpleas-
ant characteristics, *sullenness* and *hyperactivity,* that are related to our
sense of homelessness and advanced poverty. Buried in that sullenness is
callousness, the manifestations of which are private affluence and public
squalor. Mainstream economists, writes Borgmann, "advise an increase in
taxes, in the rate of savings, in the expenditures for research and development, and for capital equipment, a reduction in consumption and government spending, and more willingness to sacrifice and cooperate."[9] Robert
Bellah comments that we need to replace sullenness and hyperactivity with
care and celebration. It's hard to imagine a whole society embracing such
an austere program for the sake of new life. It sounds like the work of
purgatory.

We need two basic kinds of institutions for love to flourish: one that
serves our inner need for community, and the other that supports our need
for food and shelter in a just and safe environment. We need communities
and corporations. We need covenants *and* contracts. We need (to use Martin Buber's language) to have both "I–Thou" and "I–It" relationships and
not confuse the two. This means giving up our deadly perfectionism in
order to look for a humane, *not* a perfect, social order. North Americans
are, after all, the inheritors of the Puritans' vision of the New Jerusalem in
which covenant and contract each had its place. Dante believed that the
church and the empire needed to work together.

Covenantal promise is unconditional. In it, we bind ourselves to one another in freedom. But it's a freedom with freely imposed and accepted limitations, like "for better, for worse, for richer, for poorer, in sickness and in
health, till death us do part." A true covenant cannot be based on, "I will
wait for you forever provided you're not too long. I will love you forever

until someone more interesting shows up." In one of the made-up wedding ceremonies of the seventies a couple promised to stay together "while love lasts."

The path up the mountain, then, is a movement from "I" to "we," from "me" to "us." It is a pilgrimage for the sake of discernment, for the sake of being able to tell the difference between covenants and contracts. We see old resentments—when nursed over the years—rise up again and again in the children and the grandchildren. Recent history has taught with startling clarity that old animosities still have their power to poison. They can still cramp the soul and disease the imagination. At a recent reunion of some veterans who survived the building of the famous bridge over the river Kwai in Thailand, there were also some Japanese who had gone there to offer prayers. They were ashamed of the atrocities committed by their countrymen and had made the pilgrimage in the hope of healing. One Japanese let it be known that he would like to meet the veterans. One veteran said, "It's better that we don't meet. I would want to punch him in the face. What they did back then was unforgivable." This response is as understandable as it is tragic. The cruelty of the past was horrendously real and there seemed no way of stopping its poison from infecting the present. Stories like this, however, force us to take history seriously. In a survey at the end of the 1980s it was discovered that only 17 percent of the Bosnians considered themselves religious. Most Muslims, Serbs, and Croats were only nominally and culturally in one tradition rather than another (a bit like many Americans celebrating Christmas). But lying in wait in the depths of the soul are ancestral memories of resentment and fear ready to be resurrected and exploited.

The journey up the mountain of transformation has, however, a greater power than resentment. Love, when properly ordered, can neutralize the energy of the mean-mindedness that our fear and self-contempt stir up in us. The hardest part of love is having the imagination so healed that we are able to reach out in untried ways to others, even to those who have hurt us or whom we have hurt.

We talk a great deal about empowerment in our culture. It is a good goal for a society—the empowerment of its citizens. But it isn't enough. Empowerment that is blind to the imperative of forgiveness—of the self and of others—cannot deliver the happiness it promises. We need to accept a kind of powerlessness as well as demand appropriate empowerment. We are all mortal. We are all dependent on a host of others we cannot control. We all rely on countless others not only for our sustenance and well-being but for being alive at all. This is why going down the spiral of hell and struggling up the mountain of Purgation is vital. They shatter the illusion of self-sufficiency. Purgatory calls for the recovery of civic disciplines involving the recovery of trust.

Vaclav Havel in his *Summer Meditations* (1991) looks for a community of trust and calls for the recovery of what Dante called *cortesia* (courtesy), for raising the general level of public manners. Havel sees the need for a revolution in personal covenants and social contracts. By that he means the kind of relations that exist among ordinary people, "between the powerful and the weak, the healthy and the sick, the young and the elderly, adults and children, business people and customers, men and women, teachers and students, officers and soldiers, policemen and citizens, and so on."[10] Havel questions our relationships to nature, to animals, to the atmosphere, to the landscape, to towns, to gardens, to our homes. Can we develop a politics of trust with a vision of the state as an expression of that trust? In order for this to happen, people will have to repent (as Havel puts it, they will have to come to their senses).

> All my observations and all my experience have, with remarkable consistency, convinced me that, if today's planetary civilizations have any hope of survival, that hope lies chiefly in what we understand as the human spirit. If we don't wish to destroy ourselves in national, religious, and political discord; if we don't want to find our world with twice its current population, half of it dying of hunger; if we don't wish to kill ourselves with ballistic missiles armed with atomic warheads or eliminate ourselves with bacteria specially cultivated for the purpose; if we don't wish to see people go desperately hungry . . . then we must—as humanity, as people, as conscious beings with spirit, mind and sense of responsibility—somehow come to our senses.[11]

Coming to our senses (called conversion) is another way of talking about the discipline of the mountain. Is Havel a romantic? He is and he has a word for his postmodernist critics:

> So anyone who claims that I am a dreamer who expects to transform hell into heaven is wrong. I have few illusions. But I feel a responsibility to work towards the things I consider good and right. I don't

know whether I'll be able to change certain things for the better, or not at all. Both outcomes are possible. There is only one thing I will not concede: that it might be meaningless to strive in a good cause.[12]

Robert Bellah worries that we have exported the worst aspects of the American dream to every corner of the globe, including the countries of the former Soviet empire. The version of the dream for export has little to do with liberty and justice for all and everything to do with casino economics and consumer greed. Bellah quotes Erazim Kohak, an American-Czech philosopher who now teaches in the United States and at Prague.

The Americans of popular Czech imagination are people who never have to deny themselves anything, who can charge anything that strikes their fancy to their credit cards without ever worrying how they will pay for it. They live in an enchanted land free of all mundane cares, a land where wishing makes it so. Most of all, they live in a land which is totally dedicated to the unlimited expansion of individual material affluence.

That is what many people in the world think of as the American dream and, more dangerously, believe to be the rewards of democracy. It is a dream of a freedom made up mostly of irresponsibility, unreality, and instant gratification. It leads straight to hell. The simple truth is that happiness is not to be found in collecting "stuff" but in self-simplification, not in exploitation but in caring, not in self-gratification but in finding ways to give ourselves away.

The path up the mountain isn't easy because there is great risk in recovering the life of the passions. In a recent conversation, Chris Brain, an innovative priest from Sheffield, England, talked about bringing desire back into worship—real passionate desire. He is right to identify our malaise in the West as ennui—the nagging boredom of the self saturated with itself. We need to recover our passion for life—our elemental desire for justice, creativity, peace, and love. Many people passively experience life as bewildering and fragmented. "We can't leave eroticism," Brain says, "to the pornographers or film stars who create lying images and ultimately dehumanizing models. We need all the passion we can get to save the planet from extinction."[13]

Passion and trust go together because passion opens us up to risk. It requires a great deal of trust to act in the hope that others won't attack us at the moment of increased defenselessness. I need others to allow me to be me but at the same time to set me free from enslavement to myself. This is tricky. How do we learn to confirm and revere one another's existence, which, after all, is what love does?

One way is through sexual love. Art and sex teach us lessons about sharing and attachment. Sex, as lust, is one of the things that undermines our ability to imagine the otherness of other people, but sexual love also enables us to honor it. Think of the things that fed Dante's imagination. Think of the images that feed ours and those of our children. Images *matter*. They give shape to our desires. Metaphors are political and social. In Dante's time, a gloating hatred of sex set men against women and women against men. The erotic was both wounded and distorted. In our own day, the battle goes on in a different form. The atmosphere around sexual relations continues to be stormy and dangerous. Anita Hill's appearance before the Senate Judiciary Committee to testify against the nomination of Clarence Thomas to the Supreme Court had a whole nation riveted to its television sets.

In Dante's time, sexuality was played out in a culture of crude violence. One contemporary vision of the damned portrayed women of loose life who were made to ride on sidesaddles spiked with red-hot nails. Bodies were abused sexually and the flesh of criminals shown no mercy. Murderers in Florence were executed by being buried alive upside down. If we think that Dante's descriptions are fanciful, recall Frederick II's revenge on his enemies. He cloaked them in lead and then melted it on them. Dante himself would have been burned at the stake had his enemies caught him.

On a daily basis, what feeds *our* imagination? Aren't our lives played out more and more against the backdrop of a corrosive violence? It's not that we are to protect ourselves from the dark truths of existence. Rather, we need an imaginative tradition to help us negotiate the hells and purgatories of everyday existence in such a way that we do not create *actual* infernos to which we consign *real* people: in Northern Ireland, the Middle East, Africa, the former Yugoslavia, and, God knows, elsewhere. Violence mixes well with sex. It mixes even better with religion.

For Dante's contemporaries, many streams of horror-laden guilt had flowed into their imaginations from both Christian and pagan sources "to congeal their inner natures with fear."[14] There were, for example, tales of Nordic and Celtic beasts that tore people and the world apart. I cannot help but think of the bombardment we receive from television and movies of horror and violence. It is naive and irresponsible to think that those images don't matter. Our imaginations are as wounded as those of Dante's contemporaries and need as much healing. Dante took the late-medieval doctrine of eternal damnation and reworked it in such a way that "he helped to rid the European imagination of some of its worst fears and of its mindless acceptance of cruelty."[15] I believe our imaginative work is no less significant in our own day. The world's future depends on our being willing to reimagine the world.

Love brings with it the fear that one might be caught in a situation from which there is no escape. The good news that we dread is that there is no escape from love. Dante's God,

> the Supreme Goodness,
> breathes forth your soul directly
> and falls in love with you,
> so that from then on you always desire God.[16]

Calling Christianity erotic could be thought to be dangerous because of the violence lurking beneath the surface of a life that we fear will easily race out of control. There is certainly a great gap between the Christian mystical understanding of love and desire and that of the contemporary world. Much of what passed for love during the period of the so-called permissive society was ignorant of the shadow side of loving. We are now paying heavily for that naïveté. It is hard for us to grasp the fact that faith is an erotic quest that never ends. We find it difficult to imagine the lure and longing of unutterable beauty. We suffer from a coarseness and flatness of soul and are afraid to think in large terms about human destiny. Faith is not a feeling, but an opening of the heart to all of reality. This is another way of talking about the deep human longing for the really real. The erotic is the strongest image we have for our longings.

We all possess or are possessed by a desire to know and be known, to love and be loved. But who needs to go to school to learn about love? We are carried away by passion and one night of it makes us experts. We confuse love with emotions, just as we confuse faith with feelings. Falling into love is only the beginning, and we soon find that we are both helpless and ignorant when faced with the mystery of love. We can never get to the bottom of it because love moves on to an ever-expanding horizon. We need to be initiated into love's mysteries. We need help. We dread and yet long for the divine ordering of our loving.

Henry, in Tom Stoppard's play *The Real Thing*, tries to explain to his daughter what sexual, romantic love is all about. It has to do with knowing and being known. Carnal knowledge is knowledge gained only when we give ourselves to each other.

> Knowledge of each other, not of the flesh but through the flesh, knowledge of the self, the real him, the real her, *in extremis*, the mask slipped from the face. Every other version of oneself is on offer to the public. We share our vivacity, grief, sulks, anger, joy . . . we hand it out to anybody who happens to be standing around, to friends and family with a momentary sense of indecency perhaps, to strangers without hesitation. Our lovers share with us the passing trade. But in pairs we insist that we give ourselves to each other.

Charlotte, his ex-wife, replies:

> There are no commitments, only bargains. And they have to be made every day. You think making a commitment is *it*. You think it sets like a concrete platform and it'll take any strain you want to put on it. You're committed. You don't have to prove anything. In fact you can afford a little neglect, indulge in a little sarcasm here and there, isolate yourself when you want to. Underneath it's concrete for life. I'm a cow in some ways, but you're an idiot. *Were* an idiot. . . .

Henry responds:

> No commitments. Only bargains. The trouble is I don't really believe it. I'd rather be an idiot. It's a kind of idiocy I like. I use you because you love me. I love you so use me. Be indulgent, preoccupied, premenstrual . . . your credit is infinite, I'm yours, I'm committed. . . . It's no trick to love somebody at their best. Love is loving them at their worst. Is that romantic? Well good. Everything should be romantic. Love, work, music, literature, virginity, loss of virginity.[17]

Is it nonsense to say that everything should be romantic? The more I read the play, the more sympathy I have for the ex-wife, Charlotte. But I continue to hope that she is wrong. Where is Henry? In heaven or in hell? Love is wildly disorienting, and experiencing it for the first time can be shattering. Erotic love does two things. It makes you notice your body! In fact, for the first time in your life, perhaps, you *are* your body. Love also throws you into a whirlwind—Dante's *bufera*—so that you don't ever know quite where you are. How reliable is Tom Stoppard's Henry? Did he understand what marriage is all about? Did he know that it "images" other relationships? Marriage "images" our relationship to the world. It doesn't inhibit desire but reveals how desire is meant to work in fidelity in relationships, in the continuity of commitments. We can't be blamed for confusing the metaphor of marriage with the institution. That is why so many marriages end up on the rocks. But marriage is also a metaphor for the unmarried and married alike—a metaphor of integration and wholeness. And some actual marriages move into being a spiritual path for both partners, in which are explored the freeing but purgatorial questions: How are we free? How are we contained? How are desire and stability related to each other? What are the laws that set us free?

Joseph Campbell rightly pointed out that Dante was "one of the medieval writers who brought about a revolution in the uses and purposes of myth, from being a means to *maintaining* stability in societies as the repositories of beliefs and symbols by which each society was guided, to turning myth into a means of *changing* society through altering emotional attitudes, so that one great individual's rediscovery of the inner meaning of myth became a radical instead of a conservative force."[18] In effect, Dante provided us with a new spiritual architecture for the soul.

What were Dante's distinctive contributions to the life of the imagination for the sake of the education of desire? One had to do with his concept of the individual and another was his vision of the goodness of creation. Dante was creating in his own day a new language for the soul. R. W. Church in the middle of the last century spoke of *The Divine Comedy* as "the beginning of a language." Dante "had an eye to see the true springs and abysses of this mortal life."[19] William Anderson suggests that Dante believed that "a Christian style of language should reflect the ineffable humility of the Son of God in taking on Himself human form," because the ability to speak and communicate is the most human of characteristics and the one in which we share most clearly in the divine life. The claim is that "the Incarnation transformed the possibilities of language . . . as it did the possibilities of humanity in this life and the next." Redemption through language is a very important idea. Today we fail to take language seriously, or perhaps we take it seriously in a shallow way. Dante believed that the spiritual and the moral were fused together in the proper use of language.

Vision and action needed to be in harmony. If you could see clearly, you would be able to desire purely and act accordingly. Speaking the truth with integrity was in itself redeeming because it was the way a human being shared in the life of God. But the truth of the incarnation is that God shared in the fully human life. Divinity is present with us even in our hells and purgatories. Christ descended into the inferno, into the damnable place of our lostness and rejection, and, holding up a lamp to the dark places of the mind and harrowing hell, brought "to the light of consciousness new and forgotten areas of physical and psychological experience, begging for redemption through language and the transmutation of art."[20]

Hence the importance of naming and renaming on the various stages of our spiritual pilgrimage. As Jacob wrestling with the angel is given a new name, so are we after our struggles. We go into the depths for the sake of naming, for the transmutation of identity, for the ordering of our loving, and for the formation of character. The purpose of Dante's poem, then, is to educate his readers in what it is to be human beings, what it is to be awake and aware.

Poetry becomes the dish of an imaginative telescope capable of gathering images of our origins. Dante's distant world is still sending its messages to our own. He was no hermit meditating on timeless truths. He saw the universal in the particular, and came to his sublime vision by being involved in the bitter feuds of his day.

Just as there is no escape from love, there is no escape from myth. We are always being liberated or enslaved by the patterning power of myth. The irresistible power of myth captures the human imagination and satisfies deep psychic needs. "Mere fact pales in comparison. And myths are potent, often carrying with them an irresistible power to change lives, change nations, change history."[21] Our intense need for myths, and our imprisonment by them, is illustrated by the example of Charles Lindbergh. At age twenty-five, Lindbergh flew across the Atlantic to Paris with a quart of water and five sandwiches: two ham, two roast beef, and an egg salad. *The Spirit of St. Louis* took off, clearing the electrical wires at the end of the field by less than twenty feet, and disappeared into the fog. It landed in France thirty-three hours later. Lindbergh was welcomed back in New York as a hero. He was awarded the Congressional Medal of Honor, the French Legion of Honor, and the British Air Force Cross. Four thousand poets composed verse in his honor. He received 100,000 telegrams and cables,

14,000 packages, and 3.5 million letters; requests for funds, proposals of marriage, the Award of the Silver Buffalo from the Boy Scouts, a German shepherd, an airplane, and a lifetime pass from the National Association of Professional Baseball Leagues.

Lindbergh had joined the pantheon of Greek heroes. But it is a grievous thing to be the carrier of a myth for one's contemporaries. He was free in the air but on the ground he was a prisoner of people's projections. "The crowds believed he belonged to them. He wished to belong to no one. . . . In St. Louis women fought over a corncob he had gnawed." He fell from grace. It was his increasingly strident isolationist speeches that brought him down. In a *Reader's Digest* article just before the war, Lindbergh wrote, "Aviation seems almost a gift from heaven . . . only a Western wall of race and arms can hold back the infiltration of inferior blood and permit the White race to live at all in a pressing sea of Yellow, Black and Brown."[22]

I have a friend who helps me understand why we need to keep reinterpreting the past by telling it over and over again in story form. He struggles with spiritual homelessness, a sense of exile. He is sometimes pained by the memory of choices made decades ago. My friend is learning to remember, learning to recover a lost pain. He wrote to me recently about a significant moment in his past when he was deeply in love. We're about the same age and, although we come from radically different backgrounds, we find that the "stuff" one of us is going through has a remarkable resonance and consistency with what the other is experiencing. I don't think this is particularly unusual or profound, but there is something reassuring and comforting about one person trusting another with his or her experiences and discovering similarities and echoes. The incident happened one summer over thirty years ago, and the memory of it came flooding back in all its startling clarity when he revisited the city where it happened. The location hadn't changed much. There was the bridge over which they had walked and the avenue down which they had sauntered hand in hand. My friend realized that the *memory* of past feelings—thirty-year-old feelings—was clearer to him than his *present* feelings about the past. The past had been hastily put away all those years ago, and a different path—a good one, as it happened—had been taken. The memory raised questions that came from a raw and deeply alive place inside him. He had recovered a deep pain. He had also recovered a lost and neglected part of himself. He had returned from hell, with news about himself that he could not have found any other way.

Can one fall in love with someone and then fall in love with someone else without retaining something of that first love? We walk away from love all the time when we say Yes! to someone else. We choose one path over another. If we don't choose honestly and clearly, there's hell to pay. And yet life is full of unconsummated affairs, unfinished conversations, loves from whom we've turned. They all speak to our sense of homelessness and our wanting to find our way forward, which is our way back home.

The monk who influenced me most when I was studying for the priesthood used to say that the most convincing argument for heaven is that we have to have somewhere to finish all those spirited conversations and intimate encounters. Sometimes a memory comes back to us, triggered by a place or a smell, filling us with the original emotions. "Yes, I still love him." "Yes, I still ache for her." "Or do I? Is the pain that I feel a sign of an even deeper longing?" The feelings are still there, intact. Perhaps we weep. Perhaps we're too embarrassed to share the experience with others because it seems foolish. Perhaps we turn away in anger and impatience. The love is still there but the road was not taken. What did I turn my back on and why? Is this a stupid question? A useless speculation? Yet I wonder and it aches. Why does it disturb me so? What does it say about me now? What really happened all those years ago? Can I find out? Should I bother to retrace my steps and recover the abandoned and lost bits and pieces of myself? Should I probe the pain? In one sense, I have no choice because these bits and pieces of the past are still at work and insist on being attended to. They are all "me" and desire to be gathered together.

I think that is, in part, what Dante's journey was about—the unfinished business of the soul that was awakened by love, lost its way, and had to retrace its steps to find the right path. But I do not believe that we can ever recapture the past *accurately*. We can get to the truth only through inference—through myth and poetry, through metaphor and storytelling. There is no such thing as "what actually happened." This simple truth often causes an earthquake in people who look at the world with a literalist squint. Apocalyptic times demand the revival of storytelling. But we have to be able to listen to more than one kind of story and more than one version of the same tale. The hardest thing of all is to be prepared to listen to other voices tell *our* story from another point of view. The great stories are always pushing us into community by challenging us to find or accept a moral framework for our life together. Dante is a perfect guide for those who have the beginnings of a conscious spiritual life that is marked by an openness to imaginative and intelligent storytelling.

In spite of its impossibility, we are always trying to rewrite history (our own personal story as well as national and international history) in the hope that we will be able to get to the bottom of what "really happened," so that we can, somehow, stop the pain of longing and come home from exile. It's our way of trying to understand our confusion and incompleteness.

Our need to tell stories raises the important apocalyptic question of the relationship between myth and reality. Parents often ask a child suspected of lying, "Have you been telling stories?" Discernment here is very important, because a child knows that some stories that are not literally true are true on another, deeper level. Some fundamentalists want to ban all stories that are not literally true. There would be no hobbits, no Aslan, no unicorns—nothing fantastical or mythological. When the world is falling apart, the question of how myths are tested and regulated becomes a matter of life and death. How do we preserve the vitality of life-bearing myths and undermine destructive and harmful ones? How do we choose between conflicting stories? We are all in the business of mythologizing our lives. We cannot help it, but our mythologies need challenging and correcting from time to time in the light of a great myth or story that has been tested over time.

We need startling and powerful images to rescue us from the place of exile to which our despair sometimes brings us. Margaret Drabble, in *The Gates of Ivory*, writes about Good Time and Bad Time, between which is an apocalyptic gulf. Where these two times meet, there are conflicting and horrifying stories. She asks us to imagine standing by a bridge over a river on the border between Thailand and Cambodia. In Thailand we can see a society crammed with all the material benefits and communications technology of Good Time. Across the bridge is the Bad Time of Cambodia.

> Good Time and Bad Time coexist. We in Good Time receive messengers who stumble across the bridge or through the river, maimed and bleeding, shocked and starving. They try to tell us what it is like over there, and we try to listen. We invoke them with libations of aid, with barley and blood, with rice and water, and they flock to the

dark trenches, moaning and fluttering in their thousands. We are seized with panic and pity and fear. Can we believe these stories from beyond the tomb? Can it be that these things happen in our world, our time?[23]

We, with our stories set in Good Time, can take in all the horror stories from Bad Time over breakfast with our toast and coffee. It would be simplistic and unjust to say that we don't care, that "we thrive on atrocities, that we eagerly consume suffering. It is not as simple as that. We need them as they need us."[24] The stories interact and interrelate—so much so that we fear that Bad Time could be waiting for us, not in Cambodia or Central America but right there in the next room. The membrane separating the rich and the poor is getting very thin.

Dante spent most of his life in exile on the bridge between Good Time and Bad Time. His images provide me with "ironic points of light" to negotiate the ups and downs of a life largely lived somewhere between waking and sleeping. He does for me what Virgil did for him. He brings me into a community that I would rather avoid. The Bad Time is brought horribly close. The community of God includes undesirable aliens, strangers, and criminals. The metanarrative is all-inclusive, as all stories have to be heard for the great story to be true. Dante helps me move from a safe but isolated "I" to a communal but risky "we," from a grasping "me" to an inclusive "us." Robert Pogue Harrison accurately describes Dante's achievement: "Virgil the poet of history, empire, and epic, brought about for Dante a reorientation from the personal to the communal, the existential to the historical, the private to the public . . . and made possible for the first time the transformation of the single self's *vita nuova* into the *nostra vita* of the *Commedia*'s first verse."[25] The *new* life becomes *our* life. The shared life is the divine life, and our life is the vision of God. We move up the mountain, having come to our senses and found one another, and are ready to be reconciled to the One who has been longing for and desiring us.

EIGHT

RECOVERING THE VISION OF GOD

"The vision of God" is an odd expression. I've used it for years without having much of a clue to its real meaning. We can get some idea of what the expression signifies by thinking about our lives in stark terms of mortality and meaninglessness. Some go to their deaths in denial—wondering what happened. They have no sense that life is a series of passages, all related to one another in the form of a story. Life seems more of a futile catastrophe than a movement through a narrative. The once powerful are rendered powerless, and those of us left alive realize that it is better to be "a live dog than a dead lion." Others catch a glimpse of the bigger picture. Looking back over their lives, they are able to say to themselves, "Ah! That's where I've been. That's who I am!" Their lives are given a focus and goal because they were able to see within it the lines of a story with three basic motifs: being lost (separation), turning around (initiation), and finding home (return). They have a vision that they are part of a larger story—a more generous and expansive reality—than that of their own limited experience. Recovering the vision of God is a matter not only of recovering the narrative framework of our own lives, but (if we are in positions of power) of backing off and allowing others to have their story. These passages are not merely *mine* or *yours*; they are *ours*. "Heaven" is making room for others and celebrating their significance. There is no humanity without story, no narrative without God. There are no stories without storytellers, and storytellers are not always reliable. The whole purpose of the journey is the reordering of the imagination in the direction of an all-inclusive story. Dante's is a story about that ordering in a dramatic framework of homecoming from exile. His themes are error and homelessness. He writes from direct experience. His exile from Florence is significant because it connected him with all those who have experienced rejection and exile; it connected him also with the exilic mentality of the Old Testament, as well as with the New Testament affirmation that here we have no abiding city. Our citizenship is in heaven (Philippians 3:20); there is no final resting here. We are driven by a longing to know how the story works out "in the end." We long for resolution. There is something satisfying—even right and proper—when the words THE END appear on the screen in large letters at the conclusion of a movie.

The themes of exile and homelessness are the staple fodder for humankind's storytelling. They are recurring motifs in modern literature of "passage." We are homesick and sick of the home we have. Dante's poem is about his being made a stranger by his own people and his longing to return to his native city. Dante was a master at expressing the pathos of homelessness. He was also the poet of homecoming. The physician of our return to our spiritual home is often the artist or the poet. The wounded and exiled need a new vision that will help them to convalesce. To convalesce means to gain enough strength to return home. We are all convalescents—people on their way back home. We are birds of passage.

The journey, then, is prompted by a vision of a home from which we have strayed. We wake up in a dark and foreign place and long to return home. We have "memories" of heaven and are prompted and goaded to make the journey downward (because the way up is the way down) by a vision of our Origin, which, for Dante, is the Blessed Trinity (a symbol of love in which unity and identity are celebrated and held in balance), and with our high calling as images of the divine. It is the sublime vision of our true destiny that necessitates our facing the truths of damnation and purgation. We are on a journey to heal and restore our imaginations through *una bella menzogna*—a beautiful lie, a guiding fiction—a text, a story. The *Commedia* is the drama of the soul learning how to look and look well, to choose and choose well that for which it truly longs. It is an exercise in attentiveness. We travel with Dante to the hell where there are no real stories, only the screaming boredom of repetition, because we need to see what it means to be stuck in a place where no plot develops and no characters are formed.

There is nothing sentimental about the journey, and the pilgrim is not always outstandingly attractive. She does not necessarily draw others to herself. She is, rather, a window to something beyond herself. She does not dazzle us with her fascinating personality but draws us to an allegiance that, in Dante's case, is clearly liberating. The journey isn't for the sake of forming a better-defended ego. We are weaned away from seeing ourselves as the center of attention to discovering our dependence on an Other. Our personality is derivative, and to be a person most fully is to point to the One in whom we live and move and have our being. We are who we are because of a love story that began before the foundation of the world.

Before we leave Purgatory, we need to take one more look at the importance of *error* in the spiritual life. There is an ever-present danger of our taking guides like Dante literally and co-opting them for our own purposes. We may even find ourselves analyzing our friends and acquaintances and assigning them particular places in either hell or purgatory. We can easily slip into the role of a diagnostician who knows the ills of the world and their cure. "If only she would do X, if only he would learn Y, all would be well." "The trouble with Sally is that she will fall in love with the wrong men." "You know Mike's problem? Booze. If he could get a handle on his drinking everything would be okay." A great deal of harm is done by those who, having made some progress, think that they have come to the end and, therefore, know what's best for everybody else. The closer we get to the heart of things (and here we are in the Earthly Paradise), the greater the risk of error. People who claim to know God and the divine ordering of things are in the greatest danger. A humbling event, and if not humbling, then a humiliating one, is required to push us off the pedestal of thinking ourselves better or more advanced than others. We want to control and measure out the divine, but religion is never more sick and dangerous than when it seeks to measure out the holy, quantify the sacred, and control the Spirit. Dante would have none of it and found a strange salvation in insisting on keeping one eye on the possibility that he was mistaken.

In our dreaming is our rising and our falling. Many great works of literature have acknowledged the prophetic possibilities of dreams. They somehow anticipate the dreamer on his life's journey. At the same time, they are not completely to be trusted. When Virgil's hero Aeneas descends to the underworld, he meets his father, who reveals to him the future but in an ambiguous way. The word is, be careful when you look for pattern and order in human life. Learn the way of irony. The House of Sleep has two gates: one is of ivory and the way through for delusions and dreams that lie; the other gate is of horn and can be trusted to be the portal of true images. It is peculiarly ironic and poignant that Anchises, Aeneas's father, having shown him his future, sends him away through the gate of *falsehood*—the gate of polished ivory.

Dante, well aware of the hazards of his vocation, is careful to alert the reader to the importance of error. Between writing *La Vita Nuova* in his late twenties and pouring himself out in the *Commedia* in early middle age, he had gone through a significant inner transformation. By the time he had reached "the middle of life's way," he knew that he had to allow the poetry in him to speak for itself *and* be at odds with itself. Pattern was there but it must not be too neat or predictable. The possibility of disruption had to be part of the ordering of things. Chaos theory in science speaks to the same kind of concern: at the heart of the universe is both freedom and relationship, randomness and connection. Dante gets out of the dilemma of wanting to celebrate and honor a divine patterning of the universe and human events without invoking rigidity of form by turning statements into questions, by reopening questions that were thought to be settled, and by writing a *poem*.

Thus, the divine pattern, insofar as it can be discerned, is revealed in irony, humor, and poetic form. The pattern for us is in the divine imprint on all of us as images of God, who is, by definition, the One who cannot be manipulated and controlled. That's where the irony and the humor originate—in God's inexhaustible mystery and unknowability. In our longing for community, for connection, we may lose sight of our need to be free. In our desire to be free, we may ignore our need for relationship. Playfulness is important when searching for pattern. "You want to know my theory?" asks a character in Michael Malone's novel *Time's Witness*. "Bring back all the old feast days, harvest festivals, jousts, guild pageants. Make ritual, not war. Societies that play together stay together."[1] This gives us a clue as to what heaven—the vision of God—is all about.

Let us take a look at the spiritual exile's need for both a strong story and the honesty to admit the possibility of error. If we can bring the two within sight of each other (there's neither hope nor need for absolute reconciliation), perhaps we can live with enough focus and light in the accelerated world of chaos and change. The stories of people and nations show us how complex, ironic, and ambiguous life can be. In personal and international relations we know what a mess we get into when we fail to respect others' stories. The downtrodden rise up and tell their story. Empires crumble. Old stabilities lie in ruins. Attentiveness is everything. In the struggle for power, it doesn't make any difference whether the stories are literally true. Many want to reduce our stories to the struggle for control as seen through the prisms of race, gender, and class. The one (person, nation, corporation) who controls the narrative controls everything. The moral contradictions and inconsistencies are intense, and our inner ones reflect and resonate with those in our society. We are at war with our stories. The outer and the inner reflect each other. We see the drama of our psyches played out in our nation's politics and in our culture wars. Every interest group and oppressed tribe has its story to tell. Can we learn a language that will bring us together, a story that could bring us all home?

First, let us look at the need for a world that can be told as a story. The West received its narrative structure from the Bible, and bits and pieces of that structure can be discerned in the imaginative retelling of stories by those who, long ago, abandoned the Great Code (as the Bible was once called). Can there be a narratable world without a vision of "the end" as the vision of God? Dante's answer is a resounding no. There can be no universal story without a universal Storyteller. We cannot make narrative sense of life on our own. For people who neither understand nor even appear to live in a narratable world, existence is makeshift and ad hoc—day to day and to no purpose.

I like arguments, but arguments (as opposed to brawls) have to proceed along certain lines. I once refused to get into an argument with a man because he had little regard for the truth. He didn't play fair. "Playing fair," he replied, "is middle-class bullshit." It's easy to make fun of rules about civility (described to me once as "the tyranny of dead white males") and "decent" behavior. There's a kind of spiritual terrorism that justifies its tactics because "they" at last have the truth. Every story must be told as an example of the victim-versus-predator "truth" of human history. Members of modern tribes and ethnic groups are struggling with stories—some of which need to be abandoned.

When we invoke God as the great Storyteller and Poet of the world, we invoke a mystery that needs to be honored and guarded for the sake of human worth and dignity. Some people with rich imaginations have slipped so deeply into relativism and irony, however, that any story will do. Texts are *not* interchangeable. I cannot say, "I'm playing in the Christian drama but the atheist text would do just as well." We shouldn't mistake intellectual laziness or moral sleaziness for an appreciation of ambiguity. The issue is always discernment. The acknowledgment of error is not the divinizing of ambiguity. It is simply an act of humility as we proceed through life by a process of trial and error. Nowhere is trial and error more apparent than in our attempts to love one another.

Loving makes us peculiarly vulnerable to others because it involves living in the thrall of another who might make us subservient to a story not our own. We step back and are willing to listen as well as speak. I love you and love myself in you and you in myself. Lovers are always making fools of themselves by getting lost in their attraction to each other. We appreciate the multiplicity of possible stories, and, to please those we love, we seek to play a role in the drama that delights them. There is, therefore, a deep relationship between desire and identity. Passion "fools" us into desiring to play more roles than we can bear, and contradictory ones at that—like Bottom in Shakespeare's *A Midsummer Night's Dream*. "The bumptious Bottom is reluctant to confine himself to a single part in his drama, wishing to play several at once; and this, of course, is precisely what the lovers do in the forest, exchanging roles with dizzying speed."[2] Demetrius and Lysander, Hermia and Helena experience the unruliness of love and the destabilizing effect of desire.

Are the objects of our desire accidental? This week I long for a particular thing or person, but by the time next week comes around, my desire has moved on to something or someone else. Can anything be exchanged for something else? No wonder we distrust our emotions. We cannot do without one another and yet we are not sure of one another. If we cannot be truly ourselves without others and if human life ceases to be meaningfully human without social bonds and personal and communal faithfulness, then we sometimes have to risk making fools of ourselves. We need an antidote to that insidious form of individualism that denies love, rejects mutuality, and wounds others on the grounds that our little ego has to be preserved at all costs. We are not self-made. We are made in interaction with others. We think we are made in the isolated laboratory of our individual psyches. We think that unbridled openness to our own impulses, "provided it doesn't hurt anyone else," is an expression of freedom. The irony is that the more open we try to be, the more conformist we look. In a culture dedicated to diversity, it is amazing how alike we look. Our world tends to be dressed in a drab diversity of "freely" chosen life-styles. When values are relative, meanings are fleeting and we think we can do very well without other people.

The discerning heart knows its need for God and for community. As we have seen, Bottom in *A Midsummer Night's Dream* loved every role in the drama of Pyramus and Thisbe that the artisans were planning to stage for Theseus and Hippolyta. Bottom wanted to play all the parts, but he wears an ass's head—a sign of a fragmented and foolish identity—because he was incapable of holding within himself the dramatic range the cast of characters demanded. We make asses of ourselves in our frantic search for a text in which we can find the part written just for us. We go to hell in pursuit of love and its many illusory objects. We see it in our pathetic attempts to deny the aging process, to transcend our limits, and to dull our pain with the aid of a needle or a miracle drug. In many parts of hell we find a frantic interchange between people and things in a world where nothing matters. Our desires mislead us into acts of false reciprocity and exchange. We have to go to hell and back to come face to face with the uncontrollable Other, with the One we genuinely desire. The contrast between Bottom (the bad actor who cannot be anything but his stolid self) and Puck (the airy spirit who cannot be merely one thing and yet has no existence outside the roles he plays) illustrates our dilemma. How can we be truly ourselves and play a role at the same time? It is the mystery of solidarity and singularity. Can desire and stability ever go together? Storytelling is a very serious business and can be the vehicle for much evil and sin. Sin might be defined as our mistaking our little world for the whole universe. It isolates us from one another and from our deepest selves.

There's a story about a frog who lived at the bottom of a deep dark well. To him this was the whole world. One day another frog (who lived by the sea) came to visit. How he found the deep well nobody knows. The frog who lived in the well asked his new companion about the sea.

"How big is it?"

The sea-frog replied, "It is vast."

"You mean it's just a fraction of the size of this well?"

The sea-frog laughed so hard that tears ran down his cheeks. The well-frog was put out about this and protested,

"You mean that the sea is nearly as big as this well?"

The sea-frog realized that the well-frog had no idea of the enormity of the sea and invited his new friend on a journey from the well to the sea. It was a long journey through the valleys of love, bewilderment, loss, and abandonment. At last they reached the sea.

"Close your eyes. Don't open them until I tell you," the sea-frog told the well-frog as they reached the top of the hill overlooking the ocean.

The frog from the well opened his eyes and saw the vast luminous sea. At that moment his head exploded into a thousand pieces.[3]

Our rational control of the story of the world has been exploded, broken apart by a new vision of reality that we could not have imagined on our own. Love is the bomb that explodes the known and controllable world and introduces us to another. Love releases us from the vicious circle of self-reference and resentful isolation, yet love too has to be tested and purified.

Love is not the absorption of the weak by the strong. Still less is it an invitation to abandon oneself to an undifferentiated unity understood as a kind of erotic blob. Love requires a separate and distinct Other who can say "I." To allow an object of love to be genuinely other than a mere projection of our desire takes art and discipline. A good love story is not without irony and humor.

As we move through Purgatory, the leaves of the book in which we read the meanings of our lives are beginning to come together in one volume. It should be clear by now that our stories provide the means for deeper inner exploration. Our stories give us access to vast areas of experience that would otherwise be hidden from us. The human soul is a divinely structured emptiness that needs to be furnished by the great epics and myths that transmit the knowledge of what it is to be human. A well-furnished soul knows what it is to live in a moral universe—a world of rewards and punishments, of good and evil. The young need to be taught that the moral struggle (without which there is no real loving) is a drama of choice. Our great texts provide us with the protagonists and antagonists in the drama of moral decision making, give us a sense of the stakes involved in such choices, and show us the despair that results when magic and wonder are taken out of the world and it is reduced to the arbitrary power plays of the spiritually impoverished. Without authoritative texts, moral education becomes the vain attempt to give children "values." Values without dreams are like sex without love, rules without any game being played.

We dream of communion. We dream about communities. Think for a moment about the kind of cities we live in and what is becoming of them and us in them. Some cities still give the illusion of being manageable, but the megalopolis of the future is anticipated in Los Angeles and Tokyo and elsewhere. The city, as the theater in which human identity is formed and played out, is something of a labyrinth, an emporium—a circus. It is profoundly alienating, a place where it is easy to get lost. Those of us who can, develop a strategy for defeating the stranglehold of conformity and collectivism by hiding in a theater of different characters. In such an environment, our sense of self gets soft and fuzzy. Which self shall we wear today? What fantasy, what disguise is available to us this week? Although this playfulness can be liberating and hilarious, it can also be stressful and unsettling (because of the ever-present threat of violence and chaos). What is liberating about living in a great city (the freedom to be what one pleases) also can be the occasion of violence and psychosis, inviting the totalitarian solutions that the city's "freedom" was supposed to prevent. We struggle to play the roles of both Bottom and Puck in our version of *A Midsummer Night's Dream*. Bottom was funnily and sadly of the earth, Puck too ethereal to be human.

The image of the city reveals to us aspects of both heaven and hell. It shows us heaven's freedom and hell's fragmentation. It reveals to us the juxtapositions of purpose and play; design and chance; hierarchy and anarchy; distance and participation; presence and absence; centering and dispersal; narrative and antinarrative; metaphysics and irony; transcendence and immanence.[4] These are the polarities of the living theater in which we play out our lives.

The heavenly side is shown in allowing the religious narratives once again to have their say. Could acknowledging our spiritual hunger mean the end of secularism as the destructive desacralization of the world? Are we ready to acknowledge the bankruptcy of the human project without God? What does our "enlightened" age have to say about the universal oppression in the name of liberation of the French Revolution? What account can it give of Auschwitz, Hiroshima, Kigali, and Sarajevo? How ripe are we for some new tyranny?

The philosopher Martin Heidegger's relationship to the Nazis is a case in point. He was a great philosopher who compromised himself politically because he was disturbed by the specter of the dissolution of people's special relationship to particular places and by the flattening out of souls, all of which seemed to be the by-product of technology. Time was moving too fast and people were getting lost. He wanted to find an antidote to the poison of nihilism. He wanted to be *grounded*, and this overwhelming desire led him into an intense nationalism and into the arms of the Nazis. He preferred the *local* myth to the universal one. He proclaimed the permanence of Being over the flux of Becoming. He wanted to be rooted in a safe tradition of continuity. The destiny and particularity of nations and tribes took precedence over universal and inclusive sympathies. The Nazis filled the bill.

We need to take warning that certain kinds of nihilism leave a political vacuum ready to be occupied by the very totalitarianism we deplore. It isn't fanciful to imagine the rise of a new fascism to "cope" with the chaos of modern life. The mythology of place and person fighting for space on the planet is destructively alive today, and the rhetoric of national liberation movements is just as enslaving as the counterrhetoric of the old imperialisms with their talk of "manifest destiny, racial or cultural supremacy, paternalism (white man's burden, for example), and doctrines of national superiority."[5] Hell on earth.

How are we to find our place in a fragmented and relativized world? In a world in which desires are easily manufactured and manipulated, who's to say what the difference is between the real and the replicated? We now have access to virtual reality. In the absence of coherent narrative, we develop frantic strategies to bolster the self and feed our nostalgic impulses. History becomes mere costume drama; religion, a trip into virtual reality; life, one great ethnic festival where we can try one another's foods. In our fear, we favor aesthetics over ethics because the latter requires a hard-won narrative framework for the moral imagination. We prefer the costume drama to the openness of a story over which we have no ultimate control.

There is also a crisis in how we experience space and time, and this affects our narrative capabilities. We're now in a kind of hyperspace, and we record "time" as if it were evenly distributed on an objective scale. But we know that "time flies." There is "family time" (raising children), "industrial time" (the allocation of our labor), a time of fate and myth. Different senses of time bring conflict. We need to challenge the idea of a single objective sense of time and space. Neither had any existence before matter. The speeding up of time, which collapses distance, brings crisis. Are some global conflicts attempts to slow time down, put the clock back, and restore old borders? Issues of time and space always have a social and political content, and space-time compression is political dynamite. There is no time to grieve, no time to agonize, no time to decide, no time for stories.

The world has been brought closer together through communications, but proximity intensifies anxiety and competition. In a shrinking world of both homogeneity and fragmentation, McDonald's hamburgers and Diet Coke are everywhere but so are terrorists. In our current situation, which should we emphasize—unity or difference? Should we choose the big story (metanarrative) and risk tyranny, or should we choose the nihilism of merely private stories and risk madness?

Two modern "virtues"—instantaneity (fast foods, e-mail, automatic teller machines) and disposability—make sustained storytelling difficult. In a throwaway society, we can throw away more than disposable goods. We can jettison a story or a value. We can throw away life-styles, stable relationships, and attachments to things, buildings, places, people, and traditions. The prospect of instant obsolescence undermines any sense of continuity, leaving no motive for delaying gratification. The temporariness of everything, combined with our sensory overload, makes long-term planning look futile and even stupid. The schizophrenic mentality is divinized. Something has to be taken to be a god, even if only for a moment.

Dante believed in a God who is the Actor in a passionate narrative of communion that includes everyone and everything. We can get along very well for a while without a big story. Advertising provides us with simple and temporary narrative frameworks to help us through the day and satisfy short-term desires. The stories have to do with the manipulation of desires and tastes that may or may not have anything to do with the product. As we have seen, the three ancient themes of sex, money, and power occupy the attention of the new storytellers. Even the images themselves become commodities. We trade in concepts and ideas.

Image making has replaced storytelling. A California firm makes imitation car telephones for those who want the *look* without the expense. "Fake it till you make it" is the slogan of one company.[6] By such means we create a phony individualism through the pursuit of signs of status or fashion, or marks of individual eccentricity. But we cannot live in a world where everything is temporary and moves into hyperspace. We are in a mess not without irony, because the more we sense that life is slipping through our fingers, that our world is falling apart, the more urgently we need signs of universal meaning.

Purgatory is a good place for a contemporary human being to be because it is the place of conversion of images. In purgatory we cannot fake it until we make it. We move from misery to conversion, from remorse to repentance, from resentment to acceptance in a process that takes us through all the fragmentations and nihilisms to which the flesh is heir. Purgatory is the labyrinth of desire where our longings are purified and liberated. Our struggle with desire makes it necessary for us to take sides (even in a post-modern world), to plunge into life and risk being mistaken. We have to *decide* how we are going to live, and the comedy of life is the drama of our deciding.

At the end of the *Purgatorio,* Dante is at last united with the love of his life, Beatrice. His encounter with his beloved at the top of the mountain in the Earthly Paradise comes as a surprise, even after Virgil's promise, when they reached Ante-Purgatory, of the meeting.[7] One would think that such a reunion would not be a terrible confrontation but a wordless embrace. Beatrice is not waiting for Dante with open arms, however. After going through the narrow funnel of Hell and climbing up the cornices of Purgation, Dante is confronted with a stern and angry woman.[8] She appears to Dante not like a woman welcoming her lover after his long and harrowing journey, but like an admiral, like a queen, like a furious and exasperated mother. (When my wife read this, she responded, "Well, of course!") "*Look* at me well," Beatrice says. In effect, she tells Dante that he has perversely and persistently missed the point, and that now, at last, he has the chance to turn his life around—to repent.

In the last canto of the *Purgatorio* we read:

> "Lady, you know my need
> to know, and know how it can be appeased."
> And she to me: "I'd have you disentangle yourself,
> from this point on, from fear and shame."[9]

Disentangling from fear and shame, Dante wanted to know who he was. Self-knowledge is the most difficult kind of knowledge because it means facing up to the catastrophe of one's life without caving in to despair. Dante's desire to know himself led him to study philosophy, write poetry, fall in love, go into politics. Beatrice tells him that his pursuit of knowledge has got him tangled up in fear and shame. So much so, he learns, that she has wept over him only a little less than Mary did for Jesus at the foot of the cross. Her words are terrifying, as she holds up a mirror so that he can see himself as he really is.

Mount Purgatory has proved to be the place of the purification of Dante's imagination. There he renounces the disordered images of hell in favor of the revelation of divine Love in which he can accept himself as whole and loved.

If this sounds a bit too grand (before we move out of Purgatory and into Heaven), I want to bring us down once again to the chaotic and dismembered earth and place Dante firmly in his own times with their tumultuous politics and petty squabbles. Dante's poem has an earthy quality that we easily forget because we place it on the plinth called literature. *The Divine Comedy* is called a comedy, not because it is funny, and not simply because it begins with sad things and ends with joyous ones. Dante called his work *La Commedia* because he cast himself as the very human hero who was neither a god nor a king. He was not made of the stuff that merited high tragedy, even though he understood the importance of facing the darkness of one's worst self. It was later commentators who added the word *Divine* to *Comedy*. It is called a comedy because it is written in the language of the people. Dante wrote in Italian (a language that was beginning to come into its own), not Latin. His language is vulgar—commonplace—even though it deals with the deepest of human longings. In this sense, the style is suitable to the subject—the incarnation; the story of God, the Artist of the world, entering ordinary human experience.

The fact that a heated quarrel developed over the disposition of Dante's bones should tell us that art—especially poetry—isn't merely an elitist exercise. Dante's poem had shaken up his world. It had religious and political content that forced people to take notice. Art is part of the choreography of the spirit in its quest for a lost intimacy and its desire for self-donation. Artists are fellow exiles who either show us the pitiable state we are in or give us a glimpse of home. The myths and stories (the raw material of artists) binding the human race together are vibrant with both horror and hope. They live not only in our depths but also close to the skin—ready to pop out, insisting on being lived when we least expect it. Most of us have to descend the ever-narrowing funnel of hell at least once in our lives and climb the strenuous mountain of purgatory. Some may even get a glimpse of the great white rose of heaven. But it's all one journey.

Our character is formed when we suffer trials and cope with our frailties and vulnerabilities. This will not be a very comforting thought for many of our contemporaries. Purgatory is the symbol of endured vulnerability for the sake of a wonderful recovery—the recovery of our true selves as beings who can feel and think responsibly. There is an old maxim: *Vita hominis, visio Dei. Gloria Dei, homo vivens.*[10] It can be translated like this: The fully human life is the vision of God, and the glory of God is a human being fully alive. We were made by God and for God. This is who we truly are. This is what Beatrice was trying to show Dante.

Desire is neither satisfied nor repressed but redirected by the discipline of the mountain. The disciplined ways for our desires to find their true end are prayer and liturgy—the surrender of the soul in adoration. It may come as a surprise that liturgy and prayer have something to do with desire. There is a mistaken notion that spiritual purity requires the abolition of desire. True worship is not repressing desire but knowing—however dimly—its true object. There is healing strength in liturgy because it recognizes and honors the longings of the soul. Prayer is the breath of the Spirit that in desiring us opens us up to the miracle of our own desirability. Another name for the Spirit is desire. Prayer is a great sighing of the heart and hints at desires we cannot yet name. The heart tells us that we have lost our way and that its deepest ache is for paradise.

Dante has provided a map for the soul's journey back to its true home. As we have seen, the spiritual journey has to do with the ordering of our desires, with setting love in order, with our struggle with "inordinate affections." We make the terrible error of turning others into divinities in the hope that they can assuage our longings. In Colin Thubron's novel about the conversion of Constantine to Christianity, his secretary reflects on the emperor's stormy relationship with his wife. Their rage and disappointment with each other are about misplaced desire. "When he's not shouting at the Empress about the villa or her coldness, he's not shouting about her at all. He's saying: 'Why are you not God? Where has your divinity gone?' He's angry with himself for being deceived by an idol."[11] Our difficulties with prayer are often struggles with idolatry. We look to others and say, "Why are you not God?" Our past is littered with failed and disappointing divinities. We long to be in touch with the One who knows our desires better than we do. The spiritual life is about the integration of desire: our personal desires, our political vision, and our longing for God. Dante believed that our desires, far from being separate or in competition with one another, ultimately spring from the same source. There's an old prayer that begins, "Almighty God, unto whom all hearts are open, all desires known. . . . "[12] Janet Morley writes, "'All desires known': this phrase has always evoked in me that distinctive stance that I associate with authentic worship: namely an appalled sense of self-exposure combined with a curious but profound relief."[13] This is an accurate description of Dante's encounter with Beatrice at the top of Mount Purgatory. She looks directly at him and he experiences her gaze as both terrifying and healing.

Prayer brings together the "appalled sense of self-exposure" with one of profound relief when we enter into our longings. Our desires drive us mad. We spend much of our time either suppressing them or trying to satisfy them. The life of faith is a response to the growing knowledge in us that nothing less than God will satisfy us. Many of us acknowledge the need for an allegiance to someone or something beyond ourselves. Desire makes the allegiance personal and inward. Who is it who makes not only the grass green and the blood red but also me me? Desire and longing make prayer personal, although not in the popular sense of an ego in full possession of itself. To pray can mean losing one's grip on one's well-defended personality. Sometimes desire exhausts itself in the many unsatisfying places where it seeks fulfillment. We feel we are going to die. It is the moment of psychological eclipse. This moment of eclipse of the homemade "personality" is known to the mystics as a descent into darkness. It feels like hell. But this darkness can be transformed into purgatory, into change. When all is said and done, it is a matter of staying awake to the longings within us, to our keeping promises, and to our obligation to show up at certain times of the day. It isn't difficult or complicated. It's as "simple" as maintaining a friendship or keeping one's word!

Prayer is a question not only of our desire for God but also of God's desire for us. God, the center outside our lost autonomous selves, believes in us. God finds me credible when I am barely present and real to myself. God finds me desirable when I can hardly bear to look at myself. That God finds us desirable raises the question of whether we believe we are intrinsically good the way a flower or a tree is good. Can we bear the miracle of our own significance?

It is said that the spiritual life begins when the soul begins to recognize its own God-given *dignity*. It begins when we accept how intrinsically good we are, not how bad we are. This doesn't mean pretending that we are perfect or that we have done no wrong. It does mean, however, giving up our low opinion of ourselves, which is the last trick of the ego to keep us concentrating on ourselves. Sin is denying our dignity, our desirability. Prayer is a daily, disciplined way of resting in God's delight in us.

Our being in heaven or hell depends on how we solve the riddle of desire. Marx and Freud tried to solve it by putting us in our place. Freud, as inflated as he was, tried to cut us down to size. He thought he knew the secrets of the human heart. He rooted around in our dreams and instead of finding *ta erotika* (love matters) of which Plato wrote, all he found was the little cherub Eros—infantile sex. He reduced our sexual longings to the mechanics of our sexual plumbing. He was aware of our aching hopes and the size of our dreams. They were too big. "So big that, for them to be fulfilled, we would have to be gods. But gods we are not. We are human beings." Reality, according to Freud, is an imprisoning chain, "a stern stoic teacher who teaches us the wisdom of abandoning our impossible desires. The raw will remain raw. No banquet will be served. Religion is an illusion which is doomed to disappear."[14] Freud's reductions still leave us hungry for transcendence. We need, now more than ever, to question both a shallow and self-satisfied secularism that fails to honor humanity's hunger for transcendence, and a dangerous and vindictive religiosity that cannot appreciate the fact that the idea of God has a history and has changed and developed over time.

Marx, like Freud, spoke in the name of reality. Reality for him was not a chain, however, but the hands that make and break it. Freud denied our divinity; Marx, in throwing off religion, affirmed it. We could have heaven on earth. He was sure that hearts, heads, and hands together would steal the Garden of Delights from the domain of the gods, where religious fantasies had exiled it, so that a real garden could be planted in the world. And religion would wither away. Religion had served its turn and could now be put away, because in Paradise there are no altars, as in the Holy City there are no temples. But the Marxist dream, at least in its Soviet and Eastern European manifestations, has been discredited. In another sense, however, Marx can claim a victory. His view of politics and the power that drives human affairs seems to be universally accepted. Power is considered the key that makes it possible to decipher the riddle of the human world.

Marx, as opposed to Freud, was optimistic about solving the riddle of our longings by the establishment of the earthly paradise. Life would be a banquet. Freud was convinced that our desire is a wound that cannot be healed. It is rooted in a tragedy that antecedes history. Our bodies are born with a void inside that nothing can fill. There is no joy—only the promise that our neuroses can be transformed into routine unhappiness. For Marx, the obscure mystery of the heart is resolved in the clear, scientific knowledge of what our hands can actually do and our will accomplish. Heaven is *now*, not later. Dreams no longer have to be interpreted, because they are not the locus wherein our riddle is revealed. There are no mysteries: we act out of power and not out of dreams. If the mystery of religion is the mystery of desire, and if the mystery of desire is resolved as power, power becomes the new religion, and the place of the forgotten dream is taken by the illusion of power: our hands can produce what the heart demands. We can make heaven on earth.

Marx has won. The romantic religion of love hasn't a chance—at least not in the world's terms. But the mountain of Purgation has its own logic. The prophets of the Old Testament denounced as an illusion the claim that our hands can produce what the heart demands; they called it "idolatry." An idol is a man-made object that is believed to have the power to bring back happiness. Theologians later named it "justification by works": the riddle of our desires is solved by the means of our action, by human get-up-and-go.[15] The riddle of desire cannot be solved by action because the riddle precedes all action. The riddle of desire is the riddle of our identity. Jumping prematurely into action by grabbing power aborts my finding out who I am. It is a disease of the soul particularly virulent in the West.

Dante's text was the Bible, and on the last cornice of Purgatory we find the biblical Earthly Paradise, the reconciliation of Adam and Eve in the Garden. Dante passes through the fire of refining passion to recover his birthright as a human being. The vision of God is not a private showing but a revelation of how all things are held in being by the divine Love. That is why the image of the city is so important to Dante.

But why does God have to be brought into the picture? Why does religion have to play a part in the story? As we have seen, without God there would be no story at all. We wouldn't exist in a universe where stories are not possible. We can get at the point negatively by looking at a storyless environment populated by storyless people. Robert W. Jenson tells of one of his students "whose reality is rock music, his penis, and at the very fringes some awareness that to support both of these medical school might be nice."[16] This tells us as much about Jenson's irritation with the postmodern age as it does about the student. I sympathize with Jenson's irritation but reject his reducing his student to rock music and a fixation on his crotch. More is going on in us—even the most imaginatively impoverished—than that. Dante, who knew the possibility of error, would have deplored the view that we live in a world where no stories can be true, and would have been horrified by a person who had no story. Heaven, as we shall see, holds all texts and gathers all stories, connects and corrects them, and binds them into one in a story that has no ending.

PART THREE

HEAVEN

W E HAVE BEEN SHOT OUT OF PURGATORY LIKE AN ARROW FROM a bow and find ourselves freely moving through the heavenly spheres. Imagine a series of not one but ten heavens, the tenth of which is the empyrean—the home of the Holy Trinity, the Blessed Virgin Mary, the angels, and the saints. They make up a great cuplike rose, the harmonious symbol of unity. On one side of the rim sits the Blessed Virgin Mary. On either side of her sit Saint John and Saint Peter, Moses and Adam. Opposite Mary on the other side of the rose is Saint John the Baptist, with Saint Anna on one side and Saint Lucia on the other. In the end, language fails, as with a flash of insight Dante's will and the Creator's are one. He sees "l'amor che move il sole e l'altre stelle"—the love that moves the sun and all the stars. This is the end of our exploring. We can rest and be still in the presence of God.

We began our journey into Hell as it was getting dark. The climb up the mountain started in the early morning. Now it is midday. The sun is at it zenith as Dante ascends to God. What could be a better time—noon on a spring day? Dante wants to instruct his readers about how the universe works and is driven by love. The physical universe reflects the spiritual and vice versa. The human spirit is embodied. To be a person means not only to have a body but to *be* a body. Thus, the resurrection of the flesh is very important to Dante. Heaven is not the realm of disembodied souls, but of holy and transfigured flesh.

God created the universe either directly or through nature. "All products of Nature are perishable but whatever comes directly from the hand of God can never die."[1] And God was directly involved in our creation. God became one of us so that we might share in the divine life. The Athanasian Creed affirms that God became one of us, not by the conversion of the godhead into flesh, but by the taking of humanity into God. Dante stands in this tradition of breathtaking anthropology that could talk of the humanity of God and the divinity of humanity. And the most precious gift God has given us is freedom. Moreover, we are physically and spiritually beautiful. Being human means enjoying free will and being *Deo congruens*—God-shaped—with a particular and unique presence. Heaven is the full restoration of our humanity as God intended it to be. What is wonderful is that God in the flesh took on the work of reconciliation—the work of restoring human nature in all its loveliness. As Dante and Beatrice move through the various spheres on their way to the empyrean (where the throne of God is), they become more and more beautiful. The closer we are to God, the more beautiful (the more truly ourselves) we become.

We have followed Dante through the various stages of repentance, reform, and regeneration. Heaven is a sign of our longing for reality—for the really real, the sacred—but the *Paradiso* is the hardest of the three realms to appreciate and understand unless one can enjoy the elegance and beauty of dogma even as one acknowledges the inadequacy of all language and formulations to do justice to the mystery. "Of the three parts of the *Commedia*, the *Purgatorio* seems to a twentieth-century reader most modern, the *Paradiso* most medieval."[2] It is hard to read because, in the first instance, it is hard to visualize, and in the second, it requires understanding of the philosophical and theological world in which Dante lived. His Heaven feels static. Using images of light, motion, and sound, Dante delights in its *unchanging* perfection. Some writers in the early church had a more dynamic view of heaven as a movement "from glory to glory" into the mystery of the infinite God. "An eternity of absolute but unchanging and unproductive happiness" is singularly unattractive to us today, particularly when described in a didactic way. It would be a mistake to think of heaven as an unending celebration of a boring blessedness. Heaven is radically and uniquely *different* for each soul; that's what makes it infinitely varied. The phrase from Saint John's Gospel, "In my Father's house are many mansions" (John 14:2), was interpreted by both Saint Augustine and Saint Thomas Aquinas to mean that there were different degrees of knowledge of God.[3] God loves everyone equally, but the love is distributed unequally because each soul is radically unique. There is no envy because each soul is content at having found its true being. Dante believed that human beings long for the vision of pure beauty, the vision of God that includes intellectual and moral fulfillment.

The soul, at last, comes to rest in finding its true home, its proper place in the scheme of things. Proper loving (true love) depends on true seeing. The more intense the seeing, the more intense the love. Love and knowledge must go together if the soul is to be truly free. This third part of the journey is meant to instruct the reader-pilgrim to *see* who and what we really are by finding our true place in the scheme of things. It is an invitation to contemplation. The end of the *itinerarium*—the end of all our striving—is the vision of God.

Heaven, then, is a place of splendor, light, and clarity. God's glory interpenetrates everything. In heaven there is no dissatisfaction or envy. The universe is *moved* by the love of God, and things instinctively act according to their own nature. Human beings "naturally" want to move toward the One who created them. Only sin (making wrong choices in our loving) weighs us down, pulls us away from our true selves. When all the weight is removed, the soul moves to its proper place. That is why we, with Dante and Beatrice, are able to shoot like an arrow up into heaven. There is nothing now that holds us down.

The presence of the religious orders—especially the Benedictines and the complementary orders of Saint Dominic and Saint Francis—is significant. They represent intellectual power and passionate love. In heaven we at last enjoy the harmony and courtesy that we only glimpsed on earth. In the end, it is all gift. The criteria for a fully human life are faith, hope, and love. And "in the end we shall be examined in love" (to use a phrase from Saint John of the Cross).

The all-too-earthly and human reality of Dante's situation is never forgotten. He never gives up hope of returning home to his beloved Florence. It is very touching and even pathetic. He feels locked out by the cruelty of his enemies. His earthly hope helps him to understand his longing for a heavenly home. As Dante gazes at the brightness of Saint John the Divine, he is struck blind—rather like Saint Paul on the Damascus road.[4] While Dante is struck blind, Saint John examines him in love with a simple question: "What do you love and why?" God is the origin and source of all loving. When Dante's sight is restored,[5] he understands that seeing the glory of God in the creature (in his case, Beatrice) is what it means to be embodied. The journey has taught him the difference between the Creator and the created. Hell showed him the pain that results when the two get confused. Dante sees the glory of God in the eyes of Beatrice, who slips away just as Virgil did at the end of the *Purgatorio*.[6] Dante is now brought by Saint Bernard (the Doctor of Love and the sign of intuition) into the actual presence of God. The journey is complete. Dante is brought home to himself, to others, and to God by three humanizing energies: reason, revelation, and intuition. It is not accidental that the three energies are represented by three actual people: Virgil, Beatrice, and Bernard.

NINE

THE FREEDOM TO COME HOME TO ONESELF

E CONVIENSI APRIRE L'UOMO QUASI COM'UNA ROSA CHE PIU
CHIUSA STARE NON PUOTE.
And man should open out like a rose that can no longer keep closed.

IL CONVIVIO 4.27.4

We have reached Heaven at last. The purpose of the journey has been
for our unfolding—like a flower in full bloom. And who would not want to
open out with the spontaneous and generous unfolding of a rose? Dante,
having let go of all the dead weight that was holding him down, shoots like
an arrow from Purgatory into Heaven. He was ready for his unfolding because he knew his place in the scheme of things; he knew who he was and
where he belonged. It should be noted that the age of this opening is not at
life's midpoint (that is, at thirty-five—halfway to seventy) but at forty-five,
ten years after the entry into the dark wood as far as earth's chronological
time goes.

A human being, then, is "designed" to open up like a great rose. We
have explored what it takes to cooperate with the divine process of the unfolding of our true selves. In order for that rose to bloom, its roots must be
nourished in hell. Beatrice sent help into the depths of hell to bring Dante
back to himself so that he might blossom as a rose. No wonder the poet
was compelled to write of such a gracious rescue. In him, experience, desire, and genius combined. In Beatrice, Dante encountered "the real thing."
And, to steal Henry's words to his lover in Tom Stoppard's play *The Real
Thing*, it is as if Dante were saying, "I can't find a part of myself where
you're not important."[1] To find oneself in another is part of the pilgrim's secret that Dante discovered very early, only to betray what he had learned
and to spend the rest of his life in recovering it.

O DONNA IN CUI LA MIA SPERANZA VIGE,
E CHE SOFFRISTI PER LA MIA SALUTE
IN INFERNO LASCIAR LE TUE VESTIGE
DI TANTE COSE QUANT'I' HO VEDUTE,
DAL TUO PODERE E DALLA TUA BONTATE
RICONOSCO LA GRAZIA E LA VIRTUTE
TU M'HAI DI SERVO TRATTO A LIBERTATE
PER TUTTE QUELLE VIE, PER TUTT'I MODI
CHE DI CIÒ FARE AVEI LA POTESTATE.
LA TUA MAGNIFICENZA IN ME CUSTODI,
SI CHE L'ANIMA MIA, CHE FATT'HAI SANA,
PIACENTE A TE DAL CORPO SI DISNODI.

O Lady in whom my hope finds strength and who for my sake left the mark of your footprints in Hell, of all things that I have seen, I realize that what grace and strength I have comes from your energy and goodness. It is you who took me out of slavery into freedom by all those ways that were in your power. Guard your kindness within me so that my soul which you have restored to health, freed from the body, may be at home with you.[2]

Dante's *bella menzogna* becomes the vehicle by which the soul discovers its true identity. The "beautiful lie" of the poetic imagination is the instrument by which we climb down the hairy legs of the devil and are thus taken out of the terrifying and isolating chill of hell into the place where we can move, breath, and change. We climb the mountain and enter the harmonious mystery of the white rose. Without such lying truths and truthful lies, we die.

Dante's is a journey that is concrete and particular. His vision of heaven is a unity based on the spiritual ecology of infinite differentiation. Paradise is absolute unity in unimaginable diversity where the riddle of the relationship between desire and stability is resolved—at least in the visionary moment. Love unites. Freedom not only allows but celebrates diversity. The power of the one is unity. The power of the other is difference. Mutuality is restored. The unity of the divine glory is revealed in the brilliant variety of creation. God makes all things new and animates everything living. Dante catches a glimpse of what the recovery of the will (our freedom to choose) means. We become free insofar as we are able to enjoy being chosen.

Heaven is the vision of the true self in relation to God. Dante's legacy to us is his way of recovering religion as a transformative spiritual path rather than as the swallowing of dogma or the living of a life enslaved to custom and convention. Spiritual maturity means leaving the safety of dogmatic fundamentalism (either liberal or conservative) for the risky life of faith. Another way of understanding the journey is to see it as the healing of the rift between feminine and masculine in our recovery of the glory of the divine feminine.

Faith means finding God at the center of everything. We, therefore, have to become *eccentric*, off-center. What a relief to be decentered. The burden of being at the center of everything eventually becomes intolerable. I have wasted a great deal of my time trying to run the universe—and if not *the* universe, then my own little part of it. I have tried to make others conform to my view of things, often for their own good. I have bullied friends, coerced children, and been hard on myself for the sake of wanting to be in control.

At the beginning of our journey, we saw the need to appreciate and enjoy the otherness of others. Heaven is the place where such otherness is honored to the full in a complementary way. In fact, heaven *requires* difference. Heaven is more true to itself the more beings there are who celebrate difference. Paradise is the vision of coherence—the way the universe is *ordered* so that each creature is truly itself, in full possession of its being because each has been liberated from the need to define itself *against* all the others. The structures of all the creatures resemble God, the Holy and Undivided Trinity in whom we find the twin principles of unity and difference. The more forms that are realized, the more perfectly does the universe resemble God.[3] The principle is that stability and unity require infinite diversity. Desire—or better, love—makes the world go round. This divine inner structure (of unity in diversity) to everything is what makes a family and a human community a political possibility. Dante knew Aristotle's maxim: "Man is an animal that is intended by nature to live in a *polis*."[4] Dante's political anthropology had to include a vision for our inner and outer lives—a vision of church and empire, signifying our two complementary destinies as individuals and as citizens.

Our journey through hell and purgatory has been no individualistic trip because, according to Dante, to be fully human is to be a citizen. Perhaps more of us would be truly happy if we were to stop fussing about our interior lives and indulging in bits of spiritual horticulture and instead discover our citizenly duties. Infinite diversity is required to realize all the possible forms that already exist in the mind of God. From this perspective, human beings become truly themselves and are at their greatest and best when they are citizens in one commonwealth. Communities cannot properly exist, according to Aristotle, without the greatest possible diversity among those citizens.[5] So reverence for otherness is required for the maintenance of the commonwealth. It takes a leap of the imagination to see the otherness of others and feel both safe and joyful. In heaven there is no doubt—only enjoyment. Meanwhile, we have to live in and through time and with our memories. As we get older there is more to remember and, therefore, more to regret, as well as more for which to be thankful.

Hell is easy to describe. Heaven defies description. Perhaps that's why we disagree with one another over the vision of heaven—the definition of the good life. Our torments and terrors unite us, but each of us is bent on getting to a different heaven, either alone or with a select few. We get tongue-tied when we are asked to put into words an ecstatic experience. Describing something or someone radiant with an integrating beauty is well-nigh impossible. Dante tried and got himself caught in trying to say it all. Even he is reduced to silence. Poetry is the only vehicle suitable for the task. Poetry is the art of calling things by their proper names, yet respecting them in their ineffable mystery. Dante expresses what he can discern of the loving purpose of God with the intellectual tools available to him. These tools were formidable: the tradition of Plato and the new formulations from Saint Thomas Aquinas using the insights of Aristotle. Dante was well educated and articulate. In the end, though, he comes to the silent adoration and contemplation of the One whose *eros* not only made the sun and the other stars but also drew the divine down to earth to be with us. Dante believed that we are deeply related to and connected with God. Our irresistible longing (*eros*) has moved us through the circles of hell and up the terraces of purgation toward the uniquely Desirable One. The divine *Eros* finally unites us with the One who desires us.

Paradise is suffused with light—the light of presence and mutual recognition. Here light and life are identical. Light makes every person alive, rendering us visible and present to one another. Hell is the place of darkness where solitude reduces each of the damned to the ultimate terror of self-reference. Hell's darkness is not passive. It is passive-aggressive and hides active and resentful resistance to the light of life. In hell there is an eclipse of real content, palpable presence. Light in this heavenly sense is not the optical phenomenon. It is the revelation of the face of God. There is a heavenly progression: light, revelation, communion. *Light reveals communion* as the purpose of the journey. The divine light reveals how all things are related one to another. The drama of the soul's choice comes to an end with Dante choosing to participate in the glory that was his from the beginning. For Dante, of course, communion was supremely symbolized in the sacrament of Holy Communion, the Mass. Human beings are most truly themselves in this sacrament: the whole human family gathered around one table at a feast of communion.

We catch a glimpse of the glory and the beauty of heaven when we worship, when we participate in the liturgy. Legend has it that Prince Vladimir of Kiev sent ambassadors to search out a suitable religion for the realm. They sent word back to Kiev from Constantinople after attending the Byzantine liturgy. The ambassadors confessed, "We did not know whether we were in heaven or on earth for on earth such beauty is not to be found. We thus do not know what to say, but we know one thing for sure. God dwells among us."[6] The conviction that God is enfleshed in us is basic to Dante's vision.

Saint Nicholas Cabasilas imagines the Second Coming as Christ appearing above the clouds as "a beautiful choir master (coryphaeus) in the midst of a beautiful choir" who will draw us all to God in a great movement of love. The vision is not unlike Dante's white rose. "An assembly of beautiful creatures, surrounding God himself to form a crown around the One who is supreme Beauty."[7]

While all the above may be spiritually true, it sounds fanciful and remote from our everyday experience. Could we feel at home in such a place? Is it possible to understand heaven as a coming home to oneself? The issues raised by an embodied divinity seem insuperable. We seem to be afflicted by two identities: a heavenly and an earthly one. We are supposed to be at home with limitation, with boundaries, with the here and now. But we continually try to transcend limitation and move beyond the restraints of the present moment.

One of the advantages of living in the video-rental age is that we can watch a favorite movie over and over again. I know of two movies that bring heaven and hell down to earth in a way that we can understand. The films *Blade Runner* and *Himmel über Berlin (Wings of Desire)* explore the meaning of being human—of existing within the limits of time and space and yet longing to transcend both.[8] The marriage between flesh and spirit is uneasy. Heaven and hell coexist in all of us, and it is essential that we not identify spirit with heaven and flesh with hell. Things are more complicated than that. The relationship between flesh and spirit is played out in both realms.

Blade Runner explores the limits of time and space in individual human history. The suggestion is that to be human, one has to have a story to tell. Set in the future, it is a tale of the fate of some brilliant human replicants who have been programmed to live only four years. In this way their human inventors can control them. A few renegade replicants escape and want to find out who made them and if something can be done to alter their short lifespan. But it is difficult to tell a replicant from a real human being. They are human in every respect save one: they have no real memory. One way they can be caught, therefore, is by interrogation. Because they have no personal history, they have no story to tell. One of the replicants tries to hoodwink her interrogator by producing a photograph of her "mother" as proof that she has a past. In this future, images are taken as proof. We take the image to be the proof of the reality. That's why image makers have such power over us. They know that images can be manufactured and manipulated. The hero, Deckard (whose job is to hunt down renegade replicants), reflects that they are just like most of us. Even replicants want to know "where they have come from, where they are going, and how much time they've got." But they are living life on a very different timescale from ours. Their fate is to be born fully grown, without memory, and to be given only four years to live. But everything can be replicated, even history and relationships. Who is to tell the difference between a human being with a history and a replicant with an acquired one? To be human is to exist in time, to have a memory, to engage in relationships. Perhaps replicants can be programmed with the required elements. Deckard falls in love with a replicant who is not programmed to expire in four years. The film ends romantically with their forging a new story together. True romance truly discerned is the key. The way to tell heaven from hell has to do with the ability to tell a true story.

Wings of Desire (a pretentious, boring, yet thoughtful movie by Wim Wenders) shows how flesh and spirit desire and need each other. Two angels, Damiel and Cassiel, watch over the flat black-and-white world of Berlin, a desolate city of drifting and lost souls. Occasionally the movie breaks into color when flesh and spirit come together, but for the most part we see the city from the angels' perspective. The angels are not so much guardians (although they do interact with human beings by restoring memories and continuities) as listening presences. They overhear the thoughts of people as they move about the city. They hear such things as, "How will I pay with my small pension?" and "Women will fuck up your life!" The angels feel genuine sympathy for the human beings on earth moving through their infernos and purgatories. They reflect that they weren't always spectators. They remember prehistory and the time when the human biped first appeared. It was a story of joy and laughter. Then came war and another tale was begun.

Throughout the movie we hear a child's questions about identity and particularity, about time and space. "Why am I me and not you? *Here* and not *there?*" The child, we are told, once "had a precise picture of paradise and now it can only guess at it." There is a kind of Fall in growing up. People are cut off from one another, each in his own country with its own borders and regulations. "Everyone carries a state within him," and yet all are refugees.

Two places of possible life are found in the tedious landscape of the city: the library and the circus. And there are two characters that struggle with the need for passion and continuity: the storyteller (an old man who we learn in the credits is called Homer) and Marion, a trapeze artist. The prisonlike library is full of people wanting to connect with traditions and memories. Yet each reader is isolated from the others. The old man (*Jedermann*—Everyman) is distressed that he has no hearers. "They no longer sit in a circle. They know nothing about each other." But the tale still rises up within him—"a liturgy for which no one need be initiated to the meaning of words and phrases." The old man has his memories of the war that took away his world. He wonders why "so far, no one has succeeded in singing an epic of peace. What is it about peace that keeps its inspiration from enduring and makes it almost untellable?" Homer wonders if he should give up storytelling. "Once mankind loses its storyteller it will have lost its childhood." We need stories to help us see what's in front of our eyes. "If everyone saw, there would be a history without murder or war."

The circus is financially on its last legs. It is an amateurish affair, yet the only place in the city that is full of life. Marion practices on the trapeze and hopes for someone who will say, "I love you." She longs to be part of a story. She thinks of going to the photolab. A photograph is a way of fixing and pinning down things that are running away from us at the speed of light. It gives the illusion of stillness, of presence, of slowing everything down. A new picture could be the start of a story. Marion says to herself, "I am happy. I have a story. And I'll continue to have one." Her "fantasies are suffused, however, by a powerful aura of desire to become a whole rather than a fragmented and alienated person. She longs to be complete, but recognizes that this can come to be only through a relation with another."[9]

Damiel watches Marion and falls in love with her. His restlessness increases. Tired of his observer role, he wants to get involved in human affairs in spite of their drabness. He is fed up with his merely spiritual existence. He wants to do ordinary things, to be "like Philip Marlowe and feed the cat." He longs for a body that can touch and feel. Damiel says to his fellow angel, "I've been outside long enough. Absent long enough. Out of the world long enough. I'll enter the history of the world! If only I could hold one apple in my hand!" He wants to enjoy and endure real human experience. "I'm going to take the plunge into the ford of time, of death!" Damiel decides to become human. There is a moment when the film changes from black and white into color and he, for the first time, is able to make his mark on the world by leaving footprints.

On his first day as a human being, he hurts himself and draws blood that he is able to taste. He learns the colors of things. He has his first cup of coffee. He learns what it is to be aware and alive. But Damiel is unused to the limitations and unaware of the pitfalls of being human. He needs a word of advice and it comes from a surprising quarter.

Peter Falk (playing himself—as the famous inventor of the role of the unkempt detective Columbo) is making a movie in Berlin. "Get a good costume. It's half the battle," he says as he tries on various hats for the role he is playing. The hats suggest to him various roles, unsuitable for this particular movie—those of an operagoer, a rabbi, a bookmaker, someone getting married, someone going to a horse show in London, somebody's grandfather. We can play any role we want but we have to decide. Falk, who, it turns out, was once an angel, helps Damiel adjust to the world of the flesh, of the here and now. "There's a lot of us. You're not the only one." He continues, laughing, "How good it is to be here. Just to touch something. To have coffee." To be joyously human is to be enfleshed, limited by time, space, and place. It's good to be human.

Damiel sets off in search of Marion. The circus has broken up and they meet in a bar over a glass of wine. They are in *this* time and *this* place. What should they do? Marion says, "I don't know if destiny exists. But decision exists!" We have to plunge in and make our lives into a story. Damiel and Marion learn, in their discovery of each other, amazement at the gift of life.

The movie ends with the old man who, as the storyteller, knows that the world needs him more than ever. The last frame reads, "TO BE CONTINUED." The movie asks the Dantean question, Is our life a story or not? If it is, who is the storyteller and what is the ending?

The two movies are unquestionably romantic. Is a romanticism possible (responsible?) in a world like ours? Dante's vision of romantic love is easily dismissed and despised, but his romanticism shows no trace of the sentimental. It is toughened by real experiences of betrayal and exile. His message is, "Love makes the world go round." It's corny, hackneyed, and unreal unless the love of which Dante speaks is different from that of the popular imagination. Skeptics worry that aesthetics will override ethics and that people will retreat even more into their private and tribal worlds. We will opt for a private heaven in order (we think) to avoid a public hell. Other things threaten the human enterprise as well—for example, our inability to cope with the speed and rate of change. There's a gap between scientific and moral reasoning in contemporary life. Things move so fast in technology and scientific knowledge that our moral sensibility isn't skilled or refined enough to cope with new discoveries. Just because something is doable scientifically, should we do it, say, in areas such as genetic engineering and the manufacture of weapons of destruction? Destiny may not exist, but decision does. Choosing heaven has practical consequences in Dante's scheme. His romanticism is down-to-earth. Heaven means choosing one another.

We have come a long way in looking at our sillinesses and our madnesses. The horrors of hell and the vulnerabilities of purgatory have shown us just how precarious our hold on reality is. Have we been simply allowing our imaginations to run wild? Is heaven simply the "place" where our raving and roving fantasies fall down exhausted, or is it a sign of the really real? Heaven is the place where the acknowledgment of the possibility of error is the most urgent.

The workings of the human imagination seem to know no bounds, and what we claim for ourselves sometimes sounds like the megalomania of a divinity. Owen Glendower asserts in Shakespeare's *King Henry the Fourth, Part I*, "I can call spirits from the vasty deep." Hotspur cynically answers, "Why, so can I, or so can any man; But will they come when you do call for them?"[10] We believe all we want, but is there any way of knowing that what we believe has some validity?

I remember a visit to Glastonbury one summer. I was impressed by the ruins of the abbey, the numinous character of the Tor, and the tacky New Age industry around it all. Tolkien to Dungeons and Dragons. I am not so bothered as I used to be about some New Agers' apparent trivialization of the human condition—the metaphysical gobbledygook that goes along with much in the modern religious supermarket. I have grown tender toward our genius for making fools of ourselves. That is why art and poetry, metaphor and image, tradition and openness are important to me. William Blake's famous question about what you see when you look at the sun is important here. Do you see a disk in the sky rather like a guinea? Or do you see a blazing sign of the Lord of Hosts? Many of us have reached the end of the line when it comes to scientific explanations that deep down explain nothing. I think of William Blake and of the reductionist scientific intellectuals he castigated.

> The atoms of Democritus
> And Newton's particles of light
> Are sands upon the Red Sea Shore
> Where Israel's tents do shine so bright.

We need protocols against reductionism. Sexuality is the means of a wondrous exchange and when it is reduced to mere carnality, we enter into hell. When human relations are reduced to matters of law, neuroses, psychoses, complexes, and dysfunctions, we add to the population of the inferno. I am wary of expressions like "It's *just* a sunset" and "It's *only* your imagination." It's like Scrooge accounting for Marley's ghost as an apparition caused by indigestion. Sometimes I need language that is exaggerated and inflated, just as I need checks and balances with regard to its use. There is a need to go beyond what most people call "common sense." The statement "Let's be reasonable" is often a prelude to our justifying doing something despicable and dishonorable. It isn't always a good idea to be reasonable. Sometimes we need to *imagine* things, to allow our dreams and longings to speak to us.

For Dante, the imagination was an image-receiving instrument rather than an image-making one. Something outside us is trying to get in touch, and it is a something or a someone that demands our attention and allegiance. The imagination is the place where we are most like God, most able to say, like God, I am! And we cannot say "I am" without a story that gives shape and direction to our identity.

Dante's spirituality is romantic. The self by definition is a narrative, and the individual's story is connected to every other story ever told. Spirituality, for Dante, is the region of the uncontrolled and unexplored self seeking to understand its longings (*eros*) by using images, stories, and metaphors to locate itself, not only in the world and in the community of other persons, but also, supremely, in some final narrative (as yet unfinished) of which God is the poet, master storyteller, and actor.

> We protect the cloud-capp'd towers and gorgeous palaces of that insubstantial pageant more fervently than we would protect the quantum theory or Newton's Law of Thermodynamics because that is where we have learnt to come to terms with life's pain and muddle, if we have come to terms, which perhaps we never shall and perhaps we should not hope to.[11]

But is the region of the uncontrolled and unexplored self merely a place of cloud-capped towers and gorgeous palaces of our imagination? Or are they intimations of something more substantial than even our world of the here and now? Are they signs of an even more robust reality than our palpable world?

Some of our contemporaries have reached a point on their spiritual journey that causes them to affirm the images arising from the unknown self as fantasies—maybe useful, even vital ones, but fantasies nonetheless. I confess that I am in a quandary. Irony has its limits. Even the notion of *la bella menzogna* has to be relinquished in the final intuitive affirmation of the truth. I often feel that I betray everything I passionately believe because I don't know how to find the words I need to affirm the great truths of my faith (which I do believe) and at the same time (like Dante) acknowledge the slipperiness of language and the possibility of being mistaken. For example, I've sometimes annoyed people because I wouldn't or couldn't give what they regarded as a straight answer to the question of whether hell exists. I often mumble something about Dante, metaphor, and levels of meaning, and my questioner looks at me in disappointment if not disgust. For him or her, there is no waltzing around the question. "Too bad," I say to myself. Now, when I am asked, I give the straight answer—Yes! I believe in hell—and hope that the conversation continues.

My questioner, however, has a genuine concern. Are we, after all, simply making it up in our heads? Do our fears, needs, and longings fabricate "religion" as a mental artifact to distance our fears and anesthetize the terror? One way out is to claim that our struggle with the transcendent, and the subsequent mess we get into when we try to put it into words, requires a different kind of discourse than our everyday conversations. When I am asked, "Was Jesus God?" I answer yes and wait to find out whether this opens or closes a conversation. Far more difficult questions might be, "Who are *you* who are asking the question? Why do you want to know?" And there are those unbelievers who tell me what I'm *supposed* to believe if I'm a real Christian. They want me to be there for them—dependably wrong and reliably stupid. I don't think I'm alone in this. Many of us find it hard to talk about the things deep inside us; we don't have the skill with myth, metaphor, and poetry to express the truths inside us.

We stand in two places at once. With regard to our religious or political affiliations, we feel stuck between those who believe enthusiastically, even fanatically, and those who barely believe anything with passion. It is as if all the wrong people were saying the right things and all the right people saying the wrong. The choice we have is of being either dangerously focused or fatuously vague about words like *God*. In 1890 the Supreme Court spoke of America as a Christian nation, a Christian people. In 1952 the Court was content to call Americans a religious people whose institutions presuppose a Supreme Being. It is prudent to be as vague as possible about spiritual matters.

I think that the great, largely unacknowledged myth that most people live with is the myth of their own significance. They live and love as if they *matter*. Although they sometimes doubt the myth, they struggle with it and put on a brave face. I live with a sense that the very subject matter of our myth (the myth that life has significance) is too hard for us to look at head on, and yet the narrative seems to be calling us to grand/grandiose visions of ourselves and our place in the universe. Why do we choose one story over another, one person over another to make connections and patterns? "Why seek the comfort of the particular, the anguish of the particular?"[12] Yet we do. We go to crazy lengths to claim a place for ourselves in the scheme of things—supposing, of course, that there is a scheme, that there is heaven.

So we are in a period of "a new world disorder"—a time for remythologizing. So far, our strategies for coping with a collapsing and changing world are a false romanticism and the flight into an idealized past. We need help. In the face of planetary disaster, hunger, and homelessness, can one have a spiritual life—seek heaven—without it sounding silly, irresponsible, and escapist?

How can we face the future without some vision spurring us on and drawing us to itself? Rival visions compete for our future. Different hells and heavens wait for us. For some, "heaven" is the phantom of an upward-spiraling standard of living—an economic and technological *Nowhere* that belongs to the strong, the lucky, and the opportunistic. Others have a different utopia—one of universal peace in which everyone has a place. I don't see how we can have a future worth living unless we see all other human beings as our potential companions. And not only human beings but all other creatures as well. This is exactly the meaning of Dante's heaven. Our society, however, tends to put us in competition with one another. A heaven that does not intend to include everyone is hell.

After a false romanticism, nostalgia is a favored strategy for dealing with the terrors of apocalyptic times. "Heaven" is a recapturing of an idealized past. At least then we knew who we were, knew *where* we were. Sometimes I slip back into an ordered and manageable world when I watch the English imports on PBS's "Masterpiece Theatre" and "Mystery." They are often set in the past—my English past of the forties and fifties. My emotions can run riot with these dramatic commentaries on English social and political life. I am filled with nostalgia, confusion, envy, and anger when I see that *other* world (now endlessly repeatable on video) where I was never at home and yet that is comfortingly familiar. At least I knew the rules from which to deviate. Agatha Christie's world was well ordered. Hercule Poirot lived in a moral universe where people knew how to behave.

Let me give a trivial example. Nowadays, men and boys sometimes wander around Grace Cathedral where I work wearing baseball caps. They don't know how to behave. In the past, there were clear consequences for failing to follow the story line. Then, the men and boys knew the rules—no hats in church. Hairline cracks have appeared in the fabric of my world—fissures in the foundations, signs of a new world disorder. It is manifested in the trivial as well as in the cosmic. We aren't all reading from the same page anymore. Perhaps it was ever thus, but when I was a child, teenager, and young adult, there seemed to be a shared vision of who we were supposed to be and how we were supposed to behave. We also knew where we were going. Or so it seems from the vantage point of today. Such is the power of nostalgia.

A few years ago, I preached at a charming little church that had been built as a replica of a parish church in England. After the service, a woman angrily voiced her frustration with a world that had changed. She longed for an idealized past, for a time of heaven on earth. "Before the new Prayer Book, before the ordination of women, before the acceptance of homosexuals, we had a *darling* little church. Now, you and others like you have ruined it!" The darling little church has gone, along with the darling little communities that supported it. For her the apocalypse had already happened. Hell had invaded heaven. She wanted a replicated reality. Perhaps each of us will be able to have what we want through the technology of virtual reality—each of us hooked up to a separate world built to our specifications.

The church can disappoint and hurt as surely as the Bible can damage souls. A friend of mine accurately and elegantly identified the mood of many who feel abandoned in our churches: "The trouble is that some people take their church *literally;* that is, they escape into it psychologically as well as physically. It becomes their fantasy, a kind of religious Disneyland, where the 1990s, the recession, their deeply conflicted lives, cannot find them. Mrs. X wants it to be the 1950s again, Eisenhower president again, the economy booming and herself young and beautiful. She would resent anyone who tried to tell her that the world is changing or that she is no longer in full control."

We try to protect our vision of heaven, to hold back the tide, but time and circumstances finally overwhelm us. In some ways it's a pity. I can remember when the fountain pen gave way to the ballpoint. My grade-school teachers said it would be the end of decent handwriting. Perhaps they were right, but they had no idea of a world of personal computers. A new generation of children is growing up unable to tie its shoelaces. Velcro is depriving them of an important skill! But an emerging new world is demanding that they learn skills scarcely imagined when I was growing up. That's progress. Rules change and the game shifts and we are left wondering what happened.

When did the world begin to slip? Was it when I got married? When we had children? When we moved to or back from England in the early seventies? The world began to slip away from me about twenty years ago and I have never recovered! I believe that the slipping of the world—when "apocalyptic" penetrated my inner life—was the true beginning of my spiritual journey. I was pushed into hell and had to move down to find my way through. There was breakdown and there was breakthrough. The road has been spiritually perilous and I have been miraculously preserved. I often think to myself that mine must be the slowest conversion in history. I may not be—like Saint Paul—the chief of sinners, but I do lay claim to being the slowest of learners. My mentors have been my children, and my spiritual path is a marriage to someone who goes on refusing to abandon me to my despair and stupidity. The courage of a spouse, the spontaneity of children, the faithfulness of friends—all have contributed to bringing me to the mountain of Purgation and even to the freedom that is heaven.

In other words, I was not left entirely to myself. I had help: guides, friends, mistakes and disasters. Even when I've struggled to evade apocalyptic truths, the truth in one form or another pursues me. Layer upon layer of self-deception has been peeled away (and it's not over). I have been pursued by the Hound of Heaven through depths, spirals, and labyrinths until I've collapsed exhausted. There have been moments of sheer grace and wild splendor when I have felt myself flying or floating. Heaven.

TEN

COMING HOME TO OTHERS IN A SHARED STORY

I can't help thinking about the pain of the human family as it lives out the consequences of stories that were begun hundreds of years ago, in Northern Ireland, Bosnia, the Middle East, and Africa. Is there a way of breaking the cycle of cause in human history? I think back to the sixties—a crucial period in my formation—when the story of the First World started to be drastically revised in favor of the emerging of what was then called the Third World. There was a lot of acting out and acting up. I applauded the openness and tolerance, but I didn't like the way the world was looked at with an ideological squint. Humanity became a mass of "victims" who needed looking after by the enlightened. In the late sixties when I taught in a high school in New York City, there was an incident in an ethics discussion in eleventh grade. A student rightly remonstrated with me that she had the right to her opinion. "Yes," I said, "of course you do, but your opinion is utterly worthless because you haven't thought about the issue or made an effort to be informed!" This might have been poor judgment on my part from an educational point of view, but the point, as unpopular and un-American as it is, needs to be made even more forcefully today than it did nearly thirty years ago. What was lacking then, as now, was the belief that becoming a human being is like learning a craft. It takes work and effort.

The sixties, of course, weren't all bad. Along with the infantilism was much that was good. At least, some idealism could be discerned underneath all the wishful thinking about ushering in a new age. Then, the true believers expected a benign apocalypse. What do we expect now? I don't see much idealism. We seem to be living in the aftermath of a revolution that fizzled out, leaving the legacy of a weakened sense of authority, tradition, and civility—all decried as "bourgeois." Perhaps we needed to be liberated from our sexual uptightness, but look at what we got in exchange: the tedious Sex Wars, Part VI. If we learned anything, it was that no matter how hard we try to avoid them, actions have consequences. The notion that the only common good is the agreement that there isn't one has brought us into hell. Discernment with regard to ideas and values matters because we are coming to realize that not all points of view are equally valid. Our drives and our longings hunger for some direction. Our actions need to be informed by ideals and values.

What drives us? And to what end? Why do we long for a perfect world of happy endings? When an enjoyable movie is over, we get a feeling of glowing satisfaction when "THE END" is displayed on the screen. We like endings. We long for closure and resolution. But we are rightly suspicious of all utopias, of stories of ideal worlds. *U-topia* means, literally, "Nowhere." And there is nothing more divisive than our differing visions of an ideal world. My heaven may be hell to others. Nostalgia for an idealized past can lead to bitterness and disappointment, and a privatized romanticism leaves most of the human family out of the picture. Dante's conviction is that there is no private heaven and if we are to reach the heaven of true identity-in-mutuality, we will have to go through our own hells and purgatories for the sake of being rescued from the thrall of disordered desire and recovering the outline of a narrative in which we can *all* take part. The driving energy of the journey to hell and back has been the longing for a story in which our lives find fulfillment and meaning. Our erotic yearnings find their focus only in some form of narrative that embraces everyone.

It is hard for us, however, not to think of religion as almost entirely a private affair between the individual and the God of one's individualistic view of the world. Dante would have found such a conception incomprehensible. The classic view of politics taught that human nature has an impulse toward *society* and that society is not necessarily a maiming or division of humanity but potentially our joy and perfection. Similarly, the ancients believed that *eros* is a natural longing for the beautiful that, given our complexity and the complexity of things, can be damaged and misled but is in itself a perfection of human sociability by way of the passions.[1] We cannot help but fall in love with one another.

The closer we get to heaven the clearer we shall need to be about the nature of the erotic, that is, the meaning of our longing. All the mystics start from this single assumption that we are driven by an *eros* placed in our hearts by the *Eros* that made the universe. It is divine Desire that holds all things in being. We are made in the image of this Desire and, therefore, nothing less than God will ever satisfy us. Our longing is immeasurable because it can rest only in the One who cannot be measured. Dante was intrigued and driven by the kind of questions Saint Augustine posed in Book 1 of *The Confessions*, which can be summed up in one phrase, "Tell me why I mean so much to you." It was Dante's sense of God's longing for him, as much as his longing for God, that sustained him through his exile. What the mystics have described over the centuries is the story of how our longings are freed from the depressing and heartrending forms of satisfaction that have so often gone horribly wrong. There is no solution to our desires, no way of fixing them so that they will shut up. The mystics knew this. That's why their version of the big story is a romance—a love affair between us, the world, and God.

WHAT'S YOUR THEORY?

Knowledge and love come together in God in a way of knowing that is unlike human ways of knowing. For us, knowledge is power, a way of having some control over our lives. For some, it is the road to manipulating and dominating others. Most of us have an incurable desire to know. Stephen Hawking's interest in physics began with a desire to find out where we came from and why we are here. Hawking points out that "we cannot distinguish what is real about the universe without a theory."[2] The mystics would say that we cannot have any purpose or direction in life without a story. Theory has the word *God* hidden in it (*theos*). It suggests a god's-eye view of things. You cannot make up your mind about the nature of the universe without an overview. You have to *stand* somewhere. Sometimes you also have to make a stand. All our seeing is theory-laden.

Dante, as master storyteller, gives us a new way of experiencing the world, by loving it. He's telling us, "You won't understand yourself or the world without love." In the end, loving is the supreme way of knowing. It used to be thought that without God there could be no true knowledge; without God there could be no purpose or value; without God there would be no right and wrong. In a way, we have come back to this old idea but in a destructive way. Now there are those who claim that there can be no clear knowledge of anything, that there are no absolute values, and that categories of right and wrong are merely matters of personal preference and arbitrary societal norms. Hell. Belief in God has something to do with a big story that frees us to trust our knowing and saves us from divinizing our doubts and mocking ourselves and others for having human hopes and aspirations.

Dante the poet makes the *theory* visible by telling the story of the false trails and pitfalls as we make our way home. He uncovers and brings to light things previously hidden. That's why poets and artists are important. They call into question our version of reality. They present conflicting theories. They introduce subplots that hadn't occurred to us. They throw doubts on our interpretation of events. They show us that we don't so much "have experiences" as experiences "have" us. They are the means by which we are made into who we are. It is unnerving to discover that our experiences are neither self-evident nor without ambiguity. And experience relies on language. It doesn't happen outside a context of some established meaning (a narrative of sorts). In other words, we don't quite know what we've experienced until we can find words to describe it. Experience is something we think we know about. It is so close to us that we confuse it with the truth. "I was there. I experienced the earthquake. Of course it's true!" But experience is a bit more complicated than that. It exists in a strange middle ground between something we have already interpreted to ourselves and something demanding interpretation. That's why we keep going over our past—trying to understand afresh. The most obvious example is found in forgiveness and repentance. The past doesn't change but our understanding of it does, and in the process we are transformed.

Many of the battles in our culture have to do with disagreements about what happened in the past. Who were the victims? Who were the perpetrators? Who was to blame? Who should be punished? What am I owed? If experience relies on language and language is breaking down, how do we know what we have experienced?

Many people find it hard to understand that our experience depends on finding language (a *theory*) to describe it. It doesn't happen outside established meaning—even if today's "established meaning" will be replaced and contradicted by tomorrow's. There is, for example, great confusion when we try to talk about sexual experience. How far can we claim continuity of experience? Was sexuality the same for people in past ages as it is for us? I'm not referring to sexual acts or procreation but to how we understand who we are from the inside. My own experience of my body and my sexuality, I'm sure, is radically different from that of my father and of his father. The point is that the issue of the continuity of human experience isn't a simple thing to understand.

Things, therefore, don't "happen" to people until someone is able to *put them into words*—to tell a story about them. That is why it is important that we take time to listen to other voices and pay attention to stories that would not otherwise be heard. It is also important not to tell other people what their lives mean. Language actually shapes the experience. Dante gave voice to new experiences of his contemporaries. In fact, his readers didn't know what they had experienced until they read his poem. He presented them with another way of reading their world. "Ah!" they were able to say to themselves, "That's the world I live in now. That's what happened to me. I often wondered. That's who I am." The poem came as a revelation. The power of that new language for the fourteenth century is far from exhausted in our own century, although we need poets and artists forging fresh images for our time.

Dante understood from experience that the world is not merely a given but one that our imagination and will can act on and change. The principle is: Consciousness precedes Being. Stories forged by the erotically driven human imagination—often coming out of intense pain and won in our struggle to love one another—keep us alive and hopeful. Dante's "theory," as expressed in *The Divine Comedy*, is of a heaven (a code word for fullness of life) of communion.

As we descend through the circles of our own particular hell, or struggle up our own mountain of purgation, or suddenly find ourselves in heaven, we gradually become aware that God made all three realms and that they are instruments of the divine Love. Love made the gates of hell. These are the words inscribed above its gate.

JUSTICE INSPIRED MY MAKER ABOVE.
IT WAS DIVINE POWER THAT FORMED ME,
SUPREME WISDOM AND ORIGINAL LOVE.[3]

Love also draws us up the mountain. Love brings us home. The goodness of God draws all things to itself. To run from such overflowing goodness is a perverse form of self-deprivation. Judgment is not so much a punishment as the inevitable consequence of such a perverse choice. This seems a simplistic approach to choice. We now know that the relationship between free will and determinism in the psyche is more complicated than an issue of simple and deliberate choices. We know it is useless to tell people simply to pull themselves together when we want them, for example, to stop drinking or to lose weight. The individual will is, of course, important, but it often takes a planned and orchestrated intervention for the person to move out of the hell of addiction and up the mountain of freedom. Dante's psychology seems, at first sight, simpler than ours. He does, however, understand the misery of the will so mired in its willfulness that it no longer knows what it wants. It cannot be said often enough: people are not sent to hell; they choose to go there, not directly perhaps, but by a series of little choices, spiteful acts, and petty negations that lead to the great "No!" at hell's center.

As pilgrims led by intuitive reason, we can choose to "go to hell" but also to get out of it. This is what strikes me most forcibly about Dante's vision: his appreciation of our irrepressible longing for transcendence and our ability to adapt and revise our understanding of life as we go along. We are wonderfully adaptable in our moving toward and through our longings. Dante is a romantic who believes that the passions can be so transformed that people will be able to develop their capacity to delight in one another, and imagine different and alternative realities and futures.

It is hard for us to accept the fact that everything must inevitably be reordered and even rewritten. Stability requires adaptability and diversity. In an age peculiarly suspicious of institutions, we need them more than ever because they are signs of a belonging that introduce us to deeper possibilities of being human than we can realize on our own. They provide the context and give us the opportunity to heal and forgive. We need a container for our vulnerability that we can trust. Institutions (as corrupt and weak as they are) bear the burden of something intensely human. It is a pity that so many people have a parasitical relationship to institutions. Many of my spiritually sophisticated contemporaries have a strong sense of their personal journey. They even have a sense of the sacredness of the earth. But they lack a devotion to the mediating institutions between the personal and the cosmic that hold us all together. Institutions are the sacraments of a larger community that includes the dead and the unborn. They put us in touch with a version of the big story and free us from the confining narrowness of our self-concerns and self-pity. They are, however, not always benign; think of the Hitler Youth movement and the emotional, charismatic power of the Nazis to tell a horrific version of the big story. For Dante, the big story has to include the dead and the unborn and have at its center a self-giving love.

When I think of the dead and the unborn as members of my community, something explodes inside me. My heart is enlarged and my sympathies extended. New meaning is given to my longings and desires. The more inclusive the narrative and the longer running the play, the more I understand the breathtaking possibilities of the human enterprise. Something happens to us when we discover a story with which to identify. "Tell me the old, old story" is another way of saying "Tell me that I matter, tell me that I am loved, tell me that I count for something." But it matters what kind of story we tell. The tale cannot be our exclusive property. Others are to be included. Without an all-embracing love story, others are turned into those who are to be dreaded—even exterminated or "ethnically cleansed." In Dante's heaven, others are not the limitation of our freedom but rather its extension. Friendship with others widens the territory of everyone's liberty. Since life is communion, we give one another life. I come to life in you and you in me. We provide shelter for one another.

The weary old motto of domination is "Divide and rule." It is also the motto of the inferno. The devil is a divider as well as a liar. Domination means division, isolation, and, in the end, despair. In heaven we are freed *for* one another. We experience God in and through one another. There is no freedom without justice and mutuality. Mutuality and solidarity establish human society, but not in some revival of Leninist tyranny. Justice is about our recognizing and accepting other people in a spirit of mutuality. Anyone who experiences the telling of God's love story (the *theoria* of hell, purgatory, and heaven) is nobody's slave. There is no private heaven, just as there is no freedom at someone else's expense. Anyone who lives and breathes in the free space of open possibility will not want to dominate others. To be free, then, is not to be isolated but to share in a diverse and complex matrix of connection. This is the kind of heaven Dante saw and described in his poem. Heaven is loving communication between unique and unrepeatable, distinct beings in a banquet of communion.

Heaven is not a place of privacy but one of diversity and freedom where we make room for one another. There can be no separate deal for the individual that leaves the others out. Alice Walker once said, "We can only be healed in community and *everybody is our community*."[4] Dante's heaven is a social and political place. Nevertheless, while heaven isn't individualistic, it is intensely personal. It provides a homecoming that is peculiar to the individual, not merely generic.

There is a Spanish word, *querencia*, "that means affection for the place one calls home and the sense of well-being that that place gives one."[5] Heaven is a *querencia*. *Querer* means to desire, and our *querencia* is the place where the heart finds rest. T. S. Eliot moved to England because he found his *querencia* there. I found mine when I moved to the United States. What Eliot found good for his soul in England, I found stifling for mine. Each of us needs a *querencia* because, as we have seen, there are no disembodied people. That is why it is deeply wicked to drive people from their homes and take away their culture. Bosnia is a hell on earth because so many of its people are permanently torn away from the ground that gave them identity. We live in a world in which thousands, if not millions, of people have had their *querencia* ripped away. According to United Nations figures, over 100 million human beings are on the move around the planet. Is there any chance of the planet becoming our shared *querencia?* Without such a sense of being at home we die. One's *querencia*, then, is a personal, specific affection for one's own place, yet it is precisely the affection that connects us to the world and to others. It takes a simple act of sympathetic imagination to see that if we are attached to particular places and people, then so are others. We easily lose touch with these basic connections. We misplace ourselves and forget our nature. Allan Bloom has suggested that "The most important reason for communism's fall was forgotten nature."[6] Communism forgot what people were like in both their sinning and their hoping. It forgot that human beings are wily creatures, adaptable in their cunning to preserve life. Communism had its ideologues, but for the most part people simply went along with the regime and tried to work around it. Bloom gives as an example the Chinese government's attempt to cope with a proliferation of crop-destroying rats in the 1950s. When the authorities put a bounty on the offending rodents, the peasants started raising rats in order to claim the bounty. Our basic instincts sometimes undermine even the most deeply ingrained ideology.

We either forget our nature or fuss over it too much. We dissect the life we are given to find out its meaning, but the process often drains out the blood. In *A Day at the Races*, Groucho Marx is fooled "by Chico, who tells him that he can't place his two-dollar bet until he has purchased a breeder's guide, and then a whole series of other guides. By the time Groucho has looked into all of them and been utterly confused, the race is over."[7] Some people seem to want things explained and settled before they feel safe enough to plunge into life—and meanwhile, life passes them by. The angel Damiel, in the movie *Wings of Desire,* was driven by *eros* to risk all and plunge into life and thus into time and death, into a story with a beginning, a middle, and an end.

We need shared rituals that speak to our experience of transitoriness. We need feasts and ceremonies that speak hopefully of the future that binds us together. This is hard because we are going through "a stage of transition and moral mediocrity" (to use Émile Durkheim's phrase) that has cut us off from one another and from God. Our world is dying. Words and ideas that excited our ancestors—honor, duty, dignity, sacrifice—seem to have lost their power over our imaginations. They often sound unreal and pompous. As yet, there is nothing to replace them. Writing in 1915, Durkheim anticipated our situation as well as described his own. "The old gods are growing old or already dead," he wrote, "and others are not yet born."[8]

Plus ça change, plus ça la même chose. Nothing seems to change much. Postmodernism is the same old story. Isn't it merely a variant on modernism itself? Isn't every age one of change and upheaval? There's a cartoon that shows Adam saying to Eve as they leave the Garden of Eden, "Remember, dear, we're living in an age of transition." Is today radically different and any worse (or better) than 1915, or 1789, or any other year, for that matter? I think our age *is* different in one important respect: the world is smaller and communication instantaneous. Time has speeded up and space has contracted. We are all closer together than ever before in human history.

As we face the transition from one millennium to another, part of us aches for a new vision of society that understands the human race as a single family. Another part is attracted to individual survival and private security. The former is the "heavenly" vision of planetary consciousness, with a divine "ecology" of sacredness and reverence, of a way of being human that involves longing for the other to be free and being able to accept the other's difference without fear, of a politics of a just society of only one ethnic group of infinite variety—the whole human family. I don't think this is naively utopian. It is simply an accurate description of who we really are as a people. The affirmation of human solidarity is found in all the great religious traditions.

HEAVEN GIVES NARRATIVE SHAPE TO HUMAN EXPERIENCE

Dante's heaven is populated by differentiated beings so radically unique that it is as if each were a separate species. We tend to judge one another by category (race, gender, class). In the *theoria* of heaven, we are judged as unique and unrepeatable individuals, not as members of a class or category. The thing that grips us about Dante's version of the spiritual journey is that the single human family is made up of *specific* people in *specific* places. It is as if we were to read a contemporary poem about hell, purgatory, and heaven and meet (in various states of misery, conversion, and joy) modern people who were still alive or from the recent past whom we knew personally or by reputation. Imagine meeting John F. Kennedy and Joseph Stalin, along with Madonna, Marilyn Monroe, and Michael Jackson. Imagine talking to Mother Teresa and Adolf Hitler, as well as less famous souls found in the columns of the local newspaper. Imagine meeting your friends, colleagues, and enemies. Imagine encountering these people in the places you would least expect! When Dante wrote about the downward and upward spiraling journey of the soul, he had in his mind specific journeys with distinct scenery inhabited by real people—people who were tormented and inspired by real desires, just as he was and just as we are. Dante knew what all great literary artists know, "that a passing gesture, an image, or mood, can form a whole network of meaning. That the coincidence, the chance remark, the unexpected meeting, can *change* a human being. The significance of a whole lifetime of endeavour can be altered by the sudden confusion of events."[9] Language matters. One's point of view is significant. It is all a matter of theory—a point of view.

Dante not only helped forge the Italian language, he reimagined the Catholic faith as it was understood in his day and gave his contemporaries a new way of understanding themselves and their place in the divine love story. Peter Ackroyd's assessment of the work of Charles Dickens makes me think of Dante's ability to reimagine his own world and make it larger and more hospitable. Dickens was rooted in his time and place and yet longed for transcendence that joined all places and all times. He was more than a brilliant chronicler of his times. In his stories, his readers *reexperienced* the world. He "made it larger, brighter, more capacious than anything they could possibly have imagined for them-selves."[10] This could be said of Dante. Every great artist creates in his or her own image but also experiences his or her own times in an intense way. Dickens went from relative gentility to manual labor in a blacking warehouse. Dante plunged from being an up-and-coming politician and poet to being an exile in fear for his life.

Like Dante, Dickens was passionately concerned with giving narrative shape to human experience. This was the way the rovings and ravings of erotic desire were educated and ordered. Dickens was passionate and tor-mented in his attachments. He struggled "to maintain a vision of the coher-ence of the world, a vision of some central human continuity. In this sense it was also a battle against all self-doubt, anxiety and division that lay be-neath the surface of his own nature, just as they dwelt beneath the progres-sive formulations of nineteenth-century power."[11] But his narrative power is a gift he passed on to the entire human family. He made his times (and, therefore, all times) larger, brighter, more capacious than anything his con-temporaries or we could possibly have imagined. Who is doing this for us today? How can we recapture the sense of our need, not only to tolerate, but to be in communion with others?

The mystery of otherness is present and around us all the time, and is most clearly seen, of course, in our relations with others—others who can be deeply close to us but who can never be possessed. Dante had an ex-alted (even inflated) view of poetry, yet a humble view of his ability to rise to the occasion. Poetry celebrated that which endures. If we believe that the supreme (indeed the only) vehicles for spiritual truth are analogy and metaphor, then perhaps Dante is not exaggerating. Some atheists and be-lievers alike are horrified by the assertion that, when it comes to articulate meaning, there is nothing but metaphor. This is not a capitulation to rela-tivizing everything but an assertion that some realities can be spoken of only by inference. Irony, we already know, is always present because there is never a complete coincidence of letter and spirit. Can we ever find lan-guage adequate to our experience? Isn't speech always veiled when it comes to the mysteries? It is no accident that La Vita Nuova ends with Dante's vowing to remain silent until he is worthy of writing about Beatrice again. He breaks into words again in The Divine Comedy, but the poem ends with a different kind of silence from that at the end of La Vita Nuova—the silence of wonder and adoration. Language always erupts out of silence and returns to it.

In order to practice his art, Dante had to learn to endure false starts and trust his intuition, his inner reality. He had to pay attention to his dreams. In *La Vita Nuova* Dante tells us about the first time Beatrice spoke to him, at their second meeting. She is eighteen years old. Dressed in white, she is walking down the street between two women. He has never heard her voice before and when she speaks to him, he is so overcome that he has to rush home to be alone in the privacy of his room. There he falls asleep and has a dream—a marvelous vision.

> In my room I seem to see a cloud the color of fire, and in the cloud a lordly figure, frightening to behold, yet with a marvelous joy. He said many things of which I understood only a few; among them were the words: *Ego dominus tuus* [I am your Lord]. In his arms I seemed to see a naked figure, sleeping, wrapped lightly in a crimson cloth. Gazing intently I saw it was she who had bestowed her greeting on me earlier that day. In one hand the standing figure held a fiery object and he seemed to say, *Vide cor tuum* [See your heart].[12]

Later on in his sleep, a young man appears to him and says, "My son, it is time for you to put aside these false images." The dream figure begins to weep and Dante wants to know why. The reply stuns him. "I am the center of a circle of which the parts of the circumference are related in similar manner, but with you it is not so!" This isn't a game in geometry. It is an accusation of infidelity, of being off-center, of a lack of integrity. Dante was off track. He had lost his way. He had entered the dark wood without realizing it.

Dante knows what he must do. His heart is destined to find itself in finding *her*. The vision had told him that his heart and Beatrice were inextricably linked. His life's work would be a romantic quest to prove himself worthy of her. But he would have to wait. He would have to discipline himself for the task. "Thus, I hope to compose concerning her that which has never been written in rhyme of any woman. And then may it please him who is the Lord of courtesy that my soul may go and see the glory of my lady, that is of the blessed Beatrice, who now in glory behold the face of him *qui est per omnia secula benedictus* [who is blessed through all the ages]."[13] By our standards this is way off—a far cry from safe and calculated sex, and a world the values of which are merely a matter of personal preference. His determination to go on a journey to discern Beatrice's true glory is made of sterner yet more romantic stuff. Human encounters are fraught with significance.

If Dante is right, we mean more to one another than we can imagine. There are no one-night stands, either physically or spiritually. Nevertheless, the nagging questions remain: Are substantial attachments possible? Can there be a story worth telling without them? Are we so scared of the erotic that we dare not risk committing ourselves to one another? Can our longings really be reduced to the mere need for private satisfaction in a temporary and risk-free environment? We turn erotic relations into contracts, and we lose touch with one another in an endless and empty demand for sexual rights. With the propaganda of the politically correct, we turn to the law court rather than the confessional or to simply saying we are sorry and trying to make amends. Human relations are reduced to a battle for power—a Hobbesian war of all against all. What Kinsey did for sex, scientism does for the spiritual life in general. We turn to science to help us understand human relations because we cannot stand the complexity of the feelings raging inside us. We think science will order and domesticate our passions.

Look at the facile way we "move from the fact of promiscuity to its legitimacy." The principle is that a *description* of actual human behavior sanctifies it. If enough people do it, it's "natural." Everything is permitted. Allan Bloom asks, "If someone tells you that sex is pleasant, that there is a wonderful variety of ways to have it, that there is no rational basis for inhibition, and that practically everybody does it, what implications for action do you suppose follow?"[14] We are sold a bill of goods, falsely identified and misleadingly labeled as "The Road to Freedom." The come-on is, "Take as much as you want when you want. There is no cost, no guilt, no after-effects." What about reason, will, and imagination—the refining and guiding principles of desire? What about our imaginative and rational contribution to our own formation and becoming? What about our accepting that becoming a human being is a craft that requires training and apprenticeship?

Sex is inseparable from the imagination. Scientism reduces our horizons and relieves us of our imaginative responsibilities. It bypasses the issue of the *meaning* of our erotic choices and the inescapable dignity of those choices by palming us off with descriptions masquerading as explanations. We are told that this is what the majority of human beings do, as if the description is a kind of permission slip. "The best you can do by neglecting or denigrating imagination is to debauch and impoverish imagination." Our horizons become narrow and parochial. We settle for the mediocre and the second-rate. Bloom writes, "There is practically nothing within our horizon that can come to the aid of ideal longing." One way of making sure that our horizon is stretching us is to read the great texts of human longing so that we may learn "wonderful things about loving and hating, benefaction and doing harm."[15]

Yet there is much more to the erotic than the narrowly sexual. D. H. Lawrence is famous for suggesting that sexual intercourse is an act of holy communion. Martin Thornton asks, "Why stick to that?" What about other pleasures? The hug of a friend, the smell of freshly brewed coffee, the smile of a child, the air on a spring day? Aren't we surrounded by possible acts of communion?[16] Thomas Traherne, the seventeenth-century poet, felt the sea coursing through his veins and felt an affinity with the stars. The mystics tell us that the big story is always available to us if we will open our eyes.

What does Dante mean by new life? Whatever it is, it isn't mere youth—the first twenty-five years, which he calls *adolescenzia*.[17] There is no place in *La Vita Nuova* where "new" means merely "young." It always refers to something "novel, recent, strange, unusual, miraculous, unexpected, surprising, exceptional, or merely different and other."[18] The new life begins with falling in love, and falling in love requires learning new music. A new life demands a new song. But what form should it take? There are, then, two things about the new life: one is a new vision of what love is, and the other, a new way of expressing it—*dolce stil nuovo* (the sweet new style). The two things go together. New vision requires new expression. But there is often a waiting period for a "sweet new style" to emerge. The period after a conversion experience is often hard because the convert is clumsy and has to learn a new way of being and a new language in which to express it. A gestation period must occur before the Word actually becomes flesh. Dante had to wait until he was ready to write his *Commedia*.

Dante, as a young man, had caught just enough of the significance of his vision of the glory of God in Beatrice to set him on the path—what was to be his life's work. Imagine the joyful intensity of such a vision and the pain and anxiety about expressing it adequately. The twin terrors of betrayal and trivialization must have haunted him. Betrayal plays a large role in Dante's journey. In fact, the young Dante, for all his pining for his beloved Beatrice, had written a poem in honor of another woman. His poetic preparation for writing the *Comedy* involved a great deal of confusion about who exactly was his inspiration. Was it Beatrice? Was it Woman in general? Or is *la donna gentile* an image of Lady Philosophy? How many women have suffered because of the hungering projections of males looking for they know not what?

Dante had to go into exile to discover what Beatrice was revealing to him—the Love that holds everything together. One of Dante's favorite authors, Boethius, wrote that we would be happy if only our "minds were governed by the love that governs the heavens."[19] Could this have something to do with Beatrice? Dante's journey is about finding out who his true love is. On the pilgrimage, he has to face the consequences of his acts of infidelity and ambition. He wanted to be a famous and successful poet as well as an influential and powerful politician. He wanted to control his destiny by containing his vision in a manageable poetic form. Perhaps all he was called to do was to write a wildly successful grand canzone in a new style that would soon become all the rage. How should he prepare himself? By studying poetry, of course (or, in our case, by taking a trip to such places as Zurich, Esalen, Pondicherry, and Gethsemani as a substitute). I left home and made the trip to America to seek fame and fortune and to escape the confines of England. All I found was my lost self, looking for itself. But the trip was worth it.

In spite of Dante's limited contact with her, Beatrice Portinari was, for him, a revelation of the One who made her—*la mirabile visione, la gloriosa donna della mia mente* (the wonderful vision, the glorious lady of my mind)—which set him on the pilgrim's way. Once he had allowed the true vision of her to penetrate his soul, he knew his life's work. It was she who inspired him to write the *Comedy*. This cannot be overemphasized. His inspiration was a person. His motivation was romantic. He was willing to go to hell and back "to see the glory of my lady." I have often wondered how women read the poem. Is the drama lessened for women because the protagonist is a man falling in love with a woman? At least one expert (the woman I live with) tells me:

Yes, it's very difficult for me to relate to Dante's poem the way you do. What about Beatrice? A man's "projection" onto a woman, making her semidivine, is very unsettling. Isn't this one more instance of what men do to women—reduce them to mere projections: the madonna, the whore, and the witch? If he had had a real relationship with Beatrice rather than two brief encounters, I could more readily respond to the idea of his coming to see the glory of the Creator through the glory of the created. This doesn't mean that as a woman I can't relate to the inner journey as depicted by Dante, but it isn't easy. I respond strongly to his experiences but not to his inspiration.

This wasn't the response I'd hoped for. I wanted her to say that there was no problem and agree that the poem is an inner drama transcending sexual differences. She also posed a question I did not want to answer: What did I have to say about Gemma Donati, Dante's wife? I had to be prepared for a surprise when I left the world of my limited imagination and asked an actual woman in the room what she thought. We agreed that the poem contains a great deal of crossover material that includes women and men in a universal human experience. We also agreed that one person can be the catalyst for growth for another and that *projection* (putting all our longings onto another) is both inevitable and good as long as it is acknowledged and worked through. It would be absurd to suggest that only women can write for women and men for men. We need many voices telling many variants of the story of communion and mutuality.

I asked a woman friend to write to me about her perspective on the erotic journey.

Life is very physical, and for too long it has been thought that one can only walk with God without a body. Also, whatever sexual issues we face, the bottom line is the same: we all desire to feel fully alive, we all desire to feel loved and lovable, and we all desire, on some level, to merge with the divine. Some early sexual experiences were emotionally devastating. I received guilt-filled family messages about sex and the body. My father directed his fear of women at me, and I've taken some time to slug it out and relax into my sexuality. Trust has been the biggest single issue, but I was saved by an inner impulse (my mystical nature, my curiosity) that helped me refuse to go dead.

In fact, I feel predisposed to love and merge with almost everything! So, there are two things that have contributed to my enjoying a healthy spirituality: a strong link to and honoring of my emotional life, and a way of living more and more in my body. When I had my baby, I was immersed in the forces and processes of the universe. I had no choice and came through it all with a sense that I can trust the stronger currents of life; I can merge with them more fully without the fear of being overwhelmed and losing myself. Having a baby was deeply erotic—a tremendous love expressed through the body that taught me that the erotic encompasses more than the sexual.

Falling in love is a vital, inclusive human experience. It has its dangers (we can get stuck in it) and its follies (we can become fixated on the creature rather than worship the Creator through loving the beloved), but falling in love is *the* great engine of the soul catapulting us into new life, into new territory. It is the appointed way in which we see the glory of the Creator in a creature. The trick is to discern the difference. Dante was an angry and disappointed man who was saved from a crippling bitterness because he was unable to forget his first love. He was unable to repress entirely the new life to which Beatrice Portinari had introduced him when he was only nine years old.

What, then, was Dante up to that has such significance for us? In *La Vita Nuova* he writes of his intention to compose a poem exalting the glory of the creature in such a way that it leads us to stand amazed at the glory of the Creator. This was Dante's gift to his contemporaries. It is his gift to us. It is a gift because in our day we confuse the creature with the Creator. The modern name for it is addiction. Another word is attachment. The old name for it was idolatry. The havoc it causes is evident everywhere.

Dante's journey to hell was necessary because he had lost himself in his addictions, attachments, and idolatries. Hell was part of his education in discernment. He had to learn that, while the erotic can be a trap—a web of illusion—it was also the arrow of life moving him to his desired end. Haven't we spent much of our time keeping the lid on our emotions and suppressing the erotic, and thereby thwarting our longed-for goal? Many of us grew up with the myth

that if we acknowledge, honor, and embrace the erotic impulses of our sensual selves we will destroy the order in our world and be

cast into chaos. This terrifies us. We turn against desire itself,
against our own erotic impulses and feelings, as well as the erotic
expressions of others. We set ourselves the task of keeping the
erotic impulse down at all cost. . . . It is a life-denying endeavor
which is emotionally exhausting—a declaration of war on our
longing for life.[20]

In our embarrassment and disappointment we turn against our longings
and even despise the objects of our desire.

Ecstasy, indeed any feeling of uncontrolled and intense wonder and
amazement, is condemned as dark and dangerous. Loss of ego
boundaries, dissolution of the discrete, discernible self—a core com-
ponent of deep sexual experience—is perceived not as an emotional,
spiritual, or even religious, opportunity, but as something to be
feared and resisted.[21]

This isn't to deny the possibility of real erotic conflict. Long-simmering
resentments and painful humiliations can make the erotic impulse go haywire. As we have seen, shadow work is a vital part of the inner life, and
work with the shadow side of the erotic is doubly important. We need to go
on a clarifying journey for the sake of *eros*. Augustine told us *Ama et fac
quod vis*—Love, and do what you like. But this doesn't give us permission
to regress into a childish rejection of the promptings of conscience. Loving
with discernment leads to a new spontaneity of life. When our lack of confidence in ourselves is taken up by a newfound confidence in God, when we
forget ourselves and remember the larger story, we become radiant. We
shine with desire for the One who desires us.

Purgatory initiates the new life by restoring our sense of mutuality and
interdependence. Heaven shows us that life is made up of intersecting circles:
"the soul in the body, the person in community, the community in the se-
quence of generations, the generations of human beings in the shared
house of the earth." Once we have seen the heavenly vision of life as something shared, "we begin to live less ruthlessly and more sensitively. Then
life *at the expense of others* is no longer possible."[22]

Heaven has a political and social agenda because it is concerned with the
interconnecting circles of relationships that celebrate a story without end.
The message of heaven is simple: Life (*bios*) is always symbiosis. Heaven is

conviviality. Paradise is a party and everyone is invited. The vision of heaven is the expression of one man's experience of human longing put into a narrative. For Dante, the story of our loving finds fulfillment only in the larger story of God's longing for us. It is this longing that we shall now explore.

ELEVEN

COMING HOME TO GOD: THE END THAT HAS NO ENDING

And there will be no more night; they need no light of lamp or sun, for the Lord God will be their light, and they will reign forever and ever.

REVELATION 22:5

Human beings cannot help but try to figure out what kind of story is being played out in their lives. I have rewritten mine over and over again in the hope that I can retrace my steps, find the wrong turns, get back on track, and, thereby, change the ending. What can be done about my mistakes, about past acts that still fill me with sadness and shame? The most disturbing yet significant moments in my life have been when my life has gone blank with a temporary but total loss of memory. The story I've been holding onto dissolves. When I try to remember, all I can get are fragments of a forgotten self: the sight of the shattered windows in the street where I was born after an air raid; the feeling of disappointment when I realized that the promise that I would be given a puppy would never be kept; seeing an aunt do something spiteful for sheer pleasure; the feeling of cold when a snowball hit my face in the winter of 1947. It would be hard to weave these trivial fragments into a story. But when the blankness disappears and my memory and imagination get to work, a narrative begins to emerge once more. The truth or falsity of it, however, eludes me. Whatever truth there is in it depends on the story's endless capacity for revision. I think this is what is meant by faith. Faith is the willingness to have one's story tested by a larger narrative that one takes on trust. Seeing my life as a movement through the three passages of hell, purgatory, and heaven has helped me understand myself and what I am about. It has also kept me from ultimate despair (although on occasion I have come close). This generous and truth-telling threefold scheme allows me to hope because it gives my life moral bite and a sense of direction. My mission—like that of every other human being—is to be available to and an agent of the movement through the passage of isolation, into the transitional passage of "a change of heart," and then into the passage that never ends of communion with all things and with God.

I have been drawn to Dante because of his vision of the plot of the human story. In that version, our longing finds rest in a story of God's longing for us. Without a narrative, there is no life. Is there really a thread of a story running through the wonder and mischief of history? Terry Waite, who was held hostage in Beirut for 1,763 days—many of them in solitary confinement—describes one of his methods of survival. With nothing to write with, he composed in his imagination, reviving his memories and rehearsing his life. When his isolation grew unbearable, he often feared for his life and his mental stability, but the story sustained him. "I always managed to return to my story and thus was enabled to preserve my sanity and identity."[1] I have no way of measuring the truth of Terry Waite's narrative (or anyone's, for that matter) except by setting it side by side with other stories I have heard. We spend a lot of our time sifting stories to see if they ring true or can be used to make us feel safe.

We have seen how Dante preserved his sanity and identity through personal trials by writing a poem. His imagination shaped human experience in a three-part narrative. *Inferno* tells the tale of misery—the loss of mutuality and community. It is a vision of time as the death-bearer (history in the negative sense—like one gangster shooting another in the movies: "Take that, you dirty rat! You're history."). Hell, which begins in the dark wood of our tangled wills, is the story of our being stuck with our history in a cycle of hopeless repetition.

Purgatorio is the story of history going someplace. The pilgrim is given the grace to change, to be converted, to be transformed. Dante's purgatory is the mountain up which the soul must labor in order to recover sanity and identity. *Paradiso* is the story of homecoming. It is a tale of delight in knowing who and whose we are. Dante's unifying metaphor is the great white rose. Each soul has a unique place in the divine glory and is radiant with its own true identity. The *Comedy*'s shape is important because of the narrative structure of human life.

THE STORY/THEORY OF THE CALL TO BE HUMAN

The felicitous thing about the journey to heaven is that when we try to put it into words we are taken by surprise. The end isn't the end in any sense we could imagine. Something happens to us, to our self-understanding, when we place ourselves in a certain kind of story. Our stories *make* our world. Our theories determine our experiments with life. If we hold the theory that human beings are a rotten lot and the world a hostile place, we will find "experiments" to fit our theory.

A friend of mine claims that people have either a fortress or a banquet mentality. They see everything in terms of either defense and protection or sharing and celebration. Sometimes we need to defend and protect, but today we need to cultivate the other mentality if we are to survive. Fierce energies running loose in the world deny the sacred character of our lives and find the "theory" that we do not belong to ourselves laughable. In the end, I reject as a form of willful madness what is loosely called postmodernism, because it rules out the possibility of transcendence. It shuts out any prospect of gracious energies and powers that, while being above and beyond us, are nevertheless capable of transforming us.

But does faith in a Someone or Something other than ourselves make sense? I am skeptical about common sense and about what people acting "reasonably" can accomplish. I'm not arguing for irrationality but expressing frustration because the "sensible individual and the refined skeptic" see the person of faith as "something between an idiot and an outlaw."[2] "Sensible and rational" people cannot give an account of the depths and contradictions of human experience; they don't understand that we are not deep enough on our own.

The life of faith pushes us into a stance of patient and hopeful availability. Faith is able to bear the provisional character of our personal, social, and political arrangements. We dare fall in love and go on adventures. In spite of many setbacks, we plunge into existence and take delight in the surprises and opportunities of life. We are free to live with the for-the-time-being character of all human arrangements, both personal and institutional. Nothing, except God, is forever. We have to learn to be in two places at once: (1) grounded on the earth, accepting the limits of time, place, and space as the gracious, nonpunishing conditions of being human; and (2) defined by our destination in heaven, living into an identity that is open to and formed by God. In short, to be human is to be embodied and engodded. We take our attachments seriously and refuse to let our exile keep us away from our true destination. Yet what will happen next? And in our hearts the assurance: You haven't seen anything yet.

I know that we need protecting from fanatics and dreamers, but at what cost? What should sensible people do to protect themselves from the zealots in their midst? For an understanding of heaven-centered visionary faith, however, we should turn the question on its head: What should people of faith do with regard to the faithless people around them? Perhaps we should point out the superstition of believing that technology will save us. Perhaps we should mention the faithlessness of our relationships. We might point out how flat the world becomes when it is robbed of its wonder. We might draw one another's attention to our unspoken longings.

If we don't have a vision of heaven or a sense of the transcendent, we tend not to see any reality or value beyond the little world of our narrow experience. The "real" world is only what we can see. We grow up thinking that our parents and then our own opinions and prejudices are *objective* truths and that the social and political structures of our society are natural, part of the given order of things.

In spite of the fact that Dante is a brilliant diagnostician of the human condition (a condition that would incline any "sensible" person to pessimism), he is a man of hope. He believes that we were made for glory. But his is not a cheap glory. Glory needs a point of entry in us. Its privileged point of access is our weakness. The glory of heaven, as being-in-all-its-fullness, is not as we imagined. The road down into hell and up the mountain of Purgation has been for the sake of learning what an awesome and wonderful thing it is *to be*. Glory, then, is not an achievement (as in earthly glories), or the receiving of a kind of merit badge for spirituality. It is a free gift. Hell and purgatory teach us to make room for glory, because it requires of us a receptive emptiness. In our anxiety, agony, and loneliness, the emptiness is formed. Our weakness is an opening that can let the glory in.

Much of the time, a crack in our well-protected lives is the only way that an opening can be made for the glory to get in. Our glory is being who we really are. It is finding our true image. Do you "remember" your glory? In the economy of love, ours is a shared glory uniquely enjoyed. In heaven, we find that our mutual longing and our shared risk converge. At last we understand that our dangers and anxieties are shared, that our vocation is to support and care for one another in the ecology of the Spirit. This is Dante's *theoria*. This is how he *sees* things. What you see is what you get.

If we see humanity in godly terms we end up with a different kind of story than if we look at God in human terms. A humanity related to the infinite has a different story to tell than one related only to itself. When God is reduced to human terms and our desire confined to the private or tribal, the stories we tell tend to be narrow, prejudiced, and often bigoted. When, for example, we use masculine and feminine imagery about God, we usually begin by thinking we know what men and women are. But if we turn the process of exploration upside down, we end up with a view of humanity that is deeper and broader than we could have imagined on our own. We call God Father or Mother not so much because human mothers and fathers teach us what God is like but because the mothering of the divine Father and the fathering of the divine Mother teach us how to be mothers and fathers to our children. The metaphor is turned upside down to help us reimagine the roles we play in the drama. So, when the tradition tells us that we are made in the image of God, rather than "explaining" God in human terms, the reverse is true. Human self-understanding is broken open and we acknowledge that there is more to us than we will ever understand.

In the New Testament we read what Dante might have taken as his text: "Thus he has given us, through these things, his precious and very great promises, so that through them you may escape from the corruption that is in the world because of mistaken desire, and may become participants of the divine nature" (2 Peter 1:4, RSV). It is the plot summary of the poet's version of the drama of how our desire is educated. The goal of the journey? Our sharing in the divine nature.

The Eastern Christian tradition has its own version of the story. Truly human life is a process of divinization. Rather than thinking, as we do in the West, of a drama of creation and redemption, the Eastern church thinks in terms of creation and re-creation. The story goes like this: We all share in the divine nature. God's nature is generous love in complete freedom. God has made us, therefore, both loving and free. We are free even to betray our own nature and go against the grain of our being. God so longs for us that the divine entered into our time and space as one of us to bring us home. Through the radical work of Christ's cross and resurrection, the human race is reconstituted and made a partaker of the divine splendor.

A human being is made up not simply of body, mind, and spirit, but of body, mind, and *Holy* Spirit. Bereft of God, we are not fully human. Hell is our saying no to our own best selves, to the divine Spirit within us cooperating with us in our own becoming, in the telling of our own story. It is the terrible mystery of our settling for less for the sake of control. It is not that Christ was somehow superhuman but that we are still in the process of becoming human. Human beings don't just happen. They are made every day in the crucible of a thousand decisions: shall I do this or that, say this or that, go here or there? Some of our decisions send us spiraling down into hell; others move us up the mountain. The doctrine that we are made in the image of God tells us that our defining reference point is transcendent and unknowable (at least unknowable in our narrowly rational terms).

Two issues about the way we tell God's story have arisen in our own day and have to be faced head-on. The first has to do with inclusive language, especially with regard to the pressure to speak of God in feminine as well as masculine terms. The second has to do with our attitude to religious traditions other than our own.

With regard to the first issue, the Christian story of God is Trinitarian—it is the revelation of *relationship and relatedness*. The vision of the Trinity with the central figure of Christ gave Dante the insight to see what is *permanent* yet *dynamic* in humanity. It is "the *imago Dei*" that enables each of us to say "I am." Knowledge of God and knowledge of self are two sides of the same coin. Toward the end of the *Paradiso* Beatrice speaks of creation in these words. She knows Dante's longing to know.

> I ask not what thou long'st to hear,
> But tell thee; I can all thy longing name
> Here, where is centred every *when* and *where*.
> Not increase of His own Good to proclaim
> (Which is not possible) but that His own
> Splendour might in resplendence say *I am;*
> In His eternity, where time is none,
> Nor aught of limitation else, He chose
> That in new loves the eternal Love be shown.[3]

Dante understood the formula (popular in the Middle Ages), "Love is a form of knowing." We are good at knowing specific things for specific tasks (technology) but not good at the higher form of knowing, which desires to see how everything fits together, how the various truths are related. In the *Paradiso* Dante's desire is set in order. The strange sound and light that he encountered in heaven inflamed his desire to know their cause. Desire, even in heaven, came upon him like a sharp pain. Saint Benedict refers to Dante's *alto disio*—his exalted desire that would be satisfied only in the final sphere of heaven where "every wish is perfect, ripe and whole."[4] At the very end, Saint Bernard prays to the Blessed Virgin Mary, after which Dante recollects:

> And I, who was now nearing Him who is
> the end of all desires, as I ought,
> lifted my longing to its ardent limit [*l'ardor del desiderio*].[5]

This *ardor del desiderio* is everywhere, not least in the groaning of the heart in prayer and in the agony of purgation. *Domine, ante te omne desiderium meum, et gemitus meus a te non est absconditus:* "O Lord, you know all my desires, and my sighing is not hidden from you" (Psalm 38:9, VULGATE). Psalm 42 is also a key text here: "Like as the hart desireth the waterbrooks, so longeth my soul after thee, O God." Saint Bonaventure reminds us that, in the end, the mystery of longing is a question of "grace not instruction; desire not understanding; the groaning of prayer, not diligent reading."[6] The vicious circle of disordered desire is transformed into the blessed circle of the rose of fulfilled longing. The intellect desires to see, the will desires to possess. Through the discipline of the triple adventure through the three realms, our desires are educated. Heaven is the place where intellect and will meet in a desiring that sings in tune with the divine Desire that called us into being in the first place.

God makes humanity in the divine image. We are beings able to shine back to God in the divine splendor and say, like God, "I am!" This is a reference to the name of God given to Moses at the burning bush: "I am; that is who I am. Tell them that I am has sent you to them" (Exodus 3:14, NEB). Why is it that human beings cannot find themselves in themselves? What is it in me that is more me than myself? What is it about being human that requires self-donation in order to be fully alive? Why do I need you in order to be me? Unlike God, we cannot say, "I am who I am." We have to learn to say, "I am because you are: you are because I am." We are able to say "I am" only in relationship. In chapter 22 of the *Tao Te Ching* we read, "The person who looks at himself does not shine. But the person who does not look at himself will be filled with light." The image of God is marked by two special gifts in human beings—the intellect and the will—"the means of knowing and of choosing freedom." And because of these gifts exercised in freedom, we can do with them what we will.

I continue to use as my primary speech about God the Trinitarian language of Father, Son, and Holy Spirit precisely for this reason. God in *this* story is a community of persons. That is why I find talking about God creating, redeeming, and sustaining inadequate as far as the Trinitarian communion goes. But I also recognize difficulties with the constant references to God only as Father. I believe that this language needs explicating and deepening by the inclusion of the feminine in the divine. That is why I am attracted to Dante's unashamed focus on the feminine on the journey. Three women are the inspiration for the journey: Beatrice, Saint Lucy, and Mary, the Mother of God (the God-bearer).

Virgil at the beginning of the *Inferno* asks why Dante is afraid of the journey.

> Why are you not daring and liberated
> When three such blessed ladies have sued
> on your behalf in the court of heaven
> and my own words to you promise so much good.[7]

The fullness of the vision requires the coming together of the masculine and the feminine. There has always been a strong, if until recently repressed, feminism in the Christian tradition. According to Heraclitus, war or strife is the father of all things; harmony, accord, and beauty are the mother of all things. Traditionally, one holds a bow; the other, a lyre. The bow and the lyre complement each other. The Greek word *bios* (life) can also mean bow. The suggestion is that the aggressive masculine is to be harmonized by the feminine and changed into a life-bearing liturgy of glory and beauty. We might even go so far as to say, "At its perfection, this beauty is the *Theotokos*, the Mother of God" and thus the Mother of all of us. She is the one who brings us close to the mystery.[8]

It is a great error (and has always been regarded as such) to assume that God is male, just as it is an error to assume that God is female. Relationship, communion, and community are the key words in appreciating and understanding the love story of Christianity. The pressure toward complementarity of imagery is a movement of the Spirit to greater and greater *ad-*

equacy in our talk about God, so that our story may include everyone. It is, therefore, highly appropriate to talk of the divine Feminine. There is an old theological principle about the work of God in Christ: what has not been assumed cannot be redeemed. This simply means that the humanity of God includes all that human beings are—male and female. If the feminine isn't as present as the masculine in God (who is also beyond both), the story not only falls apart, it is not worth telling.

The second issue I mentioned earlier has to do with the revelation of God in traditions other than the dominant one. This issue is related to that of inclusiveness. God is always at work in the world, and the divine light lightens everyone coming into the world. In the way I receive and tell the story, Christ comes to meet me in the other traditions. Father Bede Griffith used an image to illustrate how the great religious traditions are related. He pointed to the fingers of his hand as representing the great traditions: Buddhism, Judaism, Hinduism, Islam, Christianity. At the extremities of the fingers and the thumb, the traditions are very far apart. As one moves down the fingers toward the palm of the hand, they begin to meet and converge. This isn't to say that deep down all religions are the same. They are not. But their stories do resonate with one another. The moral test is the same: adoration, compassion, and communion. Another aspect of the way I heard and now retell the story is that the Holy Spirit is forming the human race into one family by drawing the religious traditions closer together. There is also a countervailing force of separation and division that cannot easily be dismissed as "demonic," although I believe much of it is. The more liberal among us need to respect the genuine concern about principles and distinctions in the various religious and secular traditions. The more conservative need to be less embarrassed by the divine generosity and hospitality that invites everyone and everything into communion.

I find that I am often disappointed with the religious traditions, particularly with the one I know best. But I feel tender to anyone who shrinks back from plunging fully into the fearful and wonderful process of becoming a human being. I am more concerned with human solidarity than with the warring factions of the various traditions and their fights about the big story. It's not that these disputes are irrelevant, but we already have much more in common with one another than could possibly divide us. The Holy Spirit cannot be confined by institutions and traditions, and the truth, from whatever source, is of the Holy Spirit. The Spirit blows where it will—unevenly in and through us all, regardless and sometimes in spite of our allegiances. We learn this from Dante's heavenly vision about being human: to be human is to be embodied and to be in relationship with others. The body is good and is to be held in reverence. As human beings, however, we are limited by time and space, by history and geography, by the particularities that bind us to being *here* and not *there*. Such limitations are the means of grace. We have a history and we are a story. Dante was concerned with the resurrection of the body as the means of thinking about the continuance of a distinct personality with actual, concrete relationships with people who can be touched and handled. Basically, if you're going to love, you need a body. Heaven is an embodied existence. This stretches our imagination and asks us to think of a different kind of body not subject to all the earthly limitations. Dante puts much of his vision in the mouth of Solomon (no doubt because Solomon was thought to be the author of the Song of Songs). The king speaks of *la festa di paradiso* (the banquet of paradise) where we shall put on *la carne gloriosa e santa* (the glorious and holy flesh) and we shall be whole and complete.[9] In heaven the soul becomes more personal and individual—more true to itself, in harmony with all creation.

I think Dante would have responded with delight to the modern notion of earth as a single life system. Simple ecology teaches us that created beings live in systems and move toward the complexity of communal relationships. The theory is that creation is a community. We are destined for others and find our identity only in relationship with one another. The experience of God in the experience of the self must not be turned into opposites, as if they were alternatives. But these relationships aren't immutable. They can, they must, change over time. Human beings need institutions (the church and the empire), and these institutions are called to be always engaged in a process of reformation. Human beings affect their world. Their choices and decisions matter. The most important choice is the decision to place one's individual story in the context of the divine drama. The vision is this: every willing heart that is open to the divine will can see the web linking each to all. The love of God as joyous goodwill holds and binds, breaks open and sets free, at the same time.

HEAVEN IS A ROMANCE, AN END WITHOUT AN ENDING

How can we talk of the story coming to an end? What kind of story ends with no ending? The "end" of the story (like the end of the world) celebrates

God's big story of participation with us in freedom, in faith, hope, and love. In that sense, there is an end to the story. The future has been disclosed to us. We know what we're supposed to be up to. For one thing, the story tells us that we're not trash and we weren't made for nothing. This story tells us that Christ entered into our life with a sympathetic understanding of its fragility and unsolved enigmas. Because he is human, he knows just how it is with us. He knows our longings and temptations. God gazes at us from every human face, because we are all brothers and sisters of the divine. We see God in all people, and since we play host and guest to one another on the planet, "we are to receive all guests as Christ" (as the Rule of Saint Benedict has it). God is seen in the hungry or angelic face of a child, in the hopeful, resigned, or resentful faces of the poor, in the strained features of someone who has begun to face up to the consequences of his own sinning. God is seen even in the faces of those we fear and hate, and looks back at us through their eyes. And those eyes reflect love in both its merciful and angry aspects.

The journey to heaven widens and deepens our range of anticipation of what it might mean to be human. It points to our true end as persons. The process brings with it an ever-greater wealth in the forms of individuality that can be minted. Ever-richer forms of social relationship develop, and there is a continual expansion of the scope for free behavior. No two snowflakes are exactly alike, and a human being—a being with a history—cannot be cloned. We have seen that, for Dante, heaven means a richer variety of examples and species. The "end" keeps revealing more and more possibilities.

There are, I suppose, people who find life easy. They are not wracked, even occasionally, by difficulties and doubts, not stretched by large longings and wild passions. I am not one of them. Some years ago, Karl Barth wrote a letter to Mozart—a great pattern maker—thanking him for re-ordering and enlarging the world.

> *My dear Mozart:*
> *What I thank you for is simply this: Whenever I listen to you, I am transported to the threshold of a world which in sunlight and storm, by day and by night, is a good and ordered world. Then, as a human being of the twentieth century, I always find myself blessed with courage (not arrogance), with tempo (not exaggerated tempo), with*

*purity (not wearisome purity), with peace (not slothful peace). With
an ear open to your musical dialectic, one can be young and become
old, can work and rest, be content and sad: in short one can live.*[10]

This is how I feel about Dante. He takes the whole breadth of human experience and places it in the context of hope. He gives our lives direction,
but each of us has to play out the drama in his or her unique way. Dante
understood that our basic yearnings are signs of our longing for God. But
how to have order *and* freedom, structure *and* liberty? Christianity is basically a religion of longing and romance—no matter how hard some Christians have tried to disguise and distort the truth. The poetry of passionate
romance is the proper language for the spiritual journey.

The romance of the journey through the pit of hell and up the mountain
of Purgation shows us some of the consequences of our choices. In effect,
the damned, the converted, and the blissful say to Dante, "This is what our
choices have done to us." Judgment is self-imposed, punishment self-
inflicted by reason of the use and abuse of the gifts of intellect and will. We
suffer, however, from spiritual amnesia. We forget who we are. Ulysses in
the *Inferno* tells how he fired his last crew with desire by appealing to their
true identity, by getting them to remember who they were:

> CONSIDERATE LA VOSTRA SEMENZA:
> FATTI NON FOSTE A VIVER COME BRUTI,
> MA PER SEGUIR VIRTUTE E CANOSCENZA.

"Consider well the seed that gave you birth: you were not made to live
your lives as brutes, but to be followers of worth and knowledge."[11] But
take note, Ulysses is in hell for using his gifts of persuasion for deceitful
purposes.

The great principle of the *Paradiso* is that each of us is sent out into creation "to individuate itself among new loves." Heaven reminds us of hell
because here we catch a glimpse of what we can lose or have lost. "This is
what we have done to our souls." Dante gives us instances of those who exercised their freedom in different ways. There are examples of wounded humanity (pathetic and terrible in some cases—like a Bertran de Born or a
Manfred) bearing pains that recall the incessant suffering of Amfortas, the
wounded king in the Parsifal story. Particular wounded human beings in
the poem have significance because humanity as a whole is wounded in

both will and intellect. Amfortas could be healed only by the right question being asked. In hell, we see the consequences of our missing the point.

In the *Inferno*, we find Guido da Montefeltro (a Ghibelline warlord who, in old age, became a friar). Saint Francis tries to rescue him from hell but a demon points out the unsentimental logic of damnation, which cannot tolerate *la contradizion* of a soul who refuses grace to enter heaven. Guido was unrepentant and, therefore, unabsolved. There is no way that a soul can repent and will the sin at the same time. You can't have it both ways. There is nothing more pathetic than a resourceful person, full of ambition and ingenuity, having his own inconsistency and stupidity pointed out to him. Hell is the awful revelation of character in one act. We see "all the accumulated habits of mind and formed attitudes that make up the inner life" manifest themselves in a meanness of soul. But it is all *one* reality of fire, flame, and light. Heaven and hell are made and maintained by Love and it is "the *same* divinely created element that tortures one soul and irradiates another." For those who refuse love, being touched by its fire is hell. It is "l'amor che move il sole e l'altre stelle" that permits the hells we choose for ourselves to exist. Perhaps heaven and hell are not so far apart as we imagined. Purgatory exists as the mediating middle realm where the soul wakes up to what it has chosen. There it looks for mercy and forgiveness for having barely lived and for refusing life when it was offered. In hell, self-recognition is horror; self-knowledge is torment. In heaven, they are joy and love. One realm reflects the other.

At the end, Dante "describes the binding by Love of all the scattered pages of the universe into one volume, the understanding of all relationships as *un semplice lume*, one simple light."[12] And the lesson? Love is not diminished by sharing. The souls in heaven greet Dante with the words, "Ecco chi crescera li nostri amori"—Behold one who will increase our loves.

This is the vision, but can we see its significance? Have we learned anything from life? Do we know anything more about the code or signal or DNA of what it is to be human? Has our being human anything to do with the beauty of heaven? It is the place worth hunting for. That's why we struggle to talk about our heart's desire. The longing for it can break our hearts. Heaven is the revelation that everything we've ached for is available to us and that, in the end, the lost are found. Can we live with the longing? I don't find that hope takes away my longing. Rather, it sharpens my feelings of incompleteness and causes me distress when I see the state of the world. There's heartbreak in the vision of it as well as hope and fulfillment because it shows us God's intentions for us—the intentions of a God who journeys with us and who is calling the whole of creation into a new relationship. Abraham Heschel wrote, "God means: No one is ever alone."[13] The vision of heaven is the great and graceful pressure in us toward health, clarity, sanity, wholeness, justice, joy, hilarity, delight. It is painful when we set it alongside the tearing reality of the world and its millions of starving, bruised, and brutalizing people. But such dark truths do not invalidate the facts of human solidarity and sacred ecology.

Heaven celebrates the holiness of persons and things, and is a political and social place of practical implications for everyday life. Saint Bernard of Clairvaux, Dante's final mentor, defined wisdom as "the taste of things as they really are. The wise person is the one who savors all things as they are in reality." So, while it cannot be denied that Dante's *Paradiso* is a happy ending to a long journey, it is neither sentimental nor unreal. There is always a provisionality, a radical openness, about the final vision that guards against the chilling lies of sentimentality and wishful thinking. There is also a challenge. If this is our goal, our purpose, our end, how should we behave *now?* Dante celebrates a God who is involved in his creation all the time. Creation is a constant outpouring of the active love of God. If this is so, what should our social and political agenda be?

The *Paradiso* also shows how impoverished we become when we think that we are an end to ourselves, when we have nothing outside ourselves to act as a reference. The result of having no compelling beliefs and patterns of meaning holding us together is enclaves of fanatical and exclusionary passion but no unifying energy. We seem to be left with two unacceptable solutions: a disintegrating pluralism or an intolerant unity. In our postmodernist world, people do not have a deepening theory or a text in which to locate themselves. There is an absence of resonating images to help the soul understand itself. Once upon a time, when people walked into a cathedral or even caught a glimpse of the towers of a city, "a deep spectrum of emotions, fears, and hopes was triggered" in them and they were enriched immeasurably by what they saw. Mark Helprin comments, "When these people saw the lights of stained glass, they felt the presence of God. The aesthetics of the structure and everything within were a road to that, not as they are now, an end in themselves."[14]

CHOOSING HEAVEN NOW

We have seen how our choices—even the smallest of them—have consequences. Our choices accumulate and form themselves into patterns, which in turn become habits. Habits eventually become ingrained into characteristics. One habit we need is what Dante and his contemporaries called *cortesia*, which is more than courtesy; it is an array of humane rituals of recognition and regard. It has to do with treating one another with reverence and respect. Our character is formed by choices and our choices are revealed on our faces.

Our unacknowledged despair for the world and its future (for my world and my future) erupts into violence—both outward and inward. We imagine that the world is fixable on our own terms—terms favorable to us (too bad for the others). The affluent West has exported a version of reality ("democracy" tied to consumerism) that is returning to haunt us. There is a coming world *disorder*. We *either* agitate, protest, and mobilize our resentments—mouth old platitudes as if they were invented for the occasion; indulge in a frenzy of litigation—*or* embrace a deadly fatalism about our intractable problems.

The *Comedy* is the drama of our choice. Which is it to be? Misery, conversion, or delight? Each of us can, with a little imagination, locate ourselves (or aspects of ourselves) in one or more of the great circling spirals of desire—hell, purgatory, or heaven. So which is it to be? Misery, conversion, or delight? Is Dante right to claim that the choice is ours? What of those who appear to have no choice? Dante would insist that people in the most dire circumstances still have choice, no matter how small.

There is, for example, the story of Maria Rutkiewicz, a member of the Polish underground in the Second World War. She tells of a terrifying moment after she had been taken by the Gestapo. She was standing with her back toward her captors in a yard, certain that she was about to be executed.

> I was sure that this was my last moment, and as I stood in front of the tree, something unbelievable happened. I have never since had such a feeling, but I remember it very well. Every leaf of the tree was separate, every patch was like a picture, separate and big. I could see every detail of the little flowers in the grass. I was sure that this was my last view, and that in a moment I would feel the bullet in my head, here in the back of my neck.[15]

Viktor Frankl, in his account of his concentration camp experiences, speaks of the "intensification of inner life" that came over the prisoners, so that sunsets, remembered lines of verse, and even the most ordinary actions of the past (taking a bus, answering the telephone, turning on the lights) became filled with beauty and longing. Frankl records the words of a young woman who knew that she would soon die.

> "I am grateful that fate has hit me so hard. In my former life I was spoiled and did not take spiritual accomplishments seriously." Pointing through the window of the hut, she said, "This tree here is the only friend I have in my loneliness." Through that window she could see just one branch of a chestnut tree, and on the branch were two blossoms. "I often talk to this tree," she said to me. I was startled and didn't quite know how to take her words. Was she delirious? Did she have occasional hallucinations? Anxiously I asked her if the tree replied. "Yes." What did it say to her? She answered, "It said to me, 'I am here—I am here—I am life, eternal life.'"[16]

There is always choice, however small, and in our choosing the soul is formed or deformed.

THE EROS THAT MADE US AND MAKES THE WORLD GO ROUND

Spiritual journeys or quests are initiated by two things: a vision of beauty accompanied by a sense of dissatisfaction, and our wonder about the fate of the dead. Where do they go—if anywhere? The restless heart mopes in exile. We recognize a lack in the soul, and the soul goes on a journey to seek *another.* That's where the trouble starts, but it is the kind of trouble we need. Our hearts feel cramped. They get us into trouble because of the pretentious immensity of their longings to be in communion with the whole universe. It is a dangerous and inflationary exercise. Our search for knowledge or happiness—winning the lottery or finding the man or woman of our dreams—stimulates in us wild flights of imagination, both beautiful and horrible. Off we go to hell in the hope of reaching heaven! The place where human longings and desires meet is one of vulnerability and possible exploitation. Spirituality must be focused on truth-telling and be committed to accuracy. We need to be purged of our illusions if we are to enter the real world of heaven.

As we have seen, Dante's education of desire began with a gasp of astonishment—an encounter with a specific human being at a particular time and place. His boyhood vision never left him and it drove him deep into the funnel of hell, where he discovered that large parts of himself were already there, stuck and fixed. If there is to be a clear vision of reality, the dark side of the erotic cannot be edited out.

The life of faith is the adventure of desire and its transformation, and heaven is the white rose of the fulfillment of our desire. It is an encounter with the God who miraculously desires us. Our faith is that God yearns for us. Our longing needs direction and discipline. That is why we can talk about the *education* of desire. Dante, then, stands in a long tradition of those for whom the erotic (in the proper sense of the word) was central. Behind him stands Saint Augustine, and behind Augustine stand Plato and his disciples. What, then, is "the erotic" in the proper sense of the word?

One of the most famous passages in Plato's *Symposium* is the speech in which Socrates recounts Diotima's instruction in "love matters" (*ta erotika*). Love had a mediating function connecting spirit Heaven and Earth. Love naturally longs for the Beautiful and the Good. Love, in short, is our longing response to God's longing for us. Two of the Platonic characteristics of *eros* are movement and giving birth (and not just in the physical sense) to the *beautiful*. All true loving is a kind of begetting. Love's "madness" is not to be despised but seen as a gift from the gods—a gift, however, that needs "ordering." *Eros*, then, is not merely an expression of human need, like an itch. It is a universal energy holding all levels of reality in being and drawing them up toward the One who is God.

The trouble is that no one (not even God) can *make* us good. We have to desire it. One can easily imagine an evil dictator, but there can be no such thing as a good one, because goodness, by definition, cannot coerce. Happiness cannot be imposed, not only because it must be freely chosen but also because it is multiform. There are as many forms of happiness as there are people.

How does the soul wake up to love and to love's responsibilities? Through "falling in love"; through the manifestation of beauty. The journey begins with erotic *amazement*—the desire to connect with the glory one has seen in another. It is this sudden *shock* at the sight of the beautiful that starts the soul on its journey. Dante's vision of Beatrice was the jolt that caused him to plunge in and go on a pilgrimage. The pilgrimage involved the education of his passions, not their suppression. Without them, the soul would never find its way home. The ancient principle is: Like is known by like. Longing responds to longing. The philosopher Philo even wrote about our being "agitated and maddened by a heavenly passion."[17] The early Christians, influenced by this tradition, understood the story of the fall of Adam and Eve as that of the disordered soul that has forgotten its true nature—as the image of the God understood as communication, Word, Logos, Story. Our desires go haywire and we don't know who or where we are. We're like someone who has been knocked on the head and now suffers from amnesia.

Dante identified the pursuit of wisdom with the pursuit of happiness. He found that, while he could not separate himself from his desires, they were both unruly and muddled. The true meaning of his pain, he believed, lay in the ordering of his unruly will. He identified with his longing. "I am my longing," he thought. "I cannot be happy unless I know who I am. My happiness depends on my knowledge of my true nature. I know I exist for a greater purpose than myself and my life's task is to go on a pilgrimage to find out who I really am and to find joy in it. I am called to enjoy myself."

God, however, gives us the freedom to wander off, to be eccentric—off-center with regard to our own true selves. When I feel centered, I think that nothing can take my faith away. But the mystery of my freedom is that I can, by God's terrible grace, cease to be myself if I so choose. We can, if we choose, cease to be our God-ordered selves. Being human means that we continually rethink and thus reexperience what love truly is—not immediate emotional indulgence but the discovery of a larger love with something of the otherness and terror of God in it.

Whatever Dante was on, it wasn't a private trip. The spiritual journey as the transformation of *eros* is not solitary. It is rooted in the life of the human community. Dante's is a pilgrimage from isolation to participation.

Only one question remains for those of us who are in purgatory (and who isn't?). Who, then, devised the torment? And for what reason?[18] Can the fire through which we pass at the top of the mountain of Purgation have anything to do with the great white rose of heaven? The reason for the journey has been to set love in order. The pilgrimage has been about the crafting of persons in the apprenticeship of love. In Charles Williams's *Shadows of Ecstasy,* there's a scene in which the archbishop of Canterbury is celebrating the Mass, the Holy Communion that gives us a taste of the feast in heaven.

The sacrament was a special kind of *work*, and the archbishop knew exactly what he was doing and was up to the task. It was a kind of spiritual surgery—a work of cutting, setting right, and binding together again, based on the conviction that the human will could be as surely set right as a broken arm or leg. The human heart could be raised from its deadness and deadliness in a spiritual operation. It could be rescued from the hell of its own choosing. The archbishop's "voice lingered on and intensified the formula of two thousand years, the formula by which Christendom has defined, commanded and assisted at the resurrection of Man in God."[19]

The theory is that to be human is to be both embodied and engodded in a communion in which the will is restored. We seek a revelation of the self that is no longer the "me" of our presuppositions. The discovery of meaning requires a sense of wonder and our seeing ourselves in a relational circle with all other creatures. The circle of our longing, at last, wheels around the longing of and for God. We finally see God's desire for us and are changed by what we see.

Is there a unity underlying the messiness of the world? Is there a unifying circle? What's your theory? The glorious example of the spiraling circle in the *Paradiso* is the feminine and unifying rose—symbol of the vision of an engodded universe. It is based on the conviction that the universe is coherent and intelligible. This is hard for us to believe with any consistency back here on planet earth because, for us, the circle of meaning keeps breaking. The larger and more inclusive the circle, the greater the need for tolerance and differentiation. The greater the differentiation, the greater the need for a way of holding things together so that the differences are "managed" with authority. We cannot do without authority and discipline, but the more high-handed authority becomes in the process of management, the greater the possibilities for dissent and revolt. There are rules for storytelling (the disciplines of adoration, compassion, and community), but there can be no limit to the variations of the story.

At the end of the poem, we find that conversion leads to delight—the glimpse of heaven, the patterning and ordering of things that is truly liberating. Dante is "transhumanized" by discovering the secret of our yearning dread.

> TRANSUMANAR SIGNIFICAR PER VERBA
> NON SI PORIA; PERO L'ESEMPLO BASTI
> A CUI ESPERIENZA GRAZIA SERBA.

"*Transhumanizing*—its meaning to convey in words cannot be done; but let the example suffice to whom grace grants experience."[20]

What of the vision of heaven and the apocalyptic threat and promise of the future? Hell, purgatory, and heaven are not so much future states as present realities. What are we to do in the face of questions of survival? Heaven is an energy inside us calling to new life. Its other name is the Holy Spirit. We also know it as *Eros*. The Chinese call it Chi.

Heaven is the "broad place where there is no constraint" (Job 36:16, NRSV). Like Dante, we cannot contain ourselves when it comes to the promise of heaven, which we can anticipate in this present life. In the end, it takes the trust of the open and receiving heart to see the vision. Love requires an extravagance that embarrasses us. We make fools of ourselves and make wild claims about love even as the cracks in our structures (which we try to hide) let the light in, in spite of us.

In the end, God fills all things. God is totally present in all things and at all times. As we repair the world together, we will learn that there is no place that is not God. The point of the story is joy. Its message is: Do not be afraid to be happy. At the end of Dorothy L. Sayers's *Gaudy Night*, Lord Peter Wimsey says to Harriet: "I have nothing much in the way of religion, or even morality, but I do recognize a code of behaviour of sorts. I do know that the worst sin—perhaps the only sin—passion can commit, is to be joyless. It must lie down with laughter or make its bed in hell—there is no middle way."[21]

The end of this story is silence and adoration. The passages of life are for the sake of adoration, which is our raison d'être. Adoration isn't stupefaction in the face of an all-consuming divinity. Adoration is the amazement at being our true selves in the divine Presence. In fact, the last great simile of the *Paradiso* likens Dante's stunned amazement to that of Neptune on seeing the shadow of the first boat, the *Argo*, on the sea. The poet is kneeling before the Virgin of the Assumption.[22] The masculine and the feminine images of a great adventurer (Jason with his Argonauts) and the Mother of God, adored by the poet and his beloved, Beatrice, who drew him back into the circle of divine love, come together in one story and leave us dazed and silenced. The final passage has no ending. The passage through hell may be over, but this final one explodes into eternity. We've come home—embodied and engodded for our living in the here and now.

The soul's apocalypse is not its destruction but the revelation of its destiny—its final passage. We must never stop telling stories about our longing. While we do, there is always hope. Adoration, compassion, and community are possibilities. And while these are possible, so are we.

> Ring the bells that still can ring.
> Forget your perfect offering.
> There is a crack in everything.
> That's how the light gets in.[23]

NOTES

CHAPTER 1

1. *New York Times*, November 19, 1993; C. G. Jung, unpublished letter to Ruth Topping, November 12, 1959.

2. Leunig, *Common Prayer* (Victoria, Australia: CollinsDove, 1990).

3. Lewis Thomas, *The Fragile Species* (New York: Macmillan, Collier, 1993), 80.

4. Thomas Merton, *Conjectures of a Guilty Bystander* (New York: Image, 1968), 144.

5. See, e.g., John Ciardi, *The Divine Comedy*, 3 vols. (New York: New American Library, Mentor, 1954); C. H. Grandgent, *La Divina Commedia*, revised by Charles S. Singleton (Cambridge: Harvard Univ. Press, 1972); Daniel Halpern, ed., *Dante's "Inferno": Translations by Twenty Contemporary Poets* (Hopewell, NJ: Ecco, 1993); Allen Mandelbaum, *The Divine Comedy*, 3 vols. (Berkeley and Los Angeles: Univ. of California Press, 1980); Dorothy L. Sayers, *The Divine Comedy*, 3 vols. (London: Penguin, 1949); John D. Sinclair, *The Divine Comedy*, 3 vols. (Oxford: Oxford Univ. Press, Galaxy, 1939); and Charles Singleton, *The Divine Comedy*, 6 vols., Bollingen Series (Princeton, NJ: Princeton Univ. Press, 1975).

6. Helen Luke, *From Dark Wood to White Rose* (Pecos, NM: Dove Publications, 1975).

CHAPTER 2

1. A phrase of Osip Mandelstam, quoted in Allen Mandelbaum's *Paradiso* (New York: Bantam, 1982), xiii. Italics mine.

2. *Purgatorio* 32.101–2.

3. Elaine Pagels tried to find a pure Christianity—a golden age—but "From a strictly historical point of view . . . there is no single 'real Christianity.'" See Daniel C. Maguire, *The Moral Core of Judaism and Christianity* (Philadelphia: Fortress, 1993), 86.

4. *Paradiso* 26.

5. *La Vita Nuova* 2.4.

6. See Robert Pogue Harrison, *The Body of Beatrice* (Baltimore: Johns Hopkins Univ. Press, 1988), 39ff., for a fine discussion of *La Vita Nuova*.

7. Harrison, *Body of Beatrice*, 41. See also James Joyce's *Portrait of the Artist as a Young Man* (New York: Viking, 1965), 207f.

8. William Anderson, *Dante the Maker* (New York: Crossroad, 1982), 391.

9. Carl G. Jung, *C. G. Jung Letters 2: 1951–1961*, ed. Gerhard Adler, Aniela Jaffe, and R. F. C. Hull, Bollingen Series 95:2 (Princeton, NJ: Princeton Univ. Press, 1975), 578.

10. Peter Ackroyd, *Dickens* (New York: HarperCollins, 1992), 360.

11. George Steiner, *Real Presences* (Chicago: Univ. of Chicago Press, 1991), 231–32. Italics mine.

PART 1: HELL

1. John D. Sinclair, *Dante's "Inferno"* (New York: Oxford Univ. Press, 1939), 108.

2. Grandgent, *La Divina Commedia*, 227.

CHAPTER 3

1. From the introduction of Dorothy L. Sayers's translation of *The Divine Comedy* (New York: Viking Penguin, 1955).

2. Anderson, *Dante the Maker*, 380.

3. Martin Thornton, *Prayer: A New Encounter* (London: Hodder and Stoughton, 1972), 69.

4. *Cui servire regnare est*—whom to serve is to reign.

5. See Ray L. Hart's essay, "The Dialectic of Home and Homelessness: Religion, Nature, and Home," in *The Critique of Modernity*, ed. Julian Norris Hartt (Charlottesville, VA: Univ. of Virginia Press, 1986), 39–40.

6. Giuseppe Mazzotta, *Dante, Poet of the Desert: History and Allegory in "The Divine Comedy"* (Princeton, NJ: Princeton Univ. Press, 1979).

7. See *Purgatorio* 19.22.

8. *The Cloud of Unknowing*, ed. James Walsh (New York: Paulist, 1981), 252–53.

9. See *Brendan* by Frederick Buechner (San Francisco: Harper & Row, 1987), 166, 207.

10. Edwin Muir, *The Story and the Fable* (London, 1940), 263, quoted in David Daiches, *God and the Poets* (Oxford: Clarendon, 1984), 177–78.

11. Mazzotta, *Dante, Poet of the Desert*.

12. See Aldous Huxley essay "Substitutes for Selfhood," in *Huxley and God*, ed. by Jacqueline Hazard Bridgeman (San Francisco: HarperSanFrancisco, 1992), 117.

CHAPTER 4

1. Margaret Drabble, *The Gates of Ivory* (New York: Viking, 1992), 124–25.

2. Roberto Unger, *Passion: An Essay on Personality* (New York: Free Press, 1984), 205.

3. "From Here to Eternity" (interview with Ivan Boszormenyi-Nagy), *Psychology Today*, March–April 1993, 12.

4. Christopher R. Browning, *Ordinary Men: Reserve Battalion 101 and the Final Solution in Poland* (New York: HarperCollins, 1992).

5. See David Harvey, *Condition of Postmodernity* (Cambridge, MA: Blackwell, 1989), 100.

6. Harvey, *Condition of Postmodernity*, 352.

7. Harvey, *Condition of Postmodernity*, 102.

8. Quoted by David Jasper, *Rhetoric, Power, and Community* (Louisville, KY: Westminster/John Knox, 1993), 157–58.

9. Vesle Fenstermaker. Unpublished manuscript. Used by permission.

10. *Inferno* 5.31.

11. George Steiner, *Antigones: The Antigone Myth in Western Literature, Art, and Thought* (Oxford: Oxford Univ. Press, 1984), 17.

12. Josephine Hart, *Damage* (New York: Ivy Books, 1992), 1.

13. Hart, *Damage*, 30–31.

14. Hart, *Damage*, 34.

15. Hart, *Damage*, 36.

16. James J. Thompson, Jr., "Does John Updike Write Dirty Books?" *Image*, Spring 1989, 76ff.

17. Thompson, "Updike," 77. The reference is to Updike's "One's Neighbor's Wife," a sketch that appeared in the *Transatlantic Review*.

18. Thompson, "Updike," 77.

19. Dorothy L. Sayers, *Gaudy Night* (London: New English Library, 1974), 439.

20. A. N. Wilson, *Daughters of Albion* (New York: Viking, 1991), 7.

CHAPTER 5

1. William Golding, *The Paper Men* (New York: Farrar, Straus and Giroux, 1984), 123–25; see also Alan Jones, *Soul Making* (San Francisco: HarperSanFrancisco, 1985), 126, 139–40.

2. Stanley Elkin, "The Conventional Wisdom," in *The Best American Short Stories* (New York: Houghton Mifflin, 1978), 38–39.

3. *Purgatorio* 27.104–5.

4. See James Hillman, *A Blue Fire* (New York: Harper & Row, 1989), 76.

5. See Patrick O'Brian, *The Nutmeg of Consolation* (New York: Norton, 1991), 121–22.

6. Newsletter, Society of the Sacred Mission, Milton Keynes, U.K., November 1992.

7. Newsletter, November 1992.

8. *Paradiso* 13.

9. Charles Corn, *Distant Islands: Crossing Indonesia's Ring of Fire* (New York: Viking, 1991).

10. Huston Smith, "Postmodernism's Impact on the Study of Religion," *Journal of the American Academy of Religion*, Winter 1990, 661.

11. *Matthew Barney: New Work* (San Francisco: San Francisco Museum of Modern Art, 1991).

12. See Roger Scruton's article in the *Times Literary Supplement*, December 18, 1992, 3–4.

13. A. S. Byatt, *The Game* (London: Penguin, 1983), 38.

14. Byatt, *The Game*, 40.

15. Byatt, *The Game*, 85.

16. Anderson, *Dante the Maker*, 284.

PART 2: PURGATORY

1. From Grandgent, *La Divina Commedia*, 438.

2. Grandgent, *La Divina Commedia*, 5.

CHAPTER 6

1. See Luke, *Dark Wood to White Rose*, 40. For a harrowing description of hell from a peculiarly Irish Catholic perspective, there is no better version than James Joyce's in *A Portrait of the Artist as a Young Man*, 119ff.

2. Anderson, *Dante the Maker*, 283.

3. Robertson Davies, *Murther and Walking Spirits* (New York: Viking, 1991), 26.

4. Davies, *Walking Spirits*, 269.

5. Davies, *Walking Spirits*, 321–23.

6. See Gerd Thiessen, *Biblical Faith: An Evolutionary Approach* (Philadelphia: Fortress, 1985), 122; Maguire, *The Moral Core of Judaism and Christianity*, 113.

7. See Maguire, *Moral Core*.

8. *Purgatorio* 23.124–26.

9. W. H. Auden, *For the Time Being: Collected Longer Poems* (New York: Random House, Vintage, 1973), 138, 175.

10. Auden, *For the Time Being*, 153.

11. Auden, *For the Time Being*, 173–74.

12. Josephine Hart, *Damage* (New York: Ivy Books, 1992), 19, 23.

13. Maguire, *Moral Core*, 123.

14. I am indebted to my friend Robert Kirschner for this story. It is from the Yiddish writer Isaac Loeb Peretz.

CHAPTER 7

1. Unger, *Passion*, 222.

2. *Purgatorio* 25.65–67.

3. Richard Ellman, *Oscar Wilde* (New York: Random House, 1988), 313, quoting "The Soul of Man Under Socialism."

4. Quoted in Ellman, *Oscar Wilde*, 504.

5. *Patrologia Graeca* 51:255, cited in Maguire, *Moral Core*, 152.

6. Fritz Kunkel, *Selected Writings*, ed. John Sanford (Rahway, NJ: Paulist, 1984), 53; see also Jones, *Soul Making*, 186ff.

7. H. G. Baynes, *Analytical Psychology and the English Mind* (London: Methuen, 1950), 69.

8. Robert Bellah, "Discipleship and Citizenship in the Workplace" (Annual Mark Gibbs Lectureship of the Vesper Society Group, Fuller Seminary, Pasadena, CA, April 27, 1990); reference to Albert Borgmann's "Beyond Sullenness and Hyperactivity: Prospect for American Culture," unpublished.

9. Quoted by Bellah, "Discipleship and Citizenship."

10. Quoted by Bellah, "Discipleship and Citizenship," 14.

11. Vaclav Havel, quoted in Bellah, 115–16.

12. Quoted by Bellah, "Discipleship and Citizenship," 17.

13. Personal communication.

14. Anderson, *Dante the Maker,* 382.

15. Anderson, *Dante the Maker,* 382.

16. James Collins, *Meditations with Dante Alighieri* (Santa Fe, NM: Bear and Co., 1984), 15.

17. Tom Stoppard, *The Real Thing* (Winchester, MA: Faber and Faber, 1983), 63–67.

18. Quoted by Anderson, *Dante the Maker,* 382. Italics mine.

19. R. W. Church, *Dante and Other Essays* (London: Macmillan, 1897), 1. Dante essay, 1850.

20. Anderson, *Dante the Maker,* 388.

21. Stephen Ives, "Myth and Discovery in the West" (Lecture at 1992 Annual Conference, California Historical Society, Sacramento, September 18, 1992).

22. Quoted in Ives.

23. Drabble, *Gates of Ivory,* 3–4.

24. Drabble, *Gates of Ivory.*

25. Harrison, *Body of Beatrice,* 168.

CHAPTER 8

1. Michael Malone, *Time's Witness* (New York: Simon and Schuster, Pocket Books, 1989), 128.

2. Terry Eagleton, *William Shakespeare* (Oxford: Basil Blackwell, 1986), 22.

3. This story from Tibet is retold by Andrew Harvey, with Mark Matousek, in *Dialogues with a Modern Mystic* (Wheaton, IL: Quest Books, 1994), 48–49.

4. I. Hassan, quoted by David Harvey, *The Condition of Postmodernity* (Cambridge, MA: Basil Blackwell, 1989), 43.

5. Terry Eagleton, quoted by Harvey, *Condition of Postmodernity*, 209.

6. Harvey, *Condition of Postmodernity*, 289.

7. *Purgatorio* 6.46–48.

8. *Purgatorio* 30.73ff.

9. See Allen Mandelbaum's translation; *Purgatorio* 33.29–32.

10. Saint Irenaeus.

11. See Colin Thubron, *Emperor* (London: Penguin Books, 1978), 115.

12. *The Book of Common Prayer* (New York: Church Hymnal Corporation, 1979), 323.

13. Janet Morley, *All Desires Known* (Wilton, CT: Morehouse-Barlow, 1988), 5.

14. Rubem A. Alves, *The Poet, the Warrior, the Prophet* (Philadelphia: Trinity Press, 1990), 106–9. Alves is a professor of philosophy and a psychoanalyst in São Paulo, Brazil.

15. The preceding discussion is largely a paraphrase of Alves, *Poet, Warrior, Prophet*, 106–9.

16. See Robert W. Jenson, "How the World Lost Its Story," in *First Things*, October 1993, 36:21.

PART 3: HEAVEN

1. See Grandgent, *La Divina Commedia*, 683.

2. Grandgent, *Commedia*, 625.

3. Grandgent, *Commedia*, 626.

4. Acts 9:3–9; see also 2 Corinthians 12, where Paul writes of being caught up into paradise.

5. *Paradiso* 26.

6. *Purgatorio* 30.46–54.

CHAPTER 9

1. Stoppard, *The Real Thing*, 77.

2. *Paradiso* 31.80 ff.; see also John D. Sinclair's *Paradiso*, 451.

3. *Paradiso* 1.111–14.

4. *Politics* 1.2.8.

5. See Edward Peters, "Human Diversity and Civil Society in Paradiso VIII," *Dante Studies* 109 (1991): 65.

6. Paul Evdokimov, *The Art of the Icon: A Theology of Beauty*, trans. Steven Bigham (Redondo Beach, CA: Oakwood, 1990), 9.

7. Evdokimov, *Art of the Icon*, 16–17.

8. This discussion owes a great deal to Harvey's *Condition of Postmodernity*.

9. Harvey, *Condition of Postmodernity*, 318.

10. Act 3, scene 1.

11. Wilson, *Daughters of Albion*, 189.

12. Drabble, *Gates of Ivory*, 138.

CHAPTER 10

1. See Allan Bloom, *Love and Friendship* (New York: Simon and Schuster, 1993), 21.

2. Stephen Hawking, *Black Holes and Baby Universes* (New York: Bantam, 1993), 44.

3. *Inferno* 3.4–6; see also Seamus Heaney's translation, in Halpern, *Dante's Inferno*, 12.

4. Alice Walker, public conversation at Grace Cathedral, San Francisco, 1993.

5. "Talk of the Town," *New Yorker*, early in 1993.

6. Bloom, *Love and Friendship*, 31.

7. Bloom, *Love and Friendship*, 31.

8. Émile Durkheim, quoted by Mark C. Taylor, "The Politics of Theory," *Journal of the American Academy of Religion*, Spring 1991, 11.

9. Peter Ackroyd, *Dickens* (New York: HarperCollins, 1991), 1082.

10. Ackroyd, *Dickens*, 1081.

11. Ackroyd, *Dickens*, 1082.

12. *La Vita Nuova*, 31.

13. *La Vita Nuova*, 99.

14. Bloom, *Love and Friendship*, 18.

15. Bloom, *Love and Friendship*, 18.

16. Thornton, *Prayer*, 105–6.

17. See Dante's *Convivio* 4.23.12.

18. C. G. Hardie, *Dante's "Comedy" as Self-Analysis and Interpretation* (London: Guild of Pastoral Theology, 1959), pamphlet 104, August 1959, 128.

19. The closing line of the final poem in book 2 of his *Consolatio*, quoted by Patrick Boyde, *Dante Philomythes and Philosopher: Man in the Cosmos* (Cambridge: Cambridge Univ. Press, 1981), 24.

20. David Steinberg, *The Nature of the Erotic Impulse* (Los Angeles: Tarcher, 1993), xvi.

21. Steinberg, *Erotic Impulse*, xvii.

22. Jürgen Moltmann, *The Spirit of Life: A Universal Affirmation* (Minneapolis: Fortress, 1992), 173.

CHAPTER 11

1. Terry Waite, *Taken on Trust* (New York: Harcourt Brace, 1993), from the foreword.

2. Unger, *Passion*, 242.

3. *Paradiso* 29.10–18; see also Anderson, *Dante the Maker*, 389–90.

4. *Paradiso* 22.61–65.

5. *Paradiso* 33.46–48; see also Mandelbaum's translation, 292.

6. Bonaventure, *Itinerarium Mentis* 7.6.

7. *Inferno* 2.123–26; see also Heaney translation, 10.

8. Evdokimov, *Art of the Icon*, 13–14.

9. *Paradiso* 14.37–45.

10. Karl Barth, *Wolfgang Amadeus Mozart* (Grand Rapids, MI: Eerdmans, 1986).

11. *Inferno* 26.112–20; see also Mandelbaum translation.

12. Anderson, *Dante, the Maker*, 399; see Bonaventure's *Itinerarium Mentis* 6.7.

13. Abraham Heschel, *Man Is Not Alone* (New York: Farrar, Straus and Young, 1951), 109.

14. Mark Helprin, "The True Builders of Cities," in *Visionary San Francisco* (San Francisco Museum of Modern Art, June 1990), 105.

15. Quoted by Catherine Madsen, "Revelations of Chaos," *Crosscurrents*, Winter 1991–92, 489–90.

16. Madsen, "Revelations of Chaos."

17. Bernard McGinn, *The Foundations of Mysticism: Origins to the Fifth Century* (New York: Crossroad, 1991), 39.

18. T. S. Eliot, *Four Quartets* (London: Folio Society, 1968), 53.

19. Charles Williams, *Shadows of Ecstasy* (Grand Rapids, MI: Eerdmans, 1973), 102–4.

20. *Paradiso* 1.70–72.

21. Sayers, *Gaudy Night,* 437.

22. One of the great illuminators of the *Paradiso* was Giovanni di Paolo (born ca. 1403). He shows Dante, accompanied by Beatrice, kneeling in adoration before the Virgin of the Assumption. Jason's boat is sailing on the sea, to the right of which is the astonished figure of Neptune. See John Pope-Hennesy's *Paradiso: The Illuminations to Dante's "Divine Comedy" by Giovanni di Paolo* (New York: Random House, 1993).

23. From the song "Anthem," by Leonard Cohen. I am indebted to my friend the Reverend Donald Harris for this quotation.

SUGGESTED READINGS

ENGLISH EDITIONS OF *THE DIVINE COMEDY*

Ciardi, John. *The Divine Comedy*. 3 vols. New York: New American Library, Mentor, 1954–1989.

Grandgent, C. H. *The Divine Comedy*. Revised by Charles S. Singleton. Cambridge: Harvard Univ. Press, 1972.

Halpern, Daniel, ed. *Dante's "Inferno": Translations by Twenty Contemporary Poets*. Hopewell, NJ: Ecco, 1993.

Mandelbaum, Allen. *The Divine Comedy*. 3 vols. Berkeley and Los Angeles: Univ. of California Press, 1980, 1982.

Musa, Mark. *The Purgatorio*. Bloomington: Indiana Univ. Press, 1981.

Pinsky, Robert. *The Inferno of Dante*. New York: Farrar, Straus and Giroux, 1995.

Sayers, Dorothy L. *The Divine Comedy*. 3 vols. London: Penguin, 1949.

Sinclair, John D. *The Divine Comedy*. 3 vols. Oxford: Oxford Univ. Press, Galaxy, 1961. A straightforward translation.

Singleton, Charles. *The Divine Comedy*. 6 vols. Bollingen Series. Princeton, NJ: Princeton Univ. Press, 1980–1982.

Also of interest are Dante's *La Vita Nuova* and *Il Convivio*, both in Penguin Classics.

BOOKS ABOUT DANTE'S LIFE AND WORKS

Anderson, William. *Dante, the Maker*. New York: Routledge, 1982.

Auerbach, Eric. *Dante: Poet of the Secular World*. Chicago: Univ. of Chicago Press, 1988.

Bergin, Thomas G. *From Time to Eternity: Essays on Dante's "Divine Comedy."* New Haven: Yale Univ. Press, 1967.

————. *Perspectives on "The Divine Comedy."* Bloomington: Indiana Univ. Press, 1967.

Berrigan, Daniel. *The Discipline of the Mountain.* New York: Seabury, 1979.

Bonaventure, St. *The Soul's Journey into God.* New York: Paulist, 1978.

Boyde, Patrick. *Dante Philomythes and Philosopher: Man in the Cosmos.* Cambridge: Cambridge Univ. Press, 1981.

Church, R. W. *Dante and Other Essays.* London: Macmillan, 1897. Dante essay, 1850.

Collins, James. *Meditations with Dante Alighieri.* Santa Fe, NM: Bear and Co., 1984.

————. *Pilgrim in Love: An Introduction to Dante and His Spirituality.* Chicago: Loyola Univ. Press, 1984.

Eliot, T. S. *Collected Essays.* See his essay on Dante.

Freccero, John. *Dante: A Collection of Critical Essays.* Englewood Cliffs, NJ: Prentice-Hall, 1965.

Harrison, Robert Pogue. *The Body of Beatrice.* Baltimore: Johns Hopkins Univ. Press, 1988.

Houghton, Rosemary. *The Passionate God.* New York: Paulist, 1981.

Luke, Helen. *From Dark Wood to White Rose.* Pecos, NM: Dove Publications, 1975.

Mazzeo, Joseph. *Medieval Cultural Tradition in Dante's "Comedy."* Westport, CT: Greenwood, 1968.

————. *Structure and Thought in the "Paradiso."* Westport, CT: Greenwood, 1968.

Mazzotta, Giuseppe. *Dante, the Poet of the Desert: History and Allegory in "The Divine Comedy."* Princeton, NJ: Princeton Univ. Press, 1979.

Sayers, Dorothy L. *Introductory Papers on Dante.* London: Methuen, 1954.

————. *Further Papers on Dante.* London: Methuen, 1957.

Singleton, Charles S. *Dante Studies I and II (The "Commedia": Elements of Structure and The Journey to Beatrice).* Baltimore, MD: Johns Hopkins Press, 1977.

Toynbee, Paget. *Dante Alighieri: His Life and Works.* Edited by Charles S. Singleton. New York: Harper Torchbooks, 1965.

Williams, Charles. *The Figure of Beatrice.* London: Dacre Press, 1948.

OTHER BOOKS OF INTEREST

Ackroyd, Peter. *Dickens*. New York: HarperCollins, 1992.

Alves, Rubem A. *The Poet, the Warrior, the Prophet*. Philadelphia: Trinity Press International, 1992.

Auden, W. H. *For the Time Being: Collected Longer Poems*. New York: Random House, Vintage, 1973.

Auerbach, Erich. *Mimesis*. Princeton, NJ: Princeton Univ. Press, 1953.

Augustine, St. *Confessions*. Translated by Henry Chadwick. New York: Oxford Univ. Press, 1991.

Barker, Dudley. *G. K. Chesterton*. New York: Stein and Day, 1973.

Barrett, William. *Time of Need*. New York: Harper & Row, 1972.

Barth, Karl. *Wolfgang Amadeus Mozart*. Grand Rapids, MI: Eerdmans, 1986.

Baynes, H. G. *Analytical Psychology and the English Mind*. London: Methuen, 1950.

Berger, Peter L. *A Far Glory: The Quest for Faith in an Age of Credulity*. New York: Free Press, 1992.

Berry, Wendell. *The Country of Marriage*. New York: Harcourt Brace Jovanovich, 1975.

Bloom, Allan. *Love and Friendship*. New York: Simon and Schuster, 1993.

Bolen, Jean Shinoda. *Ring of Power*. San Francisco: HarperSanFrancisco, 1992.

Boorstin, Daniel J. *Creators: A History of Heroes of the Imagination*. New York: Random House, 1992.

Bridgeman, Jacqueline Hazard, ed. *Huxley and God*. San Francisco: HarperSanFrancisco, 1992.

Buechner, Frederick. *Brendan: A Novel*. San Francisco: Harper & Row, 1988.

Byatt, A. S. *The Game*. London: Penguin, 1992.

Coles, Robert. *The Call of Stories: Stories and the Moral Imagination*. Boston: Houghton Mifflin, 1989.

Corn, Charles P. *Distant Islands: Crossing Indonesia's Ring of Fire*. New York: Viking, 1991.

Daiches, David. *God and the Poets*. Oxford: Clarendon, 1984.

Davies, Robertson. *Murther and Walking Spirits.* New York: Viking, 1992.

Doob, Penelope Reed. *The Idea of the Labyrinth from Classical Antiquity Through the Middle Ages.* Ithaca, NY: Cornell Univ. Press, 1990.

Drabble, Margaret. *The Gates of Ivory.* New York: Viking, 1992.

Dupre, Louis, and James A. Wiseman, eds. *Light from Light: An Anthology of Christian Mysticism.* New York: Paulist, 1988.

Eagleton, Terry. *William Shakespeare.* Oxford: Basil Blackwell, 1986.

Eliot, T. S. *Four Quartets.* London: Folio Society, 1968.

Elkin, Stanley. "The Conventional Wisdom." In *The Best American Short Stories.* New York: Houghton Mifflin, 1978.

Ellman, Richard. *Oscar Wilde.* New York: Random House, 1988.

Evdokimov, Paul. *The Art of the Icon: A Theology of Beauty.* Translated by Steven Bigham. Redondo Beach, CA: Oakwood, 1990.

Fox, Matthew. *Sheer Joy: Conversations with Thomas Aquinas on Creation Spirituality.* San Francisco: HarperSanFrancisco, 1992.

Gergen, Kenneth J. *The Saturated Self: Dilemmas of Identity in Contemporary Life.* New York: Basic Books, 1991.

Gingerich, Harold D. *Let This Mind Be in You.* Topeka, IN: Vessel Publications, 1987.

Golding, William. *The Paper Men.* New York: Harcourt Brace, 1985.

Hadfield, Alice Mary. *Charles Williams: An Exploration of His Life and Works.* New York: Oxford Univ. Press, 1983.

Hart, Josephine. *Damage.* New York: Ivy Books, 1992.

Hartt, Julian N., Ray L. Hart, and Robert P. Scharlemann. *The Critique of Modernity: Theological Reflections on Contemporary Culture.* Charlottesville: Univ. Press of Virginia, 1987.

Harvey, David. *The Condition of Postmodernity.* Cambridge, MA: Basil Blackwell, 1989.

Hawking, Stephen. *Black Holes and Baby Universes.* New York: Bantam, 1993.

Heschel, Abraham. *Man Is Not Alone: A Philosophy of Religion.* New York: Farrar, Straus and Giroux, 1951.

Hillman, James. *A Blue Fire.* Selected writings edited by Thomas Moore. New York: Harper & Row, 1989.

———. *Insearch: Psychology and Religion.* Dallas, TX: Spring Publications, 1967.

Hughes, Robert. *Culture of Complaint*. New York: Oxford Univ. Press, 1993.

Jasper, David. *Rhetoric, Power, and Community*. Louisville, KY: Westminster/John Knox, 1993.

Joyce, James. *A Portrait of the Artist as a Young Man*. New York: Viking, 1964.

Jung, Carl G. *Letters 2: 1951–1961*. Edited by Gerhard Adler and Aniela Jaffe. Bollingen Series 95:2. Princeton, NJ: Princeton Univ. Press, 1975.

Kavanaugh, John Francis. *Still Following Christ in a Consumer Society*. Maryknoll, NY: Orbis, 1991.

Kunkel, Fritz. *Selected Writings*. Edited by John A. Sanford. Rahway, NJ: Paulist, 1984.

Lapham, Lewis. *Imperial Masquerade*. New York: Grove, 1991.

le Carré, John. *The Night Manager*. New York: Knopf, 1993.

Lewis, C. S. *The Great Divorce*. New York: Macmillan, 1978.

———. *Perelandra*. New York, Macmillan, 1987.

Luke, Helen. *Old Age*. New York: Parabola, 1987.

Maguire, Daniel C. *The Moral Core of Judaism and Christianity*. Philadelphia: Fortress, 1993.

May, Rollo. *The Cry for Myth*. New York: Norton, 1991.

McGinn, Bernard, ed. *The Foundations of Mysticism*. New York: Crossroad, 1991.

Meilaender, Gilbert. *The Limits of Love*. University Park, PA: Pennsylvania State Univ. Press, 1987.

Merton, Thomas. *Conjectures of a Guilty Bystander*. New York: Doubleday, 1968.

———. *The New Man*. New York: Farrar, Straus and Giroux, 1961.

Moltmann, Jürgen. *The Spirit of Life: A Universal Affirmation*. Minneapolis: Fortress, 1978.

Moore, Sebastian. *Let This Mind Be in You*. San Francisco: Harper & Row, 1985.

Morley, Janet. *All Desires Known*. Wilton, CT: Morehouse-Barlow, 1989.

Murdoch, Iris. *The Good Apprentice*. New York: Viking, 1987.

O'Brian, Patrick. *The Nutmeg of Consolation*. New York: Norton, 1991.

Percy, Walker. *The Thanatos Syndrome*. New York: Farrar, Straus and Giroux, 1987.

Pope-Hennesy, John. *Paradiso: The Illuminations to Dante's "Divine Comedy" by Giovanni di Paolo.* New York: Random House, 1993.

Rahner, Karl. *The Great Church Year.* New York: Crossroad, 1993.

Sayers, Dorothy L. *The Mind of the Maker.* San Francisco: Harper & Row, 1987.

Smith, Huston. *Beyond the Post-Modern Mind.* Wheaton, IL: Theosophical Publishing House, 1989.

Steinberg, David. *The Erotic Impulse.* Los Angeles: Tarcher, 1992.

Steiner, George. *Antigones: The Antigone Myth in Western Literature, Art, and Thought.* Oxford: Oxford Univ. Press, 1984.

————. *Real Presences.* Chicago: Univ. of Chicago Press, 1991.

Stoppard, Tom. *The Real Thing.* New York: Faber and Faber, 1983.

Thomas, Lewis. *The Fragile Species.* New York: Macmillan, 1993.

Thornton, Martin. *Prayer: A New Encounter.* Cambridge, MA: Cowley, 1988.

Thubron, Colin. *Emperor.* London: Penguin, 1978.

Tilby, Angela. *Soul.* New York: Doubleday, 1993.

Unger, Roberto. *Passion: An Essay on Personality.* New York: Free Press, 1986.

Waite, Terry. *Taken on Trust.* New York: Harcourt Brace, 1993.

Welch, John. *When Gods Die: An Introduction to St. John of the Cross.* New York: Paulist, 1990.

Williams, Charles. *Shadows of Ecstasy.* Grand Rapids, MI: Eerdmans, 1973.

Wilson, A. N. *Daughters of Albion.* New York: Viking, 1992.

INDEX